THE

CAMPAIGN OF SEBASTOPOL

INTERIOR OF HUT IN THE CAMP.

THE STORY

OF THE

CAMPAIGN OF SEBASTOPOL

𝔚ritten in the Camp

BY

LIEUT.-COL. E. BRUCE HAMLEY
CAPTAIN, ROYAL ARTILLERY

WITH ILLUSTRATIONS DRAWN IN CAMP BY THE AUTHOR

WILLIAM BLACKWOOD AND SONS
EDINBURGH AND LONDON
MDCCCLV

ORIGINALLY PUBLISHED IN BLACKWOOD'S MAGAZINE.

PREFACE.

THE circumstances under which the ensuing narrative was written were at once very advantageous for watching, appreciating, and foreseeing the events of the Campaign, and unfavourable to the free expression of the conclusions thence arrived at.

My position on the Staff of the Artillery, first as Adjutant to the First Division of the Field Batteries under Lieut.-Colonel Dacres, up to the battle of Inkermann, and subsequently as Aide-de-camp to that officer (now risen through successive grades to be Major-General Sir Richard Dacres, K.C.B.) in command of the whole Artillery force throughout the Siege, afforded peculiar facilities for observation. Regimental officers must, from their isolated position and want of reliable information, frequently form erroneous ideas of the objects of movements, and of the state and position of the Army. In all the actions, small and great, of the Campaign, I was enabled to be spectator as well as actor ; and during the Siege, besides being necessarily well acquainted with our own trenches, there were scarcely any siege-works of the French which I left unvisited, especially after an action. Besides these opportunities, a residence at headquarters has necessarily placed me in the focus of information of all kinds not confidential.

But when it is considered that men in authority do not always look with a very friendly eye on the mere possession of opinions on their conduct of public affairs, it may be supposed that to express them critically might, especially when they implied censure, be anything but an assistance to the critic in his military career. Moreover, there are many cases in which it is the bounden duty of an officer to refrain from publishing facts or opinions which might be prejudicial to the prestige or success of our arms ; to a great extent, therefore, the reader is left to make his own comments on facts which I have been careful to verify and combine in a sequence which should exhibit only the significant features of the Campaign;

and of these I hope the narrative will be found to convey a clear idea.

Deeply impressed by the scenes and events I have taken part in, and believing the public to be so warmly interested in their progress as to need no rhetorical arts to excite its attention or increase the effect, I have been studious to deliver only a round unvarnished tale. My object has been to hang historical events and memorable scenes on a thread of personal narrative, which should at once connect and relieve them, endeavouring at the same time to render operations purely military intelligible to the general reader. And I may remark, as evidence that I have not written at random, that in no case has the course of events rendered it necessary for me to recant an opinion or alter a statement. Especially I would point to the view taken of the state of the Army and its causes in Chapter XVII.; a view entirely adverse to the state of public feeling at the time, and to the tone of the press, but borne out entirely by evidence subsequently given before the Sebastopol Committee by officers of high authority, and adopted by statesmen in the Parliamentary discussions on the conduct of the war.

The whole of the narrative has been, as it professes to be, written in camp in the intervals of military duty,—at first in a tent, and after Christmas in a hut.

An American publishing firm has done me the honour to anticipate this edition of my narrative by a piratical reprint from the pages of *Blackwood*. But I am bound to state that, like Claude Duval, Jack Sheppard, and other courteous and considerate robbers, Messrs Gould and Lincoln, of Boston, have pillaged me with great urbanity, prefixing an introductory notice, so flattering to the work and its author, that I fear the hope of an extensive sale must have had some share in the panegyric.

E. B. H.

SEBASTOPOL, *Oct.* 5, 1855.

CONTENTS.

CHAPTER I.
THE RENDEZVOUS.

Arrival at Constantinople—Halt at Scutari—The repulse of the Russians at Silistria—Causes of delay—Varna—Ravages of cholera—The encampment at Gevreckler—Gloomy scenes in camp, ... 1–7

CHAPTER II.
THE MOVEMENT TO THE CRIMEA.

Preparations for embarking—Voyage to Balchik Bay—Continued losses from cholera—The voyage—Off the Crimea—The landing at Eupatoria—Difficulties of the landing—Composition of the English force—Total strength of the Allies—The English commissariat—The ammunition and ambulance corps, ... 8–16

CHAPTER III.
FIRST OPERATIONS IN THE CRIMEA.

Peculiarities of the Campaign—Advantages of the fleet—Commencement and order of march—Foraging for supplies—The natives—First skirmish with the Cossacks—Skirmish on the Bulganak—Expectations of a general action, ... 17–24

CHAPTER IV.
BATTLE OF THE ALMA.

Arrival at the Alma—Description of the field—Progress of the French—The Russian defences—Attack of the British—Movements of the artillery—The Russian battery carried—Retreat of the Russians—Advance of the Highlanders—Capture of a Russian general—Menschikoff's carriage and papers taken—Strength of the Russian position, . . . 25–34

x   CONTENTS.

CHAPTER V.

THE BATTLE-FIELD.

PAGE

Visit to the field—Fearful wounds—Scene of the French struggle—The dead at the breastwork—The wounded—Memorials of the field,   .   35–39

CHAPTER VI.

THE KATCHA AND THE BALBEK.

Continued ravages of cholera—Advance to the Katcha—Strength of that position—Night encampment—Junction of the Scots Greys—Arrival at the Balbek—Deserted villa—A disappointment—First view of Sebastopol, ...   40–45

CHAPTER VII.

THE FLANK MARCH.

Commencement of the flank march—Unexpected appearance of the Russians —Their flight—Mackenzie's farm—Skirmish—Abandoned carriages— Arrival at the Tchernaya—Probable object of the Russian sally,   .   46–51

CHAPTER VIII.

OCCUPATION OF BALAKLAVA.

Exhaustion of the troops—Capture of Balaklava—results of these movements—Description of the place—The harbour—The fortifications, . 52–56

CHAPTER IX.

THE POSITION BEFORE SEBASTOPOL.

The village of Kadukoi—Positions of the troops—Landing of the siege material—Description of the ground—The monastery of St George— General aspect of the scene, ...   57–63

CHAPTER X.

COMMENCEMENT OF THE SIEGE.

The Malakhoff, the Redan, and the Barrack battery—Character of the ground—Peculiarities of the siege—Opening of the bombardment—The Lancaster guns—Fire of the fleet—Effects of the first day's fire—Continued fire—Sortie from the town, ...   64–71

CONTENTS. xi

CHAPTER XI.

ATTACK ON BALAKLAVA.

PAGE

Position of the Turks at Balaklava—Commencement of the attack—First success of the Russians—Flight of the Turks—Charge of the Heavy Brigade—Repulse of the Russian cavalry by the 93d—Charge of the Light Brigade—Its losses—New position held by the Russians—The conduct of the Turks—Object of the Russian attack, ... 72–80

CHAPTER XII.

FIRST ACTION OF INKERMANN.

Features of the ground—Attack of the Russians—Their repulse—Hewett and the Lancaster gun—Losses of the Russians—Their object in this attack—Forces engaged—The wounded, and surgical operations—Capture of Russian horses—Progress of the siege-works—Visit to the French hospitals—The position strengthened—Errors of the Newspapers—Field-works and redoubts—The Ruins of Inkermann—Reinforcements to the Russians, ... 81–92

CHAPTER XIII.

BATTLE OF INKERMANN.

The morning summons—State of the weather—The battle-field—Advance of the Russians—Their guns of position—Defensive measures of the British—Progress of the enemy—Arrival of the French—Heroism of the Guards — Terrible artillery fire—Renewed attack—Narrow escape of the Author—Severity of the struggle—Death of Sir G. Cathcart—Arrival of General Bosquet—The heavy guns brought up—Sir de Lacy Evans—Retreat of the Russians and close of the battle—Forces engaged—Character of the battle—Severity of the struggle—Losses on both sides—Burial of the dead—Fire of the enemy on the burial-parties, 93–110

CHAPTER XIV.

WINTER ON THE PLAINS.

Setting in of winter—Storm of the 14th November—Scenes in camp—Fall of the hospital tents—Losses among the shipping—Effects of the loss of the Prince—State of the camp and sufferings of the troops—Sufferings of the cavalry—The horses—The dogs—State of the roads—Want of fuel—The Author's hut—A night in it—Plans for warming tents, &c.—Sufferings of the soldiers—Night contests—Capture of rifle-pits—Works at Inkermann—Retreat of Liprandi—A reconnaissance—Close of the year—Supplies from England, and sympathy there, . . 111–128

xii   CONTENTS.

CHAPTER XV.

CIRCUMSPECTIVE.

View of the position of the Allies—Sufferings of the troops—Difficulty of bringing up provisions and stores—Causes which led to this state of things—The impatience of the public—Ignorance of the country—failure to provide for a protracted siege—Deficiency in means of transport—Insufficiency of the force, and difficulty of augmenting it—Deficiencies of the cavalry and artillery—Probabilities of the future—Review of the course pursued—Probabilities had the enterprise been hastened or postponed—Real cause of our losses, ... 129–141

CHAPTER XVI.

HOSPITALS ON THE BOSPHORUS.

Disposal of the sick—The officers and their tents—The ambulance waggons—Difficulties in removing the sick—Their sufferings on shipboard—The Author sent to Constantinople—Winter aspect of the city—Scenes ashore—The hotels and their inmates—The Golden Horn and shipping—Landing of sick and wounded—The great hospital, and scenes in it—Appearance of patients—The Nurses and Sisters of Charity—Miss Nightingale—The Hospital Kitchen—The other hospitals—The English cemetery and burial scenes—Visit to the French hospital—Difficulties of the hospital staff—The commissariat, . . . 142–158

CHAPTER XVII.

EXCULPATORY.

The feeling of the public at home—Ministerial changes—The comments of the press—Difficulties of road-making—Necessity of maintaining the trenches—Difficulty of providing for winter—The alleged superiority in the condition of the French—Causes of this—Inadequacy of the British force—Conduct of the commissariat—Who was really to blame for the disasters?—The alleged superiority of the French, . . . 159–169

CHAPTER XVIII.

PROGRESS OF THE SIEGE.

Second visit to the hospitals—Return to the Crimea—Adventures of a pie—Improvements at Balaklava—A reconnaissance in force—Defeat of the Russians at Eupatoria—Seizure of advanced post by the Russians—Attack on it by the French—Their repulse—Return of spring—Improvement in the state of the troops—Fire on a Russian steamer—Death of the Czar—Seizure of the Mamelon by the Russians—Death of Captain Craigie—New works—Incidents in the trenches—Sorties and night combats—Reported death of Menschikoff—Return of Sir John Burgoyne to England, ... 170–182

CONTENTS. xiii

CHAPTER XIX.

THE BURIAL TRUCE.

Sortie—Repulse of the Russians—Losses of the French—Burial truce, and scenes during it—The Russian rifle-pits—Aspect of the Russian soldiers—The Mamelon and Malakhoff—Close of the truce—Progress of the railway—Improvements at Balaklava—Retrospect of the siege—Position of the Russians—Influence of the death of the Czar, . . 183–193

CHAPTER XX.

VIEW OF THE WORKS.

Character of the besiegers' works—Survey of the whole scene—The town and its defences—The Redan and the Malakhoff—The Mamelon—The artillery practice—The North forts—The British works—The trenches—The mortar batteries—Chapman's battery—The Barrack and Flagstaff batteries—The Valley of the Shadow of Death—The French works—Descent into a French mine, ... 194–208

CHAPTER XXI.

THE SECOND CANNONADE.

Reopening of the fire—State of the weather—Feeble fire of the enemy—Night fire of the mortars—Continuation of the fire—Causes of the failure of the Russian artillery—Expected assault—Attack on rifle-pits—Death of Colonel Egerton—Difficulties of the siege—Various operations which presented themselves, ... 209–218

CHAPTER XXII.

SUBSEQUENT OPERATIONS.

Reconnaissance under Omer Pasha—Personal appearance of that leader—Retreat of the Russians—Sorties and night-combats—Visit to the field of Inkermann—Pelissier assumes the command of the French—French attack on rifle-pits—Capture of the cemetery—Renewed attack, and its success—Burial truce and losses of the parties—Expedition to Kertsch, and its capture—Occupation of Yenikale—Operations in the Sea of Azoff, 219–229

CHAPTER XXIII.

THE POSITION EXTENDED.

Reinforcements to the Allies—Arrival of the Sardinians—New aspect of affairs—Various plans which might have been followed—A ride round the position—The view from the outposts—The valley of Baidar—The view of the Euxine, ... 230–236

CONTENTS.

CHAPTER XXIV.

ASSAULT OF THE MAMELON AND QUARRIES.

Reopening of fire—that of the Russians subdued—The Quarries—Assault and capture of the Mamelon—Attempt on the Malakhoff—The Mamelon secured—Struggle at the Quarries—Their capture—Gallantry displayed on both sides, ... 237–245

CHAPTER XXV.

THE CONFERENCES AND DEBATES.

Character of the conferences—Arrogance of the Russians—Error of Russia in refusing the terms offered—The Four Points—Proposals on the third of these—Campaign proposed by Disraeli—Accessibility of the Crimea to a hostile power—Position of the parties—Mr Bright, the Peace party, and their arguments, ... 246–255

CHAPTER XXVI.

ATTACK OF THE MALAKHOFF AND REDAN.

Progress of the works—Renewed bombardment—Plan for the assault—Subsequent modification of it—Advance of the French—Attack of the Redan—The struggle at the Malakhoff, and repulse of the French—Causes of the failure—Progress of Eyre's brigade—His repulse—Defects of the whole plan—Death of Admiral Boxer, &c.—Death and funeral of Lord Raglan—General Simpson appointed to command—Further successes in the Sea of Azoff—Yenikale fortified, ... 256–273

CHAPTER XXVII.

PROGRESS OF THE SIEGE.

New aspect of the siege—Description of the Malakhoff—The Mamelon—Losses of the French—Deaths of Captain Oldfield, Commander Hammett, &c.—Fire in the town—A sunset scene—The sailors as horse-appropriators—Visit to the Mamelon—Its interior—Great explosion there, 274–282

CHAPTER XXVIII.

BATTLE OF THE TRAKTIR BRIDGE.

Expected attack by the Russians—Scene of action—Commencement of the battle—Passage of the river, and losses at it—Artillery fire—Retreat of the Russians—Losses on both sides—Object of the Russian attack—Firing on burial-parties, ... 283–290

CONTENTS. XV

CHAPTER XXIX.

A CRISIS IN THE CAMPAIGN.

PAGE

Apparent preparations for retreat—Construction of bridge across the harbour—Expected attack—The last cannonade opened—Its severity—Russian reconnaissance—Exhaustive nature of the struggle—Supposed importance of the defence to the prestige of Russia—Prospects for England, ... 291–297

CHAPTER XXX.

THE GENERAL ASSAULT.

Plan of the assault—Preparations for it—Description of the works to be assaulted—Commencement of the attack, and first success of the French—Singular escape from a mine—Capture of the Malakhoff—Repulse at the Curtain and at the Little Redan—Heroic feat of the French field-artillery—Losses at the Little Redan—Attack of the Redan—Struggle there and repulse of the British—Repulse of the French at the Central Bastion—The evening and its prospects—Errors in the construction of the Malakhoff, ... 298–311

CHAPTER XXXI.

THE LAST HOURS OF SEBASTOPOL.

The Redan found deserted—Fires in the town on the 7th and 8th—The town fired by the Russians—Blowing up of Fort Paul—Plunder—Inexpediency of burning the town—Retreat of the garrison—Burial of the slain—Interior of the Redan—and of the Malakhoff—The wounded and dead—Explosions of mines and magazines—Visit to the town—its interior—Frightful hospital scene—Destruction of the Russian steamers—Interest of the entire scene—The plateau and its associations, . . 312–326

CHAPTER XXXII.

A RETROSPECT.

Review of the policy pursued—Tactics at the Alma—The attack of the north side of the fortress—Effects of the sinking of the Russian fleet—General character of the campaign—Character of the Russian defences—The Flagstaff Bastion—Changes in public opinion—The position of the Allies on the plateau—Policy and views of the French Emperor—The losses of Russia—Prospects of the future, ... 327–339

LIST OF ILLUSTRATIONS.

INTERIOR OF HUT IN THE CAMP,—*Frontispiece*.

"You ask about the two drawings of the hut: it is the one alluded to in the narrative [page 120] in which we have lived since Christmas. The three occupants of the interior are Sir R. Dacres reading the paper—Gordon, my brother aide-de-camp, at the table—and myself in the fur-lined coat, a present which Government made us last winter. The cat is not the one I had at the Katcha, which ran away, but one which I have had since last November, when it was a small kitten: it was given me by a brother officer, who saw it on board a transport, and knowing my penchant for the tribe, brought it up to my tent in his pocket-handkerchief. She is called Topsy; and having formed an intimacy with a vagrant lover with one eye, a native of the country, who comes from nobody knows where, has been the mother of one family, and there is every prospect of another. The outer hut or burrow, where we are sitting in the drawing, is the one we took our meals and sat in; the inner was the sleeping apartment of the General and myself; but it exhibited an unpleasant tendency to fall in, so we got into wooden huts as soon as we could get them. I have been in one of the latter about two months, and find it an agreeable change, though it smells of tar. The principal difference is, that the former residence was like a grave, and this is like a coffin."

—*Extract from Author's Letter, 5th Oct.*

	PAGE
THE FIELD OF ALMA,	25
THE MONASTERY OF ST GEORGE,	61
CLIFFS AT THE MONASTERY OF ST GEORGE,	62
BALAKLAVA IN WINTER,	118
EXTERIOR OF HUT IN THE CAMP,	120

"The exterior view shows the same hut, and one or two others, forming a kitchen, stable, &c.; in a line with it, the marquee we used as a harness-room, and our live stock also resided there. The three horses are portraits of my stud; the old hunter led by the artilleryman is an Irish horse, a very good one, brought to the Crimea by Sir de Lacy Evans; the middle one is an old Spanish horse which I brought up from Gibraltar, generally known as Jones, from the name of his former proprietor, the commanding engineer there; and the dark bay is an Irish horse, formerly belonging to an officer of horse artillery, from whom I bought him; a capital fencer; he is called the Czar."

—*Extract from Author's Letter, 5th Oct.*

SKETCH OF SEBASTOPOL AND THE WORKS, TAKEN FROM THE LOOK-OUT PLACE,	194
ZOUAVES AT A WASHING PLACE,	236
VALLEY OF TCHERGOUM,	283
SKETCH MAP OF SEBASTOPOL AND THE SIEGE WORKS,	340

THE STORY

OF THE

CAMPAIGN OF SEBASTOPOL.

CHAPTER I.

THE RENDEZVOUS.

DURING the months of April and May the Allied Army continued to arrive by instalments in the Bosphorus. On their way they had most of them halted at Malta. Those who came in steam vessels made a swift and pleasant voyage, surrounded by every luxury a traveller can hope for. The visits to the palaces of the Knights and the churches of the city—the novel and striking aspect of the harbours and fortifications — the subsequent voyage through the Egean—the view of the plains of Troy, dotted with the sepulchral mounds of classic heroes—the passage of the Dardanelles—and the gay scenery of Constantinople, contributed to give the expedition rather the air of a pleasure excursion, than of the advance of an army.

The halt at Scutari, so far from the scene of action, was rendered endurable to all but the most impatient spirits, by the curious scenes of the Turkish capital, and the magnificent landscapes disclosed at every bend of the Bosphorus. A vast quadrangular barrack, capable of accommodating a small army in its numerous chambers, and of affording ample space to assemble the occupants on parade within the oblong enclosed by the four walls of the building, was made over to the English. The regiments not lodged here were encamped on the grassy plains behind. A steamer plied across the strait every hour for the convenience of the troops; and those who happened to miss it found means of passage in the numerous caïques which, gaily carved and painted, and of peculiarly graceful shape, danced everywhere on the clear water, propelled, some by one, some by two, handsome Greeks in red skull-cap and white tunic. The background to these graceful figures was especially pleasant to the eye, whether formed by the white buildings of the city, gleaming amidst the dark clumps of trees, or by the banks of the sea-river, covered with soft feathery foliage, amidst which black cypresses stood stiffly up, varied by the pink blossoms of the peach and apple, and the purple clusters of the Judas tree; while close to the water's edge extended a line of red-roofed, painted, wooden houses, many of them decaying, but picturesque in their decay.

In the mean time the Russians had crossed the Danube and laid siege to Silistria, which was expected to fall, for the fortress was neither regular nor strong, and the besieging force was disproportionately great. Consequently, the original plan of the campaign remained as yet unchanged. This was, to fortify Gallipoli, in order to prevent the Russians (who might, after turning the left of the Turks, have advanced to the Chersonese) from closing the passage of the Dardanelles; and to intrench the neck of the isthmus on which Constantinople stands, so that, should the Russians defeat the Turks south of the Balkan, the capital might still be saved from the invader. As the end for which these works were designed has never been fulfilled, and they have ceased to be objects of interest, a detailed account of them is unnecessary.

Contrary to expectation, Silistria continued to hold out, and, at the request of Omer Pasha, an English division was landed at Varna early in June. The Russians being checked in their rapid advance, the line of the Balkan might now be held, and the fortresses of Shumla and Varna covered, when the enemy should turn upon them after taking Silistria, which, though marvellously defended, was still considered as doomed to fall. The rest of the English army, including the greater part of the brigade left in Gallipoli, followed the Light Division to Varna, and was distributed on the heights south of Varna bay, and at various points on and near the Shumla road, Devna, Aladyn, and Monastir; places which, though surrounded by landscapes picturesquely grand, will long live drearily in the remembrance of the British army in Turkey. Foiled in their repeated attacks on Silistria, and suffering terribly from disease and want, the enemy made one final grand assault, and, when repulsed, withdrew across the Danube. It was now expected that the Allies would push on; but for this they were not prepared. Overrating the resources of the enemy from the beginning, an advance into the Principalities does not seem to have entered into their calculations. Various reasons for our inactivity were circulated: the commissariat could not supply us on the march; there was no transport for the reserve ammunition; we were waiting to see what Austria would do. Leaving diplomatists to attach a value to the last reason, I may say, that the commissariat would probably, if they had been called on, have found means to supply the army, but that the want of animals to carry the ammunition formed a more serious obstacle. The French, indeed, sent a division into the Dobrudscha, but it rejoined the army without other result than a fearful loss of men from the malaria of those pestilent swamps.

A new and terribly prominent feature of the campaign now disclosed itself. Towards the end of July the cholera broke out at Varna, and in a few days the hospitals were filled with cases. Some of the transports lost many men in a few hours, and were ordered to cruise outside the bay, in hopes of evading the pestilence. Changes of site seemed of no avail to the troops, and not a day passed, in any quarter, without the ghastly spectacle of many men, victims either to cholera or fever, being borne through the camp, sewed in their blankets, to be laid in the earth. At this time the troops were busily employed in manufacturing gabions and fascines from the brushwood which everywhere covers the face of the country. Huge piles of these were collected on the south side of Varna Bay; the sappers were busy running out temporary piers; the transports remaining in the Bosphorus were ordered up; and everything pointed to the speedy fulfilment of what had become, since the repulse of the Russians at Silistria proved the Turks capable of holding the line of the Danube single-handed, the true strategical object of the campaign, viz., the invasion of the Crimea. Stores were accumulated — rumours of speedy departure were everywhere repeated, and the 14th August was even confidently named as the day of embarkation. However, the 14th passed without movement; and though the preparations still continued, yet all, except the most sanguine, began to despair of an active campaign at so advanced a season.

The First Division, consisting of the Guards and Highlanders, and two field-batteries, was now encamped at Gevreckler, a dreary common on the heights to the right of the Shumla road going from Varna. The soil was stony, and covered with short wiry grass, such as geese feed on in England; trees were thinly sprinkled round the borders of the desolate plain. Going out of the camp in any direction, however, the prospect speedily became more smiling. Woods of low coppice appeared, having in the intervals vast corn-fields, spreading sometimes for miles in every direction. These were laid out in patches of wheat, oats, and barley, golden with ripeness, and of tall guinea-grass of deepest green. Amid the crops occasionally sprang up groups of trees of maturer growth than those in the surrounding woods. Bulgarian peasants, in parties generally consisting each of a man and two women, or young girls, were reaping in the patches of corn; their left hands, which grasped the stalks, being defended from the sickle by part of a bullock's horn pushed over the fingers. Quail were tolerably plentiful in these fields; and parties of sportsmen might be seen in all directions, who, taking soldiers for beaters in the absence of dogs, advanced in line across the fields. A party of three generally averaged about ten brace of quail and two or three hares in an afternoon. Crossing the common from Gevreckler, over patches of thistles and ploughed land, the position of the Second Division was reached, commanding a spreading and magnificent prospect. Distant passes near Shumla could be discerned; great woody hills of graceful form undulated in tumbled confusion through the valleys; and on the south was seen the blue outline of the Balkan range.

Such was the brighter side of the picture, affording

a temporary respite from the gloomy scenes which awaited us in camp. Accounts of friends, last seen in health, suddenly struck down with disease, and then reported dead; cries from the hospital tents of men in the agonies of cramps; silent groups of five or six digging, on the outskirts of the camp, receptacles for those who, the rigid outline of their features and feet showing through the blanket-shroud, were presently borne past, followed by the officer who was to read the funeral service; sales of the clothes, camp-equipage, and horses of those who died yesterday,—such were the dismal sights and sounds that spread a gloom over the army, and doubled its impatience for action. On that melancholy plain the Guards alone left seventy-two graves, many of which contained a double tenant. Besides the fatal cases, sickness of milder though similar type was almost universal; and it is scarcely an exaggeration to state, that not more than a tenth of the army remained in average health.

CHAPTER II.

THE MOVEMENT TO THE CRIMEA.

AT length came the wished-for order for embarkation, and the First Division moved, on the 23d August, towards the sea, the men so enfeebled that their knapsacks were carried on pack-horses during even a short march of five or six miles, and lamentably different in appearance from the splendid regiments who had marched past the Sultan on the plains of Scutari at the end of May. At the close of the first day's march, the artillery of this division halted at the base of the hills, near a Turkish village, so picturesque as to be worth describing. Its streets were green lanes, bordered by hedgerows of fine trees; on each side of the lanes were gardens, and each garden contained a mud-walled house, with thatched roof, having a farmyard attached to it, one of the invariable features of which was a great, white-washed, dome-shaped, clay oven. These lanes had a common centre in a sort of village green, but I did not observe any sports going on there; all the inhabitants seemed sedate and apathetic, except the girls at the fountains, who tittered and whispered as the martial strangers passed by, much as young female villagers of any other nation might have done. In a stackyard an old peasant, seated in a kind of sledge, with a little girl standing up beside him, was being dragged round and round by oxen, over loosened sheaves of corn. This was a luxurious mode of threshing. The oxen, according to the Scriptural precept, were unmuzzled, and occasionally stooped for a mouthful. Milk, fowls, and fruit, were brought from here to the tents for sale, though at other villages the inhabitants had kept carefully aloof. Probably they were now beginning to discover that we were not robbers.

The portions of the English army, as they embarked, sailed at once for Balchick Bay, where the greater part of the Allied fleet lay. Thither the cholera still pursued us, and every day boats might be seen leaving ships, towing a boat astern, wherein was a long motionless object covered by a flag. After a time the corpses, sewed in blankets or hammocks, and swollen to giant size, rose to the surface and floated upright among the ships, their feet being kept down by the shot used to sink them. One of these hideous visitants lingered about the foot of the accommodation ladder of one of the transports, till men going down the side passed cords with weights attached over its neck, when it slowly sank. Gevreckler Common was scarcely more depressing to the men than the bay at Balchick.

Part of the French army marched from Varna to

Balchick, defiling along the hills above the beach, and embarking from their encampment. Day after day our own transports came up with troops, and the Turkish squadron, with the Ottoman portion of the Allied army, also joined us. When all were assembled, we were still kept waiting by an adverse wind, against which the steamers could not have towed us. At length, on Thursday the 7th September, we sailed with fine weather, and, when under way, arranged ourselves, according to order, in six columns, a division in each. The Light Division, which was next the shore, was distinguished by a blue and white chequered flag; the First Division, blue; the Second, white; the Third, red; the Fourth, white and red; the cavalry, blue and red. Each steamer towed two transports; the men-of-war stationed themselves ahead and on our flanks; the French fleet was on our right. Most of the transports were East Indiamen of the largest class, equalling in size the frigates of the last war; the steamers were among the finest in the world; and though more numerous invading armies have traversed the Euxine, yet so complete and imposing an armament never before moved on the waters of any sea.

On the 9th we were signalled "Rendezvous 14," which meant "forty miles west of Cape Tarkan;" and, on coming up with the ships ahead of us at 6 P.M., we received the order to anchor. We remained at anchor the whole of Sunday the 10th, while Lord Raglan, whose headquarters were in the Caradoc,

escorted by the Agamemnon, reconnoitred the coast.
The day being fine, and the water smooth, boats were
hoisted out and visits paid to other vessels, some of
which had suffered much from cholera. The delay
was disagreeable and unexpected, as we had all
calculated on landing in the Crimea on Sunday
morning. Starting at noon on the 11th, we were
signalled from the Emperor "Rendezvous No. 9,"
which meant "thirty miles west of Sebastopol;" and
at sunset "Rendezvous 13," which meant "Eupatoria."
Squalls came on in the night, and our tow-ropes
parted; the Kangaroo, which towed us, ran into the
Hydaspes, and lost her bowsprit. In the morning of
the 12th we were sailing far from any of the other
ships, which appeared in different groups around us.
Land had been sighted at dawn, and before breakfast
we saw Cape Tarkan in the distance. On the previous day, the French, who had fallen astern, came
in sight; but on the 12th none of their ships were
visible all the morning, anywhere in the horizon.

On the night of the 12th, signal was made to
anchor in the prescribed order. We had Eupatoria
point on our right; the coast-line in front was low,
sandy, and perfectly open; a few white houses, with
stacks close to them, were scattered along the plain.
On the 13th we were not under way till long after
sunrise, when the columns, wheeling to the right,
stood along down the coast, and parallel to it, and
the signal was made to prepare for landing. At
half-past eleven we were nearly off Eupatoria point,

and we anchored for the night, while the place was taken possession of without opposition.

On the 14th we were taken in tow, and moved off at half-past two in the morning. There was a splendid sunrise. We kept near the shore; and anchoring about twelve miles below Eupatoria, the disembarkation commenced at about ten o'clock. Some French troops were already on shore, about two miles farther down the coast, when we began to land. The English disembarked on a narrow strip of sandy beach, having a lake on its other side. In front was a steep cliff, with only one path down, which led to the point of disembarkation. At the top of the cliff extensive plains spread all round to the horizon and the sea. Two or three Cossacks with long lances appeared on the cliff, who, as our skirmishers mounted the hill, galloped away, and the troops continued to land without molestation. During the morning some firing was heard down the coast, which proceeded from the Furious, Vesuvius, and some French steamers, who, seeing a Russian camp, with about two thousand soldiers drawn up before it, fired shells at long range, and struck and dispersed their columns, and afterwards sent some others among the horses and tents.

In the afternoon it rained, and a swell arose along the coast, which continued to increase. At night the rain came down in torrents, and the troops on the beach were drenched. Bad as their situation was, I envied it. At eight in the evening I had left the transport with another officer in a man-of-war's boat, which, assisted by two others, towed astern a large raft, formed of two clumsy boats boarded over, on which were two guns, with their detachments of artillerymen, and some horses — two of my own among them. The swell from the sea was now considerable, and made the towing of the raft a work of great labour. As we approached the shore, a horse swam past us, snorting, and surrounded by phosphorescent light as he plashed rapidly by. He had gone overboard from a raft which had upset in attempting to land. The surf was dashing very heavily on the sand, though it was too dark to see it. Fires made of broken boats and rafts were lit along the beach, and a voice hailed us authoritatively to put back and not to attempt to land, or we should go to pieces. Unwillingly the weary oarsmen turned from the shore. The swell was increasing every moment, and the raft getting more and more unmanageable. Sometimes it seemed to pull us back, sometimes it made a plunge forward, and even struck our stern, while the rain poured down with extraordinary violence. It was a long time before we reached the nearest ships, which were tossing on the swell, and not easily to be approached. The first we hailed had already a horse-boat alongside, with Lord Raglan's horses, and needed assistance, and two or three others which we passed were unable to help us. By this time the raft was fast filling with water, and the men on it were much alarmed; and our progress was so slow that we took at least ten minutes to pull from the stern to the stem of the Agamemnon. At length a rope was thrown us from a transport near, whose bows were rising on the swell like a rearing horse; and, getting the artillerymen who were on board her out of bed, we hoisted in our horses and guns;—but the gun-carriages, too heavy for our small number of hands, were lashed down to the raft, which was allowed to tow astern of the ship, and which presently sank till the water was up to the axles, when the Agamemnon sent a party and hoisted them on board, and the raft shortly after went to pieces. A horse, which had been swimming about for two hours, was also got safely on board. It was a grey, said afterwards to have been given by Omer Pasha to Lord Raglan.

The next morning the surf abated, and we were all landed without accident, as were a great many other guns and horses, under the superintendence of Captain Dacres of the Sanspareil, who was indefatigable in carrying out the arrangements of Sir Edmund Lyons, and who was warmly thanked by Lord Raglan for his exertions. Ascending from the beach to the level of the common, we saw the Allied army spread along the plains in front, the French on the right. Plenty of country waggons full of forage, driven by peasants in fur caps, with their trousers stuffed into their boots, were ranged alongside of the artillery camp,—some drawn by oxen, some by large two-humped camels.

THE ENGLISH ARMY.

The army being thus landed, it will be well to describe shortly its composition and material.

A division of infantry, under Major-General Cathcart, had joined from England just before we sailed from Varna. The English army in the Crimea then consisted of four divisions of infantry, each division consisting of two brigades, each brigade of three regiments. To each division of infantry was attached a division of artillery, consisting of two field-batteries, each battery of four 9-pounder guns, and two 24-pounder howitzers. The brigade of light cavalry was also embarked, the heavy brigade remaining at Varna. With the cavalry was a 6-pounder troop of horse artillery. In all, the British mustered 26,000 men and 54 guns; the French 24,000 men, and, I believe, about 70 guns; the Turks 4500 men, with neither cavalry nor guns.

The food supplied to the English troops by the commissariat was of very good quality. A ration for an officer or soldier was 1 lb. of meat, 1 lb. of bread, 2 oz. of rice, $1\frac{3}{4}$ oz. of sugar, 1 oz. of coffee, and half a gill of rum, for which $4\frac{1}{2}$d. was paid. The ration of meat was at one time increased to $1\frac{1}{2}$ lb.; but when provisions became scarcer this was discontinued. The ration for a cavalry, artillery, or staff horse, was 10 lb. of corn and 12 lb. of hay or straw; for a baggage animal, 8 lb. of corn.

A number of carts of a peculiar construction had been provided at Woolwich, to contain small-arm ammunition in reserve for the infantry. These, being found too heavy, were left at Varna, and the cartridges, packed in boxes or barrels, were carried on pack-horses, a great number of which had been purchased for the British government in Tunis, Syria, and Turkey. An ambulance corps, provided with light spring-waggons, containing layers of stretchers and seats for the sick and wounded, was also left behind; and disabled men were either carried on stretchers by hand, or in arabas, the common carts of Turkey and the Crimea.

CHAPTER III.

FIRST OPERATIONS IN THE CRIMEA.

THE campaign thus begun differed from all campaigns with which the reader has hitherto made himself acquainted, in some essential particulars.

According to the practice of war up to the present time, it was necessary for an invading army, on first entering an enemy's territory, to secure one or more defensible posts as depôts, from whence to draw supplies, to form hospitals, and as points to retreat upon in case of disaster. As the army advanced from these points, the lines of communication grew more assailable, and it became necessary either to leave a movable force to keep the road open, or to secure and garrison some other strong points on the line of march, from whence to oppose any attempt the enemy might make to throw himself on the line of communication. In advancing, it was also impossible to disregard any fortress or body of troops of the enemy stationed on the flank. The former must be besieged and taken, the latter attacked and routed; or a strong force must be detached to hold either in check, before the advance could be continued in safety;—and each of these necessary operations, of course, called for a certain expense of time or of material.

According to the old conditions of war, in the invasion of the Crimea near Eupatoria, and the advance on Sebastopol, the right flank of the army would be secure by resting on the sea, but the left would be totally unprotected. In the first place, the army, after landing its stores, must have strongly intrenched and garrisoned the depôt on the coast selected for them. As it advanced, the communication with this depôt must have been rendered secure, by detaching a force sufficient to repel any Russian army appearing on the flank of the line of march, and strong escorts must have accompanied all convoys between the army and its depôt. In order to leave, after these deductions, a sufficient force to carry on the siege, the invading army must have been far larger than that which the Allies possessed. It would also have been necessary to attack the fortress on that side on which the landing of the army was effected; because, a complete investment being impracticable, to have passed round the place would have been to leave the communications at the mercy of sallies from the garrison.

All these considerations were obviated by the presence of steam. The fleet, moving as the army moved, within sight of, and in constant communication with it, carried the supplies and received the sick and wounded; and had the Russians, advancing from the interior in overwhelming numbers, attacked the left, or threatened the rear, the army, falling back parallel to the coast, might have fought, and, if necessary, re-embarked, with the advantage of an immeasurably more powerful artillery—that of the fleet—than the enemy could possibly have brought into the field. Thus the calculations and provisions which so largely contributed to the difficulties of warfare, and its chances of mishap, resolved themselves into the simple measures necessary to keep the army in readiness for battle while marching on the point in view.

The French, as stated, disembarked at a point about two miles lower down the coast. From thence they extended their front across the plain till their left touched the right of the English light division, while the first division filled up the interval between the light and second divisions and the head of the lake. On the ground thus enclosed by the front of the army, the lake, and the sea, the other divisions were encamped at intervals down to the point where the disembarkation of the stores went on. In the plain, about two miles in front, might be seen a Russian villa, with its outbuildings and clumps of trees. Here was an outpost of English rifles and French light infantry, with some artillery; and close to this place the light cavalry bivouacked and made daily reconnaissances of the surrounding country. In a village beyond the lake, on the left of the army, was another outpost of riflemen. The inhabitants remained in this village, and, being paid for any poultry, forage, and vegetables they might possess, freely parted with them; and they also brought their camels, bullocks, and arabas on hire. The camels were especially fine animals—large, well-fed, sagacious-looking, and covered with smooth brown hair—very different from the gaunt, mangy dromedaries of Barbary. The indefatigable foraging of officers and men, who returned from the village at all hours laden with poultry and vegetables, very soon exhausted the scanty supplies the village contained, though at first it was easy to get fowls, turkeys, geese, melons, and pumpkins. On the third morning, taking with me a Turkish interpreter of the division, I rode to the village to try my fortune. Successful foragers, with strings of poultry hanging to their saddles, passed me, and assured me there was nothing eatable left. The houses were of mud, thatched, and standing within small stone-walled enclosures. The inquiries of the interpreter at the doors only elicited the assurance that the inhabitants had already parted with all they had, and that there was not a single goose, hen, or turkey left in the place. However, I got some melons, pumpkins, and a jar of butter. On repeating the visit next day, even these were scarcely to be obtained; and almost the only result of the expedition was a small lump of fresh butter, which a woman brought me in a gourd. Looking round for something to cover it with, I saw a peasant in a long gown and fur cap standing beside his araba, eating a water-melon, and made signs to him that I wanted a piece of the rind. He courteously choked himself in his haste to finish the eatable portion of the section he was occupied with, gave me what I wanted, and then, scooping out the heart of the melon, presented it to me on the point of his knife. I had not thought it possible that water-melons could be so delicious as this juicy mouthful proved then; certainly those of the Crimea may challenge the world.

In the mean time, the commissariat officers, indefatigable in their efforts, had purchased, or, where the presence of Cossacks or the absence of the owners rendered purchase impossible, had "lifted," large droves of sheep and oxen, so that the army had daily fresh meat of good quality. Water was scarce, and not good. A muddy well in the village afforded the principal supply, and over it a guard was placed.

On the 18th, about eighty of the 11th hussars, reconnoitring in front, were pursued by seven troops of Cossacks, and, retiring in skirmishing order, were fired upon; but the enemy kept too far aloof to do mischief. At midnight, on the 18th, the order was given for the army to advance on the following morning, the necessary supplies and reserves being all landed.

Accordingly, on the 19th, at about seven in the morning, the army commenced its march. The order of advance was by double column of companies, from the centre of divisions, the artillery on the right of their respective divisions. The day was cloudless, and the spectacle splendid. From any one of the numerous grassy heights produced by the undulations of the plain, the whole army might be seen advancing as if at a great review : the Turks close to the beach ; then the French columns ; next to them our second division, followed by the third ; and on their left the light division, followed by the first and fourth. On the left of all marched the cavalry, parties of which, as well as of the rifles and French light infantry, were in front, in skirmishing order. Close in rear of the columns came the trains of horses carrying the reserve ammunition, the baggage animals, the arabas with sick men and commissariat stores, and the droves of oxen and sheep. There was a road along the plain, but none was necessary ; everywhere the ground was smooth, grassy, and totally unenclosed. Perfect silence reigned in the vast solitudes around ; no inhabitants, nor any signs of habitation, were visible ; only sometimes a Cossack might be seen perched on a distant hillock, who presently vanished like a ghost.

In this way the army continued to march, halting occasionally, till, early in the afternoon, the Bulganak was reached. This stream, dignified in these ill-watered regions by the name of a river, is a sluggish rivulet, creeping between oozy muddy banks, along the scarcely indented surface of the plain. Though fordable everywhere, the army commenced filing across it by a bridge, the light division leading. Before reaching it, we had seen our cavalry gallop up to and over the ridge beyond, in pursuit of some

Cossacks who showed themselves, and a troop of horse artillery followed. Just as the first division began to follow the light across the bridge, we heard the guns open.

I obtained leave to go to the front and see what was going on. Arriving at the ridge, I found it lined with the troops of the light division, looking on at a skirmish of cavalry and artillery in the plain. All our cavalry, about 1000, and twelve guns, were drawn up opposite about 2000 Cossacks, whose artillery was just ceasing to fire; while ours continued to practise at them at a long range, probably 1200 yards. I rode down to the troop of horse artillery, and saw them throw some shot and shell, which appeared to fall short; but at the beginning of the skirmish the combatants had been much nearer. Three or four dragoon horses, killed by the Russian artillery, were lying about, and we had seven men of the cavalry wounded. After a time, the Cossacks slowly retired up the next ridge, behind which more of the enemy showed themselves, and Lord Raglan forbade any further advance. We found afterwards that the Russians lost in the skirmish twenty-five men and thirty-five horses. The army, withdrawing behind the ridge south of the Bulganak, prepared to bivouac; but there being reason to suppose that the enemy meditated a flank movement to attack our left, they having been seen extending in that direction at dusk, the divisions on the left had to abandon their scarce-lit fires, till the wing of the army, falling back till it rested on the Bulganak, showed a front in the required direction.

The night passed quietly, though the change of front had caused some confusion, and men who had straggled on the march were wandering about everywhere, unable to find their regiments. The English lay without cover, the tents having been left behind, with some few exceptions for generals, hospitals, and staff. The knapsacks, too, remained on board ship; and the articles judged most necessary having been selected from them, were carried, packed in the greatcoats and blankets.

The next morning we were under arms early, but did not move for some time. Marshal St Arnaud, riding along the front from an interview with Lord Raglan, was loudly cheered. A report went about that a general action was to be fought that day, which was shortly verified; and between nine and ten o'clock the army advanced, in the same order as on the day before, and over plains exactly similar in character to those we had been traversing.

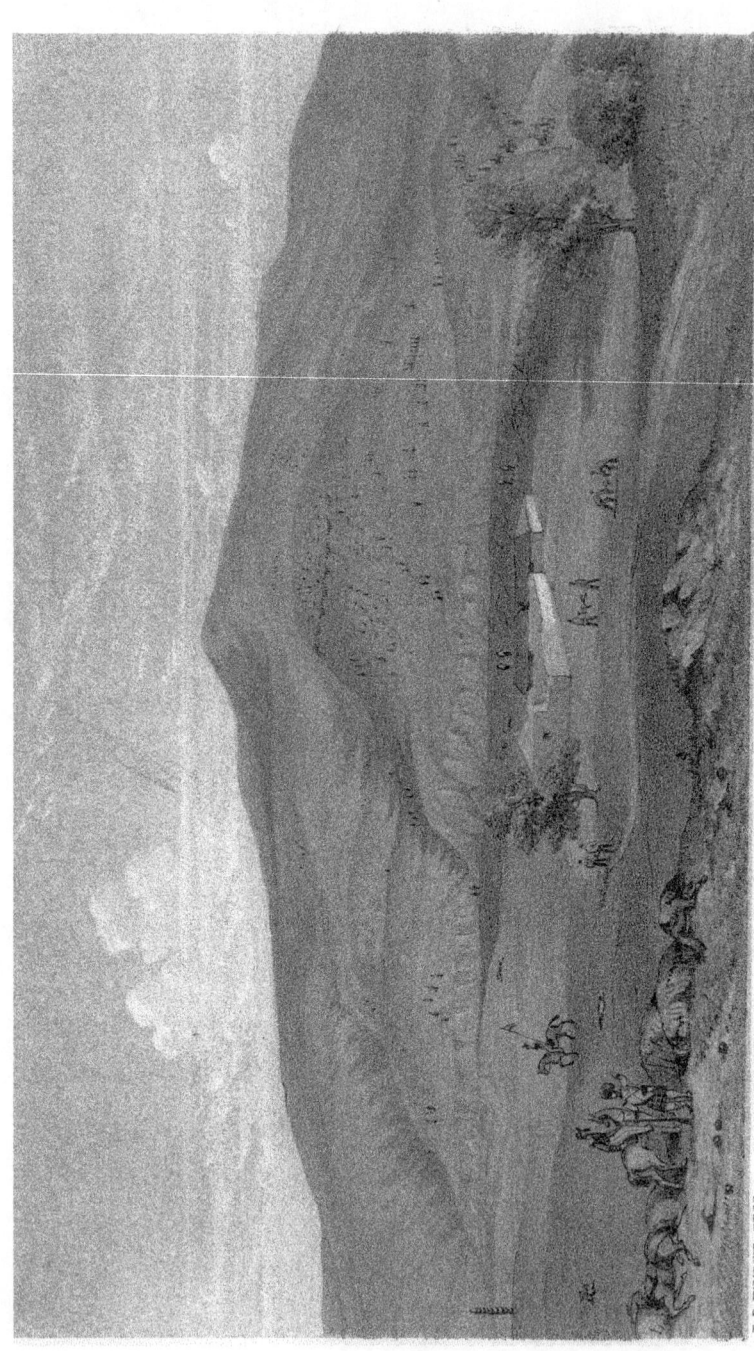

BATTLE FIELD ON THE ALMA.

CHAPTER IV.

BATTLE OF THE ALMA.

UNDER a bright sun we marched onward for about two hours, surmounting the grassy ridges which successively formed our horizon, only to see others equally solitary rising beyond. The front of the Allies was oblique, the Turks on the right being about two miles in advance of the British left.

About noon a steamer, coasting along beyond the Turks, began to fire on the land just where a sharp steep cliff terminated the shore. None of the enemy's troops were within range from the sea. The firing was precautionary, to insure an unmolested passage to the troops on the right, who were already passing the river Alma at its mouth. When the British surmounted the next ridge, the scene of the coming struggle disclosed itself.

The plain, level for about a mile, then sloped gently down to a village, beyond which was a valley sprinkled with trees, and watered by the river Alma, a narrow stream, deep in parts, and its banks very steep, but in many places fordable and easy of passage.

Between the village and the river were flat meadows and vineyards. On the opposite side of the stream the banks rose abruptly into high steep knolls, terminating in plateaus, behind which rose another and higher range of heights. Both these ranges were occupied by masses of Russian troops; the higher by the reserves, the tops of the knolls below by heavy guns, supported by cavalry and infantry on the plateaus behind. Such was the position in front of the British. In front of the French the first range of knolls grew more and more abrupt, so that guns could not be placed there, and, indeed, seemed unnecessary from the natural strength of the position. These were defended by infantry, and field artillery were posted, with more infantry, on the plains at the top of the heights. Following the course of the river to the sea, the lower range of heights, growing more and more precipitous, gradually merged in the upper, till all became one steep perpendicular cliff, traversed by one or two narrow paths, where the Turks passed in single file. This cliff, had it been held by the enemy, could have been shelled by the fleet; but the Russians, as already stated, trusting, probably, to the natural inaccessibility of this part of the position, did not occupy it, and our Ottoman allies saw no enemy that day.

The progress of the French against the heights in their own front was marked by the puffs of musketry as they swarmed up. Their advance was steady and incessant. On the plain at the top, a small building, probably intended as a signal-station, had been left unfinished, with the scaffolding still round it; and this was the point most hotly contested against the French. During the attack on it, the right of the British had, in the oblique order of advance, gradually come under the fire of the heavy artillery on the knolls, which now began to open, and our skirmishers in advance exchanged shots with the Russians in the village, who retired after setting the houses on fire, the smoke from which, rolling up the valley, rendered the view in front obscure for some time. Pennefather's brigade of the second division, advancing in line along the slope of the plain, lay down near the walls of the village for shelter from the fire of the enemy's guns, which was now incessant and destructive, and then moved onward to the river; while the light division, passing into the valley on the left of the second, continued to advance slowly,—sometimes lying down for shelter against the terrible fire of an 18-gun battery directly in their front, sometimes pressing on, till, passing the river nearly up to their necks, they began to ascend the slopes beyond, which were held by the Russian battalions.

The battery now in front of them, where the great struggle of the British took place, was, unlike the guns of the Russian centre, covered with an epaulment—that is, a thick low bank of earth, obtained in this instance from trenches dug between the spaces occupied by the guns. This battery swept the whole front of the British throughout its depth and length, and distributed its fire, sometimes on the regiments advancing to attack it, sometimes on the second division, while in and behind the village, sometimes on the first division, drawn up on the plain behind the light. Its fire was crossed by that of the guns from the knolls, which searched the village, and ploughed up the plain behind it. Between the first and second divisions was a wide road, bounded by low stone walls, leading to a bridge and ford ; and this point, being nearly intermediate between the principal lines of fire, was probably the hottest of the cannonade. Many of the 55th fell there, before advancing into the village ; and Captain Dew, of Franklin's battery, was killed by a round shot early in the action, near a large painted post beside the road. Many corpses, marked with ghastly wounds, were sprinkled on that part of the slope—two I noticed, while riding into action with Wodehouse's battery, as killed by especially horrible injuries ; a corporal of the 55th, whose brain, scooped out along with the back of his skull, was lying in a mass beside him, leaving his face perfect ; and a soldier with only a profile left, half his head being carried away. Shot and shells of various calibres whistled and bounded incessantly along this spot, so that it seemed a marvel how anybody escaped ; but the circumstance of the ground there sloping upward, in an opposite direction to the line of fire, considerably diminished the actual peril : for the shot, bounding high after striking, hit only those who were in their line within a few feet of where they touched the ground.

To oppose, however inadequately, this fire, Franklin's and Turner's batteries of the second division had come into action behind the village, the former suffering more severely during the day than any other. Turner's battery, while moving to the right, was ordered by Lord Raglan, who had crossed the river on the left of the French, to send two guns to the spot where he had stationed himself, from whence the Russian batteries were seen in reverse. Some delay was caused by a horse being shot, crossing the narrow ford; but the guns were at length brought successively into action on the opposite bank, and their fire took the Russian centre and guns in reverse; while the French, pressing up the heights, had driven back the left. Anderson's battery of the light, and Wodehouse's of the first division, being unable to come into action advantageously so far on the left, had joined the second division, and, unlimbering on the right of the road, directed a fire on the knolls in front of them. The Russian artillery on these knolls, attacked in front, and having their flank and rear threatened by the French and by the field-battery which had crossed the river, now began to retire in succession from the left, and the covering masses of infantry soon followed; and a few minutes afterwards the 18-gun battery also limbered up, and began to retreat. It was at this moment that a brigade of the light division, consisting of the 7th, 23d, and 33d regiments, very gallantly led by General Codrington, advancing up the slope under a terrible fire of musketry, pressed into the epaulment before the guns were withdrawn, and Captain Bell of the 23d running up to a driver who was urging his horses out of the fight, the man dismounted and ran away, and the gun was taken. But the Russian battalions were as yet too numerous, and their fire from the breastwork and the slope behind it too close and heavy for the regiments assailing them, and the brigade, with a loss of six hundred killed and wounded, was compelled to retire down the slope, and re-form under cover of the attack of the first division, which had been led across the river by the Duke of Cambridge to support them. The Fusilier Guards, going up to the breastwork with a cheer, retook and kept possession of the gun; the 33d and 95th came to the support of the 7th; the 19th and 47th also advanced; and after a terrible slaughter the Russians were driven back. The 55th and 30th regiments, coming up on the right of the 95th, drove back the enemy in their own front; and the three brigades, viz., Pennefather's of the second division, Codrington's of the light division, and the Guards, formed line on the ground they had won.

At this time Wodehouse's battery, which had been limbered up, and led across the river by Lieutenant-Colonel Dacres when the Russian guns ceased firing, came up on the right of the 30th regiment. The slopes in front were still covered with the enemy's skirmishers, obstinately contesting the ground with our own, and giving way, if at all, very slowly. Over the heights behind the contested battery the helmets of a Russian column might be seen; and presently the solid mass, apparently about 2000 strong, marched over the hill, and began to descend towards the British line. A shell from a gun, laid by Colonel Dacres himself before the gun detachment came up, dropt among the Russian skirmishers; the other guns, coming up in succession, opened their fire on the column, and struck it every time. Franklin's and Anderson's batteries, crossing the river, came up and opened on the left, and Paynter's followed; and the column, after marching about fifty yards down the hill, halted, turned about, and, disappearing over the crest, was seen no more. At this time some guns were brought to bear upon another column which halted in a ravine on the right, quite close to where the French skirmishers were pressing along the heights, and, apparently at a loss what to do, presented a somewhat puzzling aspect; insomuch that Sir De Lacy Evans twice stopt our fire, under the impression that the column was French, and sent a staff-officer to the nearest French regiment to inquire. But, it being presently apparent that a French column would not be in front of their own skirmishers, and some bullets from the troops in question beginning to drop into the battery, where they wounded a sergeant, the guns reopened and dispersed them; and there being none but fugitives now within sight, the batteries limbered up, and advanced in pursuit.

The battle, it will be seen, had thus rolled back to the right rear of the Russians. On the extreme right of their original position, at the top of the heights, was a battery behind an epaulment, with a flank for seven guns thrown back to prevent the right being turned. The brigade of Highlanders being on the left of the British line, found themselves, when the first division crossed the river, directly in front of this battery, which, before it followed the other guns in their retreat, poured upon them, during their advance, a heavy but ill-directed fire, doing them but little damage. At the top of the hill they met some battalions of the enemy still showing a front, and compelled them to retreat with the loss of a good many men; and two troops of horse artillery, which had crossed the river higher up, coming into action, played upon the retreating masses with great effect. Thus ended the battle of the Alma. The Russians might still be seen withdrawing in masses across the plain; but the troops, French and English, halted on the ground they had won; and the batteries, six in number, which, by advancing, had placed themselves at the apex of two irregular lines, found themselves with nothing between them and the enemy. Some withdrew behind the third division, which, together with part of the light, had been moved to the front, and others were covered by a detachment posted for the purpose on the plain.

In the advance, an officer of Wodehouse's battery, Lieutenant Richards, took prisoner a Russian general, whose horse had thrown him, and who was trying to hide himself. While he was seated on a gun-limber, Lord Raglan rode up and questioned him. In reply he said that the number of the Russians was about 50,000; that they did not expect we should ever take the position; and added that they had come to fight men, and not devils, as our red-coats seemed to be. When taken on board ship, he complained that one of his captors had deprived him of his silver snuff-box. Inquiry was made, and the artilleryman who had it gave it up; but it certainly seems no more than reasonable to expect that, if people choose to take such articles into action, they should submit to lose them with a good grace.

Two guns were taken, but the principal trophy was Prince Menschikoff's carriage, with his papers. In one despatch the general assures the Czar that the position selected on the Alma must detain the Allies at least three weeks, and that he confidently hoped it would be found altogether impregnable. It was taken in three hours.

But the Russian general did not overrate the strength of his position; his mistake was in his estimate of the troops who were to assail it. It would be difficult to find a position more defensible in itself, and almost impossible to select another equally strong, where the ground in front is so favourable to the artillery fire of the defenders, and so devoid of all shelter from it. However, one other position as strong, or even stronger, exists on the river Katcha, five miles distant from the Alma, on which we expected to find the Russians had fallen back.

Two men of literary celebrity witnessed the action —Mr Layard, who saw it from the ships, and the author of *Eothen*, who rode with Lord Raglan's staff throughout the day.

CHAPTER V.

THE BATTLE-FIELD.

GOING out of our camp next morning, to see where our own division lay, I heard a moaning on my right, on the bank of one of the ravines we had fired up the preceding day. Proceeding towards the sound, I found it came from a wounded Russian, who had made a pillow of the corpse of a brother soldier which lay on its back, its breast pierced, and left arm broken by a round shot. Beside these lay two other soldiers, one alive, wounded in the head, and resting, like the other sufferer, on a comrade's corpse, which lay on its face. The first man, by signs and words, earnestly begged for water, which was brought him, and a surgeon coming up, examined his wounds. The flesh of both his thighs had been torn away; he was too badly injured to be moved, or even relieved otherwise than by trying to make him comfortable as he lay; and next morning it was a relief to hear that he had died in the night. On the knoll around were about a dozen wounded men, who had lain there all night in torment, and to whom our soldiers now afforded a temporary relief.

The sides of the ravine, or rather gully, were sprinkled all the way with bodies, and with knapsacks and accoutrements thrown away by the flying enemy. On the slopes, too, and the paths crossing them, were lying dead men here and there, with scattered knapsacks and arms. One dead Russian appeared to have been lying on his back, probably wounded, or perhaps killed, when a shot from our batteries, towards which his head was turned, had carried away all his features, leaving an unsightly block, and had broken his foot short off at the instep, where it hung back as if on a hinge.

But it was not till reaching the plain on which stood the unfinished signal-tower, already mentioned as the contested point in the French attack, that there appeared signs of a sanguinary conflict. Many Russians lay dead there, and they lay thicker near the signal-tower, the hillock on which it was built being strewn with them. Three or four had been bayoneted while defending the entrance; and in the narrow space within, which was divided into compartments, were three or four small groups, slain in the defence. Another spot near contained three or four hundred corpses.

Riding back up the course of the river, we came to the slopes where the British had been most warmly engaged; and here it was that the real nature of the struggle first became apparent. The slope below the epaulment, on which the 18-gun battery had been posted, was covered with men of the 7th, 23d, and

33d, thickly intermixed with grey-coated, helmeted Russians. Within the breastwork the enemy lay in ranks. One company seemed to have fallen as it stood; there was no heaping of the bodies one on another, but it would have been difficult to step between them. Some lay with their faces buried in the soil, as if they had fallen as they turned to fly; others on their backs with bullet-holes through their foreheads; a few had their hands outstretched, as if still grasping their weapons, or grappling with their enemy. Altogether, I estimated the bodies in and about the breastwork at seven or eight hundred, of whom two-thirds were Russians; and the returns of the officers charged with the burial duty did not much differ from that conjecture.

Passing onward to the right of the Russian position, the plain was again thickly strewn with dead; the tall bear-skins showing where the Guards had fought. In a narrow hollow way I observed a line of Russians, who seemed to have fallen while using it as a breastwork. Ascending the slope to the top of the position, the bodies there bore the marks of cannon shot; this was where our fire had turned the column. In a spot to the left, fifty or sixty bodies showed where the Highlanders had poured in their fire at the close of the battle; and again, on the plains at the top of the heights, files of slain, with the round shot still in some instances sticking in the farthest body, marked the line of retreat where the artillery had last fired upon the enemy.

All over the ground, so grimly strewn, were numerous parties burying the dead, and carrying off the wounded, both friends and foes. Hospitals had been established in the village north of the river, in some empty houses on each side of the road. Here the surgeons of the army, and some from the navy, were in terribly full practice ; and as those whose wounds were already dressed were borne to the sea, others from the field took their places. Parties of sailors carrying hammocks assisted the soldiers, who were provided with stretchers for the wounded, and the road to the beach was crowded with these. Some stray Cossacks were seen during the day hovering on our flank and rear, and a detachment of cavalry patrolled the plain we had been marshalled on the day before, to protect the hospitals and burial parties. As I stood on this plain, sketching the position of the Russian army, a clergyman approached an open grave, to the edge of which a party of artillerymen brought a body wrapped in a cloak. It was that of Lieutenant Cockerell, whose leg had been carried away by a cannon shot the day before, while in action with his battery near this spot, and who had died after amputation.

Two entire days were occupied in removing the traces of conflict and carrying the wounded to the ships. The Russian arms and accoutrements left on the field were collected in heaps, from whence the curious gathered trophies to hand down to posterity, as mementoes of a famous field. The eagles on the front of the helmets of the Imperial Guard seemed in greatest request for this purpose; and though, on the second evening, I examined some hundreds of these helmets, I found all had been stript of the ornaments, so I contented myself with a pouch-belt. Some were so fortunate as to get excellent rifles, but the common muskets were very shabby in appearance, and were mostly thrown away after being broken. One English soldier was said to have found forty gold pieces on a dead body; and I heard of a drummer of the Guards who, assisting a wounded Russian officer, received from him his purse. This the man took care of, and gave to the captain of his company, who forwarded it to the Russian on board ship; but it was returned, with a request that the drummer would keep it as a token of the owner's gratitude.

On the plain near the signal-tower, where the struggle was hottest on the part of the French, our allies left a stone, inscribed "Victoire de l'Alma," with the date. The English left no monument on their fatal hill; but it needs none. The inhabitants will return to the valley, the burnt village will be rebuilt, the wasted vineyards replanted, and tillage will efface the traces of the conflict; but tradition will for centuries continue to point, with no doubtful finger, to the spot where the British infantry, thinned by a storm of cannon-shot, drove the battalions of the Czar, with terrible slaughter, from one of the strongest positions in Europe.

CHAPTER VI.

THE KATCHA AND THE BALBEK.

AMID this scene of blood, it seemed unnatural that any one could find time to die other than a violent death. But the cholera still exacted its daily tribute. Major Wellesley of the Staff died of it on the morning of the battle. Brigadier Tylden, of the Engineers, whom I met riding over the ground in good health on the following day, never left the field, but expired after a few hours' illness; and there were many others who passed unharmed through the combat, only to die a less soldierly death by pestilence.

The road between the Alma and the Katcha, traversed by the army on the 23d, lay as before over dry grassy plains. Here we expected to find the enemy awaiting us; but, ascending the ridge which overlooks the valley, we saw the heights unoccupied. The lesson on the Alma had been so sharp that the enemy never stood again in the field; and could he have found heart to hold the position, it would scarcely have been prudent for him to risk a battle where the pursuit might carry the victors into Sebastopol along with the vanquished.

The position on the Katcha is, in one respect, more advantageous than that on the Alma. Like the latter, it has a village on the north bank of the river, beyond which is a plain; but the plain, in this instance, instead of sloping upwards against the line of fire, is quite level for about three quarters of a mile; and the lower range of heights on which the cannon would have been posted being less elevated than the knolls occupied by the artillery at the Alma, every shot that bounded along the plain would have told with double effect. Except at the ford, the banks of the river were high, and as steep as the sides of a trench. It was such a position as English troops would have held against the world in arms; and had the enemy made a determined stand there, the conflict would have been no less desperate and bloody than that of the 20th.

Though it was scarcely noon when we reached the heights beyond the river, we encamped there for the night. The village extended for some distance along the narrow valley, and became, up the stream, extremely pretty, with nice white houses standing amid poplars, and surrounded by vineyards, gardens, and stackyards. The cottages had been deserted in evident haste; bedsteads were still standing; large chests which had apparently held the household gods and treasures were open and empty; and there were cradles from which the infants had lately been snatched in hurry and alarm. All the cottages were very neat and clean, and the furniture spoke of comfort. This, as well as the doors and rafters, was appropriated by the soldiers as firewood to cook their rations; and from every door-way might be seen a forager with a beam, a bench, or a chest, and under every camp-fire were blazing the splinters of some cherished Lar, or long-descended heirloom. Many cats lingered with feline tenacity about these forsaken thresholds, winking lazily at the new-comers as they suckled their kittens in the sun, and apparently indifferent, so that mice were plentiful, whether Russians or British held the village. I carried a small black one, which one of our people picked up on the bank of the river, on my holsters for some time, feeding him with biscuit; but during my absence from the saddle he made off. Many ownerless dogs made friends with the army here, and, no doubt, will long be found in the ranks, all answering, of course, to the name of Katcha. At this place the Scots Greys and the 57th regiment joined the army.

Between this river and the Balbek the Allied armies marched so close to each other, on the 24th, that the red coats almost intermingled with the blue; and the officers of the two nations rode together, Prince Napoleon conversing with the Duke of Cambridge. The Guards and Highlanders were on the right, and were much admired by the French officers, who called them "superb" and "magnificent." They also praised highly our artillery, the horses and equipment of which were certainly not to be surpassed.

A yawning rift, half a mile wide, separates the heights on the opposite sides of the Balbek. Beyond the stream the aspect of the country changes from grassy plains to hills, divided by deep ravines, and covered with low oak-coppice. A steep road, which the English and French artillery descended together, led us to the river. Down the hill we found two waggons, painted green, abandoned by the Russians: they contained a great number of copper pans and dishes, and about 20,000 rounds of rifle ammunition, the balls pointed, and fitting a two-grooved rifle. The Russian method of folding a cartridge is particularly neat and convenient: the end can be twisted off and the powder exposed in a moment.

Passing up the valley to the river, we came to a small villa, which had been plundered by the retreating Russians. I rode up the road leading to the courtyard, and, tying my horse to the garden railing, entered the house. On the steps of the porch were some broken arm-chairs covered with yellow damask. In a room on the right were broken sofas, chairs, and card-tables heaped together, and a piano, still tuneable, with the front board torn off, exposing the keys. Upstairs was a small library, where a good many French books lay scattered on the floor. Portraits of a lady and gentleman, of a very low signboard-kind-of-order of art, had been torn from their frames; and two fine mirrors, quite uninjured, in gilt frames, leant against the wall amid a heap of other furniture. In front of the house was a garden laid out in flower-beds, with fruit-trees in the midst of them. I climbed into a tree bearing still some large yellow plums, and found them delicious, though rather over-ripe. On the right of the garden was a vineyard with plenty of grapes. On the left a fence, lined with dahlias in full bloom, gay in colour, though not of high floricultural rank, separated the garden from a kind of orchard of apple, pear, and peach trees. Under the latter the fruit lay thick on the ground, and before riding off I filled my haversack to furnish a dessert.

Passing the river we ascended a narrow, stony, winding road, leading up a steep ravine; and, emerging into plainer ground at the top, pitched our tents amid the coppice, in the pleasantest camping-ground we had yet found in the Crimea. While dinner was getting ready, the allurements of which were heightened by the presence of a fine cabbage and a pumpkin from the garden of the villa, I took off my haversack to display the dessert it contained. But the transformation of the money in the Eastern tale into dry leaves, was not more disappointing to the owner than the spectacle now revealed. The ripeness of the fruit had unfitted it to bear the jolting of my horse. Plums and peaches were squeezed into a shapeless compound, and mixed with crumbs of ration biscuit; while in the centre of the mass lay imbedded a piece of dried tongue, escaped from its envelope; and the expressed juice of the fruit, partly running down the leg of my trousers, partly absorbed by my forage-cap, which was in my haversack, had turned the colour of those articles of dress from their original blue to a dirty olive-green. However, the pumpkin, mashed in the Yankee fashion, and the boiled cabbage, turned out so good, that no vain regrets were expended on my unfortunate contribution to the feast.

We were now so close to the great object of the expedition that, by going up the road about a mile and a half, the towers and fortifications of Sebastopol were seen, at no great distance, in the basin below. This was the north front of the place, to strengthen which all the efforts of the Russian engineers had been directed since the expedition had been first talked of. The whole of the ground there was supposed to be rendered deadly by batteries and mines, and the next move in the game was anxiously awaited. We had halted two nights on this ground, during which the cavalry and horse artillery, who were on outpost duty, led a hard life. The horses had neither forage nor water for forty-eight hours, all which time they remained accoutred and harnessed ; and the men and officers did not, for these and two other days, taste meat.

CHAPTER VII.

THE FLANK MARCH.

TOWARDS noon on the 26th the artillery of the First Division received orders to march immediately, without waiting for the infantry, up the road near which we were encamped. Proceeding about a mile, we came to a white house on the roadside, in front of which Lord Raglan and General Airey were seated looking at a map. His lordship motioned us to take a by-road into the woods on our left, and called out to us to go south-east. Accordingly we went on, steering by the sun, and following the main path, which was overhung with bushes. After proceeding in this way for an hour, our progress was stopped by a troop of our horse artillery, halted in the road in front. Finding themselves unsupported by cavalry, they had naturally become alarmed for the safety of their right flank and front in a spot where artillery would be taken at a great disadvantage if attacked by skirmishers, who might pick off the men and horses, and capture the guns without risk.

Presently Lord Raglan came riding up, followed

by his staff, and demanded sharply why we had halted; and, going to the troop in front, ordered them immediately to proceed, himself leading the way. Accordingly, we advanced through the wood for about three miles farther, when Lord Raglan and his staff came back in haste, inquiring for the cavalry. In an open space in front of us they had come suddenly on a Russian force, marching at right angles to our own.

Had the enemy, whose numbers were variously estimated at from ten to fifteen thousand men, known our order of march, they might, by throwing a sufficient force of infantry into the wood, have captured, or at any rate disabled, about twenty of our guns. The cavalry, some squadrons of which presently trotted past us to the front, could not have acted efficiently against musketry in a thick wood; the artillery themselves could not have acted at all; and our own infantry, with the exception of a small body of the rifles, which presently followed the hussars to the front, was still some miles in rear. Luckily the enemy, far from adopting any such bold measure, at once took to flight, the meeting being no more expected, and much less desired, by him than by us; and our horse artillery, debouching into the open space, opened at once on the rear of the fugitives, who, in their haste, left some carriages with baggage and ammunition on the plain.

On this small plain, which is surrounded by trees, stands a large white house, known as Mackenzie's

Farm. From Sebastopol a road crosses it at right angles to the one we had come by, ascending very steeply from the plains below, on the side of the city, and descending again on the left after passing the farm. Down the road to the left the troop of horse artillery (Maude's) pressed in pursuit, and came up with some infantry, who, turning on the skirts of the wood, fired a volley, which did no damage, and ran into the bushes; when the artillery, unlimbering, opened with case shot, and killed several. Some of the Scots Greys, dismounting, went skirmishing through the wood, and about a dozen Russians, throwing themselves down and pretending to be dead, rose after they were past and fired on them, for which discreditable ruse they were, as they deserved to be, all put to death.

In the mean time, all the artillery was brought into the open space and placed in position in both directions, so as to open on the force that had passed us if it returned, or on any other body which might be following it. Going to the edge of the plain opposite the side we had debouched from, we found ourselves on the edge of a steep cliff descending to the plains below, along which was retreating a train of carriages which, cut off by our advance, had turned back by the road they came. A gun was moved down this road, and some rounds were fired, with no other effect, however, than accelerating their flight, and causing them to abandon some of their vehicles.

Those left on the plain were immediately submitted by the artillerymen and dragoons to a rigorous examination. They appeared to contain the wardrobe of some luckless cavalry officer. Blue jackets, trimmed with black fur, and laced with silver, silver sashes, smart shakos, marked with the number "12" in silver, and gorgeous shabracks, were among the spoils. There were also fine shirts and other garments, a looking-glass in an inlaid tortoise-shell case, which I tried in vain to tempt the captor to sell me (he said if he was spared he hoped to look at himself in it in England), and a sort of altar-piece, in a great wooden case with folding doors, which, being thrown back, disclosed a goodly assemblage of saints and sacred personages, whose figures were gilt; while their faces, appearing through holes left in the metal, were beautifully painted on ivory behind. There was some concealed machinery by which the figures were moved. My own share of the spoil was a large bucket filled with corn attached to one of the carriages, into which my horse immediately plunged his muzzle, having had but short rations for some days past.

By degrees the divisions of infantry came through the wood, and formed on the plain. The cavalry, coming back from the pursuit, brought in a few prisoners, mounted on Russian carriages, with some pairs of nice horses. An officer was taken, to whom the Duke of Cambridge put some questions in French about the late battle. "Ah," he said, "our men fought well enough, but 'tis of no use—your infantry are the best in the world."

Before we resumed our march, a dull deep roar was heard behind us, and from amid the trees ascended a column of smoke, itself in shape like a magnificent tree, its rounded outlines spreading, like white foliage, high and wide. This was the explosion of some ammunition waggons of the enemy, which Captain Fortescue of the artillery had been ordered to blow up. Then the divisions moved in their accustomed order of march down the steep chalky hill, on the precipitous side of which were numerous carts and waggons, upset by those who had fled back by the road they came. The march was slow, and the stoppages, from the carriages and waggons halting on the steep, frequent; and, though evening was approaching, we still had to traverse some miles of plain before reaching water. These plains had a surface of chalk covered thinly with grass, amid which the white dust rose in clouds at every step, and chalky hills were all around. At length, after a long and weary march, we reached the river Tchernaya, which runs through the valley of Inkermann, and pitched our tents after nightfall, while the rear divisions and batteries did not arrive till some hours afterwards. During the night, the redness of the sky above the heights on which Mackenzie's Farm stands, showed that our allies, following in our steps, were encamping there.

It is not easy to define the object of the Russian troops in thus sallying from Sebastopol. Probably it was done with a view to operate in the woods in our rear during the siege, on the supposition that we would attack the fortress from our camp on the Balbek. But for the halt which our artillery made in the wood, it would have debouched at Mackenzie's Farm, across the middle instead of across the rear of the enemy's column of route. Had the infantry been close, in sufficient force to support us, this would have insured the discomfiture of the Russians, and the capture of many prisoners. But, under the actual circumstances, we may consider the halt fortunate, and console ourselves with thinking all's well that ends well.

CHAPTER VIII.

OCCUPATION OF BALAKLAVA.

ON the 27th we only went about four miles; but the consequences of the long and fatiguing march of the day before, showed themselves directly we started. Men, fallen out of the ranks, began to strew the roadside, many of them in the agonies of cholera; and, within a mile, I saw at least fifty or sixty Highlanders lying exhausted. On this day Colonel Cox, of the Guards, seized with cholera, was taken up on one of our gun-limbers, and, going on shipboard, died the same evening.

Before noon the first division halted at the mouth of a gorge between very lofty hills; and up the heights enclosing it, the brigades of the light division advanced, one on each side; while some riflemen took possession of a low pointed hill in the valley, crowned with a white house. From beyond this hill we presently heard some of the guns of the light division, and the smoke of others also rolled back over the heights on the left, while a shell or two from the enemy burst over the valley. The Guards were moved forward into a village at the mouth of the gorge, down which appeared a piece of water like a small lake, closed at the other extremity by a high hill crowned by a long wall with towers, looking in the distance like a respectable fort. Presently ships' guns were heard from the sea. Our own continued to fire from the height on the left, and dust flew from the walls where they struck; while the garrison, instead of continuing to reply, ran along the edge of the wall towards the sea, apparently in great agitation. A party of Rifles, moving up the slopes, entered the place and followed the garrison along the wall, and a white flag showed that Balaklava had surrendered, fortunately without any blood spilt; while a small English steamer, appearing suddenly on the piece of water below, assured us that the harbour was our own, and our communication with the fleet re-established.

The manœuvre, now successfully accomplished, of transferring the army from the north to the south side of Sebastopol, would, as before remarked, have been impossible under the old conditions of war. With a stationary depôt north of Sebastopol, convoys with munitions could not have been taken past the fortress, unless guarded by detachments of such strength as could not have been spared from the army, and then only with constant risk of interruption and loss. To transfer this depôt to the south side of the fortress, in sailing ships, the first condition must have been a favourable wind; and, when the fleet had obtained this, and taken advantage of it, the manœuvre, detected from the fortress, would have been baffled by the interposition of a Russian force on the land side of Balaklava. But, thanks to steam, the army could afford to abandon its communications with the fleet on the Balbek, confident of resuming them at the point concerted ; and the labours of the Russian engineers, long directed solely to resist the anticipated attack on the north side, were, by this unexpected movement, rendered unavailing.

As Balaklava henceforth becomes a place of importance in the narrative of the campaign, it is worth describing, and indeed deserves notice from its picturesque beauty.

The valley, extending less than a mile from the gorge to the edge of the harbour, consists of gardens, meadows, and vineyards, the latter spreading a little way up the slopes on each side till the hard rock forbids further cultivation. To the soldiers, long accustomed to eat their ration, fresh or salt, with the vegetable accompaniment of rice only, the vineyards, rich with clusters of ripe grapes, and the gardens, abounding overhead in apples and plums, and underfoot in pumpkins, tomatas, and cabbages, all of excellent quality, appeared a paradise. The last-mentioned vegetable seemed especially agreeable to the military palate ; and men of all arms of the service might be seen crossing the meadows, bearing on their shoulders long poles, on which whole rows of cabbages were impaled. Clusters of trees were intermingled with the spots of tillage, and a small stream, filling wells as it went, flowed along the meadows.

The harbour, a narrow inlet of the sea winding between steep barren heights, looked more like a fresh-water lake than an arm of the ocean, its mouth being concealed by an abrupt bend. I have seen something like it in the basins of the hills around Snowdon and Cader-Idris. Except at the upper extremity, where it grows shallow, it shelves down to an extraordinary depth close to the shore. Its greatest width is about 400 yards. In the course of the afternoon many ships came in and ranged themselves side by side close to the south shore;—the Agamemnon, towering above the rest, looked like the old puzzle of the reel in the bottle on a magnificent scale. The town, consisting of several narrow streets, stands on the south shore; the women, apprehensive of ill treatment, had fled to the opposite side, but a staff-officer crossing to assure them of safety, several boat-loads returned. Amongst them was a poor lady who told me in French that she had left Sebastopol only the day before, "to escape from the English:" she submitted with exceeding good grace to the will of fate. Outside the guardroom were ranged in order the garrison to the number of eighty, with their venerable white mustached commandant, prisoners of war, their arms being piled on the ground in front. Behind the town the rock slopes very steeply up to the wall and the towers at the top. These, built in rude times, and unrepaired for centuries, are absolutely useless for defence. The ruinous towers seem ready to topple over with the first footstep that ascends their broken stair ; huge gaps yawn in the intervening walls ; and the portions of the latter still standing show, by their thin parapet raised in front of a narrow path, that they were intended to resist an enemy who knew not the use of cannon. Nevertheless, at a distance these shattered stones wore an imposing and martial aspect, like an ancient suit of mail in an armoury. There were no guns in the place, and the shells fired at us were from a mortar.

CHAPTER IX.

THE POSITION BEFORE SEBASTOPOL.

Most of the inhabitants of the valley had left the doors of their houses locked, as if they intended to return shortly, and expected to find things as they had left them. But, notwithstanding a general order (called forth by a great slaughter of turkeys, geese, and hens, with rifles and revolvers) that private property was to be respected, the houses in Kadukoi, the village at the entrance of the valley, were pillaged, and the doors, window-sashes, and rafters for the most part taken away for firewood. Some of the chiefs of the army took up their quarters in Balaklava; a post-office was established, and ships laden with siege materials were brought into the harbour and ranged along the road in front of the houses, which the great depth of water close to the shore rendered almost as accessible and convenient as a wharf. Private speculators set up stores for the sale of grocery and clothing; cargoes of the same articles were brought from Constantinople in the hired transports; and in most instances advantage was taken of the necessities of the troops to demand shamefully exorbitant prices. Meantime the third, fourth, and light divisions were moved up to the heights of Sebastopol, and bivouacked within long cannon-range of the fortress. Some shot, pitched into their positions, forced them to move, on different occasions, a little to the rear; but, after a time, this ineffectual annoyance was for the most part discontinued, and at the beginning of October the rest of the Allied army was moved up to the position it was intended to occupy, leaving the cavalry, a troop of horse-artillery, the 93d regiment, and some marines and seamen, with guns from the fleet, to protect Balaklava.

For eight days the time was spent in landing and bringing up the materials and armament for the batteries of attack ; and these being collected in sufficient numbers, the trenches were opened. This process was rendered very difficult and laborious by the soil, which was extremely rocky, and the progress made in it necessarily slow. As the whole interest of the campaign was now focussed in this particular portion of the Crimea, it will be well to describe minutely the position which was soon to become the theatre of a series of conflicts. These would be but imperfectly understood without a fuller idea than a map can give of the whole of the ground occupied by the Allied army, and by the enemy.

Looking at a map of the Crimea, the reader will see that a valley extends from the inner end of the harbour of Sebastopol, where the Tchernaya runs into it, to that of Balaklava. From the former harbour to the ruins of Inkermann the valley is from 1200 to 1500 yards wide; then the heights on either side separate till, at the point where the road to Mackenzie's Farm crosses the Tchernaya, they are nearly four miles asunder. Here a rounded cluster of gentle eminences divides the valley into two defiles: these, sweeping round from south-east to south-west, unite in one plain, which, traversed by small hills, spreads to the gorge of the valley of Balaklava, and up to the heights right and left. Thus this valley, extending from one harbour to the other, forms a wide neck to a small peninsula, of which Cape Kherson is the extremity, and on which the Allied troops took their position. This peninsula, having steep cliffs at the sea-shore, consists of a high undulating plain, or range of plains, cleft by deep gullies that descend gradually to the basin in which lies Sebastopol. From a point opposite the ruins of Inkermann, to that where the road from Sebastopol descends to Balaklava, the range of heights bounding the valley is unbroken, except at a point easily defensible, where the Woronzoff road crosses it. But to the left of the point opposite the ruins of Inkermann the ground south of the Tchernaya slopes upward so gradually as to oppose no serious obstacle to the advance of troops to the heights, while the English division posted there was not on the ridge looking into the valley, but on another ridge in rear of it. Thus the space between the right of the Allied batteries of attack and the heights opposite Inkermann was, while unintrenched, the weak point of the position. The ground will be more minutely described in an account of the two actions of which it was the scene.

The harbour of Balaklava lies, as has been said, in a cleft between high and steep mountains. Beyond the inner extremity of the harbour this cleft continues itself for about half a mile in the small cultivated valley described in the last chapter. A row of low isolated hills extends across the entrance of the valley and up the heights on each side, to the plains of the peninsula on the one hand, and to the cliffs above the sea on the other, thus forming a natural line of defensive posts. At about 3000 yards in front of these, on the plain, sweeping, as before described, from the valley of the Tchernaya, is another range of isolated hills, the left of which is within cannon-shot of the heights held by the Allies, and the right one near the village of Kamara, which lies on the mountains forming the southern boundary of the plain. This last range of hills, crowned with small intrenched works armed with artillery, and garrisoned by Turks, formed the outposts of the Allies in front of Balaklava. Thus, the position extended from the sea-shore in front of Sebastopol round the heights of the peninsula to the Woronzoff road, and thence across to the last hill on the plain near Kamara; while an inner line of posts extended across the entrance of Balaklava valley, up to the heights of the peninsula on the left and round to the

MONASTERY OF St GEORGE.

sea-cliffs on the right, enclosing valley, town, and harbour.

Of the gullies already mentioned as channelling the plains, the principal one divides the peninsula nearly in half. Resembling at first a wide ditch between grassy slopes, it gradually becomes a deep winding ravine with steep rocky sides like the dry bed of a wide river, and descends to the basin of the inner harbour. The left of the English lines in front of Sebastopol rested on one margin of this ravine, the right of the French lines on the other. The greater part of the French troops were encamped behind their lines on the site of the ancient Khersonesus, leaving a large space by the sea unoccupied. Their supplies were landed at Kamiesch Bay, one of the deep narrow recesses of Cape Kherson, from whence to Sebastopol the coast is indented by many inlets. There a fleet of transports assembled, so numerous that their masts looked like a forest; and a wharf afforded the necessary convenience for landing the multitude of stores which crowded the beach and the environs of a small city of tents.

Half-way between Cape Kherson and Balaklava the bold coast line turns back at a sharp angle, close to the site of an ancient temple of Diana, now occupied by the monastery of St George. It stands on the edge of a high sloping cliff, and consists of a long low range of white buildings, with pillared porticoes and green roofs and domes. The cliff it stands on is of yellow clayey stone; the next headland southward, abutting far beyond it, is of extreme richness of colour—a deep pearly grey, dashed with dark red, of a tone which, even on a gloomy day, imparts to the mass a kind of sunset radiance and glow. A sergeant's guard of Zouaves is stationed in one of the buildings, and many Russian families continue to inhabit the place. Passing through the edifice by a steep flight of steps, a gallery is reached extending along the upper face of the cliff. Terraces connected by a winding path jut out below, and near its base the rock is clothed with a shrubbery of small firs. There was a sound of chanting as we passed along the balcony: the Zouave who accompanied us opened a door, and motioned us in without ceremony. The place was a very small low chapel, its walls hung with sacred pictures executed with elaborate vileness. A priest in a red garment was reading prayers to some others who sung the responses. He was bareheaded, but the rest, clad in black gowns, wore tall cylindrical caps, from which black veils descended behind. There was something strange in coming thus suddenly from a great camp into the presence of this secluded brotherhood, whose devotions, usually accompanied only by the dashing of the waves below, were now broken by the less seemly sound of the distant bombardment.

The whole of these plains are probably much the same in aspect now as in the days when Diana's worshippers crossed them on the way to her temple. A short dry turf, scarcely clothing the grey rock, which

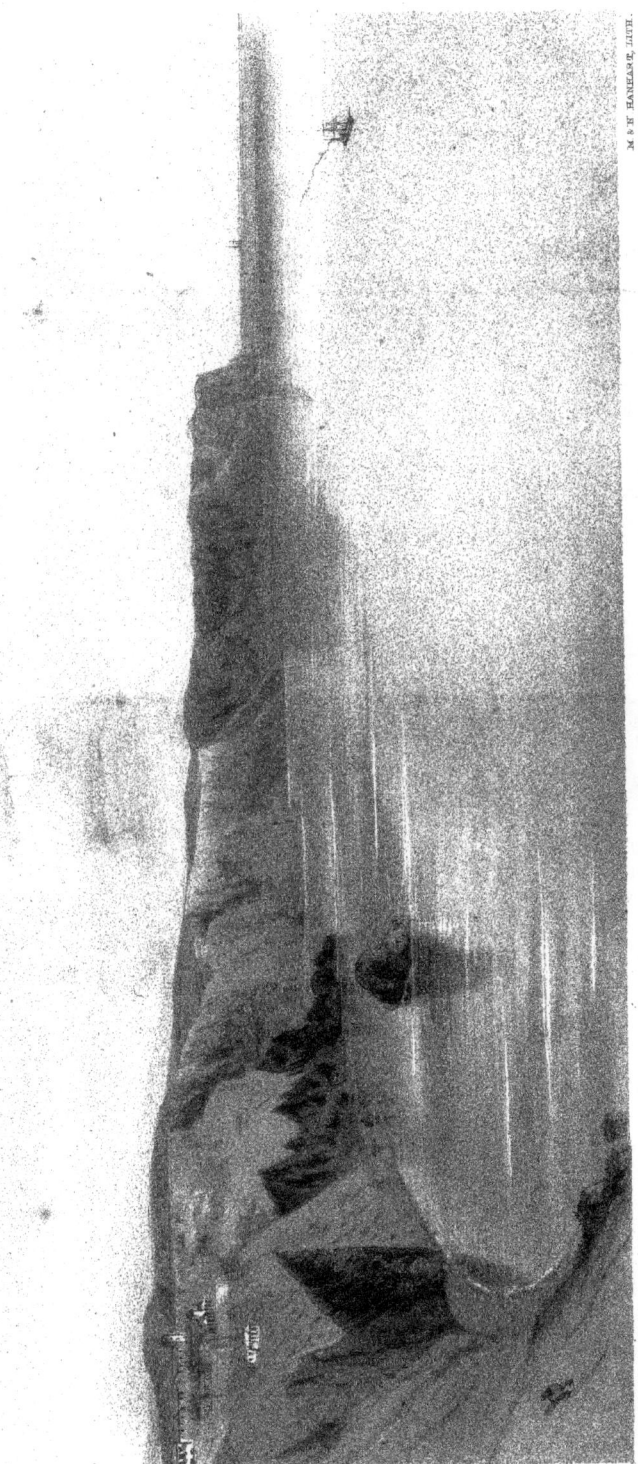

CLIFFS OF THE MONASTERY OF ST GEORGE.

everywhere pushes its fragments through, is, except the patches of coppice, the only verdure. No fields nor gardens tell of an attempt to make the soil productive, but here and there vines cling to the side of a slope where the earth is deepest, and are enclosed by walls of loose stone. A few trees, soon cut down for firewood, surrounded the farm-houses, and others grew at intervals down the course of the larger ravines. Lit by a warm sun, bounded by a blue sea, and enlivened by the view of the white-walled city, the aspect of the plains in October was fresh and almost cheerful, while, looking inland, the tumbled masses of hills always lent grandeur to the landscape. But when a north wind whistled piercingly across the heights; when the dense fogs of November hung their grey drapery along the horizon, and rested in cold white masses on the hills; when the green turf grew mire, and the leafy coppice a texture of wet brown twigs and roots, and yellow turbid pools settled along the course of the ravines, it was no wonder that the tents of the Arab, who is at least dry and warm in his desert, seemed preferable to the camp before Sebastopol, and that the hardiest soldiers turned now and then a longing thought to the firesides of England.

CHAPTER X.

COMMENCEMENT OF THE SIEGE.

THE ravines already mentioned, five in number, beginning in the middle of the plains of the peninsula, descend in courses, more or less winding, to the basin of the harbour. On the slopes of the plain, between these ravines, the English batteries were traced. In front of them, in the angle made by the outer and inner harbours, and on our right of the latter, stand some large public buildings belonging to the dockyard, and a large barrack. These, in the absence of permanent defensive works, were covered by strong and solid earthen batteries on commanding points, thrown up simultaneously with the progress of our own trenches. In front of the right of our attack on a conical hill was a round tower called the Malakhoff, surrounded by an intrenchment armed on all sides with heavy guns. Next was a very large battery, composed of two faces meeting in a salient angle; this was known during the siege as the Redan. Near the inner harbour was another, known as the Barrack Battery, capable of firing on our left batteries or on the French. These were all that were immediately opposed to us, besides the broadsides of a line-of-battle ship in the inner harbour, and the long guns of some steamers.

Between the English camps and the fortress the ground sloped upward to a ridge, and then downward towards the Russian batteries. It is evident that the farther down these slopes our trenches were placed, the more they were commanded by the enemy, and the higher must be the parapets to cover us from their fire. In such very stony and deficient soil it would have been almost impossible to obtain the requisite amount of earth very low down on the slopes, and our first batteries were placed on some spots where the ground rose gently upward for a space on the face of the descent.

From the left of the great ravine to the Quarantine Harbour the ground is comparatively flat and unbroken, and on the right portion of this space the French trenches were opened at much shorter range than those of the English. In the angle of the outer and inner harbours, opposite the French attack, stands the town of Sebastopol, protected partly by parapets of masonry, partly by earthen batteries.

The distinctive features of the campaign have been noticed in a preceding chapter; the siege now commenced had also its peculiarities.

In ordinary sieges, the place having been completely invested so as to confine the garrison to its own resources, the trenches are opened at about 600 yards, enclosing one or more salient points of the fortifications. Thus the works of the assailants being on the arc of the outer of two concentric circles described from a point within the fortress, while the defences are on the arc of the inner one, 600 yards nearer the centre, it follows that the besiegers always have space for a far greater number of guns than are mounted on the works to oppose them. When the superior fire from the batteries in the trenches has overpowered that of the place, the works are pushed forward; other batteries are established close enough to breach the walls; and the breach becoming practicable, the assault is made, and the garrison being overpowered by superior numbers, the place is taken.

In the present instance, the assailing force being insufficient to enclose the whole extent of front, the southern side of the harbour only was invested, leaving the formidable forts on the north unassailed, and the road from the interior free for supplies of all kinds. The front attacked being about three miles in extent, the space at the disposal of the garrison enabled them to reply with at least as many guns as the besiegers could bring to attack them. But had the Russian batteries been totally silenced, and the south side taken by assault, the outer harbour, acting as a huge wet ditch, presented a fresh obstacle, backed by a fresh line of batteries, and rendered a new series of operations necessary. If the harbour had remained open, the fleet might have come in to support an assault of the land forces ; but, on entering Sebastopol after the defeat at the Alma, Menschikoff had caused eight large ships to be sunk across the entrance. Henceforward, so long as this obstacle existed, the operation of the fleets was limited to making a diversion by attacking the forts at the entrance ; and this was the part they took in the combined attack.

Until the whole of the Allied batteries were ready to open together, not a gun replied to the fire which the Russians did not cease to direct, first upon our camps, and afterwards on our trenches. Hidden as the Allied camps were behind the crest of a hill, there must have been something of mystery and awe for the garrison in this strange silence, almost the only token of the presence of an enemy being the increasing height of the parapets of the trenches.

On the 17th at daylight, pursuant to the general orders of the night before, the silence was broken by such a peal of artillery as has scarcely ever before, in the most famous battles or sieges, shaken the earth around the combatants. A hundred and twenty-six pieces, many of them of the largest calibre, opened at once upon the Russian defences, and were answered by a still larger number, of equal range and power. The din was incessant, and the smoke in the batteries so dense, that after a few rounds the gunners laid their pieces rather by the line on the platforms than by a view of the object aimed at. The first visible effect of our fire was on the Round Tower, the pieces on which were soon dismounted, and its surface deeply scarred by the shot of the heavy 68-pounder guns in the naval battery on the right, practising at a range of more than 2000 yards. Several explosions took place this day—the first in a French battery, where a magazine blew up at half-past eight in the morning, killing and wounding fifty men and disabling the battery; another less serious one occurred afterwards in the French lines. In the afternoon the Russian magazine in the Redan was fired by a shell from the English batteries, which silenced a great number of its guns; and shortly afterwards a number of cases filled with powder blew up in rear of the English trenches, doing but little damage. The Lancaster guns (a new invention now tried for the first time in war), of which there were several in our batteries, sent forth their missiles with a rushing noise exactly like that of a railway train, and were distinguishable at each discharge amid the din of the cannonade.

At one o'clock the French and English fleets, whose attack had been anxiously expected, stood in, and engaged the forts at the mouth of the harbour, the former on the south, the latter on the north side; and the deep volleying thunder of their broadsides, continuing without an instant's pause, gave a new character to the cannonade, while a dense canopy of smoke, hanging heavily above the scene, hid the sea, the harbour, and the town, from the spectators on the heights in front of the English camps. The Agamemnon and the Sanspareil maintained on this occasion a position much nearer to the forts than the rest of the fleet, which anchored, for the most part, at upwards of 2000 yards.

When the fire ceased at nightfall, and the gains and losses were counted up, the result was by no means commensurate with the expectations previously afloat in the Allied army. High authority had been quoted for the opinion that we should silence the Russian batteries in a few hours. The less sanguine had prescribed three days as the limits of the contest. Our progress hitherto had fallen short even of the latter estimate. On the Russian side many guns had been disabled, the works had been much damaged, and Fort Constantine was said to be seriously shaken by the fire of the two line-of-battle ships ; but on ours, the French attack had totally ceased since the explosions of the morning. The Russian works, being of earth like our own, were repaired with equal facility, and the disabled guns were replaced by fresh ones from the arsenal. It was while watching the renewed vigour of the enemy's fire, and seeing our own wounded borne by from the trenches, that we received on the 18th the mail bringing the absurd and mischievous announcement of the fall of Sebastopol, and read the details of our own imaginary victory—an announcement happily characterised afterwards in a newspaper article as "discounting" the glory of the conquest. It was robbing success of its best rewards thus to give us our honours before they were due.

The interest excited by a contest of artillery, without decided advantage on either side, soon languishes; and in a few days the thunder of the bombardment was almost unheeded. But the troops in the trenches and batteries were hardly worked, and exposed by day incessantly to a tremendous fire. The space in the magazines in our batteries was at first insufficient to hold ammunition for the day's consumption, and to take in fresh supplies formed one of the most trying duties which artillerymen can be called on to perform. Waggons filled with powder, drawn by horses of the field-batteries, were driven down the face of the hill for upwards of half a mile, in full view, and quite within range of the enemy's guns. A shell bursting in the waggons would have blown horses and men into the air; and to the risk of this were added the usual chances of being struck by shot or splinters; yet neither the officers (often mere boys) nor the drivers ever showed the slightest hesitation in proceeding on their perilous errand. Several horses were killed by cannon-shot, and on one occasion a shell, lodging between the spokes of a wheel, exploded there, blowing off three wheels and the side of the waggon, and blackening the cases of powder without igniting their contents.

Hitherto the attention of the Allies had been concentrated on the fortress, but on the 20th October a new element forced itself into their calculations. Russian troops showed themselves on the cluster of low heights which, as before mentioned, divide the valley of the Tchernaya into two defiles. Some Cossack horsemen lounged about the meadows at about 2000 yards from our position, and about fifty infantry soldiers, emerging from a ravine in the heights, crossed to the river for water, remaining for some time on the bank of the stream, and returning with a deliberation which showed they felt secure of support if molested. A body of cavalry with some guns also posted itself on the Bakshi-serai road, near the bridge which crosses the Tchernaya there, and close to the meadow where our own artillery had bivouacked on the night of the flank march. From day to day this force seemed to be augmented, and was judged to be the rearguard of an army whose numbers, being hidden in the farther defile, were unknown.

On the night of the 20th a sortie was made by the garrison on the French trenches. The Russians, calling out in French, "*Ne tirez pas, nous sommes Anglais*," penetrated into the works without opposition, and bayoneted some of the defenders, but were speedily repulsed with a loss of six killed and four wounded. During the next few nights some Russian guns on the heights in the valley once or twice opened fire on the Turks garrisoning the outposts in front of Balaklava, without result.

CHAPTER XI.

ATTACK ON BALAKLAVA.

In the description of our position, the line of outposts occupied by the Turks was said to be on a range of low hills, crossing the plain from below the heights of the plateau to the opposite mountains near the village of Kamara. Between these hills the plain slopes upward from Balaklava to a ridge, and down on the opposite side, where the valley, as before mentioned, is divided into two defiles, the one sweeping round to the left under the heights of the plateau held by the Allies, the other passing straight on to the Tchernaya. In this latter defile, and on the low eminences dividing it from the other, the Russian army, now numbering thirty thousand men, under General Liprandi, was posted.

At daybreak on the 25th the Russian guns on the eminences and in the valley commenced a cannonade on the outposts held by the Turks. A troop of horse artillery and a field-battery, supported by the Scots Greys, were ordered up to Balaklava to the slopes between the outposts, and found themselves opposed to the fire of several field-batteries and some guns of position, which covered an advance of infantry against the hills on the right. As the troop was armed only with 6-pounders, it and the field-battery were quite overmatched, both in metal and in numbers; nevertheless, our artillery maintained the contest till its ammunition was exhausted, when it retired, having lost a good many horses and a few men, besides Maude, the captain of the troop, who was severely wounded by a shell which burst in his horse.

At about 9 A.M. the first division and part of the light were ordered down to support the troops in Balaklava, which consisted of a body of marines and seamen, with heavy ships' guns, on the heights to the right of the valley, the 93d Highlanders and a Turkish detachment in front of the village of Kadukoi, and all the cavalry drawn up behind their encampment on the plain to the left, near a vineyard. The first division, passing along the heights from the Woronzoff road to that which descends from the plateau to the valley of Balaklava, had a complete view of the attack.

The Russians, pushing on a large force of infantry, cavalry, and artillery, had just succeeded in carrying the works on the hills nearest Kamara. Two large columns of cavalry, numbering probably three thousand each, swept with great rapidity over the slopes of the other hills nearer to our position, and the Turks who garrisoned the works there, firing a volley in the air, fled with precipitation over the parapets and down the slope. The Russians passed on; and their guns, darting out from the columns and dotting the plain at intervals, fired shells at us up the heights, all of which burst short. At that moment three heavy guns—two Turkish and one French—in position on the heights along which we were passing, were fired in succession on the Russian cavalry, the right column of which, losing some men and horses by the first shot, wavered, halted, and, before the third gun was discharged, turned and galloped back. When the smoke of the battery had dispersed, we saw that the left column, passing over and down the opposite slopes, was already engaged with our cavalry on the plain. There was something almost theatrical in the grandeur of this portion of the spectacle: the French stationed on the heights, and the English passing along them, looked down, as if from the benches of an amphitheatre, on the two bodies of cavalry meeting in mortal shock on the level grassy plain, which, enclosed on every side by lofty mountains, would have been a fit arena for a tournament of giants.

The Scotch Greys and the Enniskilleners, charging in front, were impeded by the tent-drains and picket-lines of their own camp, and, advancing but slowly, though with great steadiness, were swept back for a hundred paces by the torrent of Russian horsemen, fighting as they went, the red coats, fur caps, and grey horses, conspicuous amid the dark masses of the enemy. The 4th Dragoon Guards were passing in column towards the outposts, having a vineyard on their right, as the enemy swept by. As soon as they cleared the wall of the vineyard, they formed to the right, and, advancing like a wall, buried themselves, in an unbroken line, in the flank of the Russians, while the 5th Dragoon Guards charged in support of the Greys and Enniskilleners. For a moment sword-cuts and lance-thrusts were exchanged—then the Russians turned and fled confusedly back over the slopes, pursued for several hundred yards by the whole of the heavy cavalry, the Greys and Enniskilleners having rallied in time to join in their discomfiture.

While this was going on, part of the enemy's column, throwing its right shoulder forward, made a rush for the entrance of the valley. The 93d were lying down behind a slope there; as the cavalry approached they rose, fired a volley, and stood to receive the charge so firmly that the horsemen fled back with the rest of the column, pursued as they went by the fire of the battery (Barker's), which had already been engaged in the morning.

At this stage of the action the enemy's infantry and guns held the two hills nearest Kamara, and had taken, in the works there, nine iron 12-pounders, which we had confided to the Turks. We held the two points of the ridge nearest to our own position, and an intermediate one, crowned with a redoubt, remained unoccupied. The divisions advancing to support our troops having descended into the plain, some field-batteries were moved forward, and a desultory and ineffective exchange of fire took place, at very long range, between the Russian guns behind the hills they had taken, and our own posted on the slopes in our possession.

At the same time the brigade of light cavalry, which had not yet been engaged, had advanced to the edge of the slopes, whence they could look down on the enemy rallied on their own side of the plain, who had posted there a battery, flanked by two others, to repel any attack which might be made on them in their turn. Captain Nolan, author of the book on cavalry tactics, serving on the staff, brought an order to the commander of the cavalry to charge the enemy. To do so seemed desperate and useless; but Nolan asserted the order to be peremptory, and, joining in the charge which presently took place, was struck by a shell in the breast and fell dead. Never did cavalry show more daring to less purpose. Received in front and flank by a fire which strewed the ground, for the half-mile of distance which separated them from the enemy, with men and horses, they nevertheless penetrated between the guns and sabred the gunners. Captain Lowe, of the 4th Dragoons, is said to have cut down eleven of the enemy with his own hand. This gallantry availed nothing. The whole Russian force was before them; a body of cavalry interposed to cut off their retreat; and, assailed on every side by every arm, and their ranks utterly broken, they were compelled to fight their way through, and to regain our position under the same artillery fire that had crashed into their advance. Singly, and in two's and three's, these gallant horsemen returned, some on foot, some wounded, some supporting a wounded comrade. The same fire which had shattered their ranks had reached the heavy cavalry on the slope behind, who also suffered severely. Our loss would have been greater but for the timely charge of a body of French cavalry, which, descending from the plateau, advanced up the heights in the centre of the valley, where they silenced a destructive battery.

The ridge of hills, stretching entirely across the plain, hid the occurrences on the Russian side of the ground from the view of our troops in front of Balaklava; but the nature of the disaster soon became apparent. Riderless horses galloped towards us over the hill, and wounded men were brought in, or rode slowly back, escorted by their comrades. I saw three privates of heavy dragoons riding back in this way. The middle one, a smooth-faced young fellow, hardly twenty, in no ways differed in his demeanour from the other two, sitting straight in his saddle and looking cheerful; but, as he passed, I saw that a cannon shot had carried away a large portion of his arm, sleeve, flesh, and bone, between the shoulder and elbow, leaving the lower part attached only by a narrow strip of flesh and cloth. Colonel Yorke of the Royals, too, rode past, supporting himself with his hand on the cantle of his saddle, and, in reply to an inquiry from the Duke of Cambridge, said his leg was broken.

In this unhappy affair the light cavalry lost 10 officers and 147 men killed or missing, and 11 officers and 110 men wounded, with 335 horses. The heavy brigade lost, during the day, 9 men killed, and 10 officers and 87 men wounded, and 46 horses.

When the artillery fire ceased, some rifles were moved in skirmishing order up towards the hill near Kamara, apparently as a preliminary to an advance to retake it. But none such took place, though the expectation was universal amongst our people that it was to be recaptured at once. Towards evening some rum and biscuit were served out to the men, who had had no dinner, and at dusk the first division was marched back to its own encampment on the heights. The Russians were left in possession of two of the outposts held by the Turks in the morning, and nine guns, and their columns remained in the plain about 1500 yards from our front, drawn up as if to offer battle. Much murmuring was heard that they should be allowed thus to defy us, and to keep possession of the hills. But their success was rather apparent than real, and, but for the loss our cavalry suffered, would have been even beneficial to us. While it showed us that we were holding a front more extended than was necessary or desirable, it conferred on the enemy no advantage worth fighting for. Balaklava was no more assailable after the action than before; and if the possession of the road into the mountains by Kamara was convenient to the Russians for supplies from the interior, they could, by a detour from the valley of the Tchernaya, have communicated with it.

The Turks were loaded with abuse for running away from the outposts, and losing the guns; and certainly the celerity with which they fled from the left of the position reflected no great credit on them. But the amount of obloquy seems undue. Others besides Turks would have left slight field-works attacked by an army, and having no support within cannon-range. The redoubts and works nearest our heights were so weakly constructed as to be rather a cover for the defenders than an obstacle to the assailants. Any sportsman would have considered it no great feat to have ridden his horse over both ditch and parapet. These works were held by few men; the distance from them to the scanty force covering the entrance of the valley of Balaklava was 3000 yards; and they were not all abandoned without a struggle; for an Englishman, serving with our Ottoman allies, told me on the field that he had seen thirty-seven of the fugitives from the posts on the right who had received bayonet wounds in their defence. But the combats on the Danube had procured for our Mussulman friends such a reputation for valour in defending intrenchments, that it was believed to be necessary only to throw up a few shovelfuls of earth, and any Turk posted behind them would live and die there ; and the reaction produced by the upsetting of this belief, operated a little unjustly to their disadvantage.

It is not easy to assign any precise object to the Russian attack, except that of penetrating into the village, and doing what hasty damage they could to the stores there, and to the vessels in the harbour. To attempt to hold the place without the command of the sea, and with a very superior enemy on the heights on each side, would have been madness. The Russians would have been enclosed, and destroyed or captured to a man. Nor, in any case, would the loss of Balaklava, though a disaster, have been absolutely crippling to the Allies, or effectual for the relief of Sebastopol, since the British might have landed their supplies, as the French did, at Kherson ; and the abandonment of Balaklava, as too distant from our siege-works, was once said to be in contemplation.

CHAPTER XII.

FIRST ACTION OF INKERMANN.

On a detailed map of the Crimea, a path is shown which, branching to the right from the Woronzoff road in its course towards Sebastopol, descends the heights to the valley of the Tchernaya, close to the head of the great harbour. On this road the second division were encamped across the slope of an eminence. The road, passing over the ridge, turns to the right down a deep ravine to the valley. To the left of this road the ground, sloping gently downwards from the crest in front of the second division, rises again to a second eminence about 1200 yards in front of the first; and from this second ridge you look down across the head of the harbour in front, on the town and Allied attack on the left, and on the ruins and valley of Inkermann on the right. To the right of the road, the ground, first sloping upwards, then descends to the edge of the heights opposite Inkermann. All the space between and around the two ridges, down to the edge of the heights, was covered with low coppice.

From the first, the Russians showed great jealousy of any one advancing on any part of the ground beyond the ridge. As soon as any party, if even but two or three in number, showed itself there, a signal was made from a telegraph on the Russian side of the valley to the ships in the harbour, which (though the spot was not visible from their position) immediately sent up shot and shell at a tolerably good range. As the ridge in front was rather higher than that behind which the second division was posted, and as the road, as well as the slopes from the valley on the left of it, afforded facilities to the advance of an enemy not found at any other point of the heights, this was notoriously the weak point of our position.

About noon on the day after the action at Balaklava, a Russian force was descried from the naval battery on the right of the attack, sallying from the fortress, and, shortly afterwards, the pickets of the second division were driven in. Volleys of musketry on the ground between the ridges showed the affair to be serious, and a battery from the first division hastened to join those of the second in repelling the attack, while the Guards were moved up the slope in support. Some shot from the enemy's field-pieces were pitching over the ridge, behind which the regiments of the second division were lying down, while their skirmishers met the enemy's down the slope; and the guns of the second division had come into action on the crest of the hill. The battery of the first division (Wodehouse's) ranged itself in line with them, and, the enemy's guns being at once driven off the field, the whole eighteen pieces directed their fire upon a Russian column advancing half-way between the ridges. Unable to face the storm of shot, the column retired precipitately down the ravine to its left, where our skirmishers fired into it, and completed its discomfiture. Another strong column then showed itself over the ridge, and, after facing the fire of the bátteries for a minute, retired the way it came. Presently the first column, having passed along the ravine, was descried ascending, in scattered order, the height beyond; at 1400 yards every shot and shell pitched among them, our skirmishers also pressing hard on their rear and flank. When they had disappeared over the hill, the only enemy visible was the body of skirmishers fighting with our own on the space between the ridges, and to them our guns were now turned. From the circumstance of those of our men who had been on outpost duty that day wearing their great-coats, it was difficult to distinguish them from the grey-clad Russians, especially as all were hidden to their waists in coppice, but an occasional speck of red enabled us to avoid mistakes. The Russian skirmishers, under the fire of our guns and musketry, retired, as I have always seen them retire, without precipitation, turning to fire as they went; and, in less than an hour from the beginning of the combat, the space between the ridges was cleared of them. As their columns retreated towards Sebastopol, they came within range of the Lancaster gun in the right siege-battery. The naval officer in charge (Mr Hewett) blowing away the right cheek of the embrasure, to obtain the requisite lateral sweep, fired nearly a dozen rounds into them with very great effect; and the men of the second division, pressing on their rear, were with difficulty recalled from the pursuit. The Russians left a hundred and thirty dead within our pickets. We took forty prisoners, and a great number of wounded were brought into our hospitals. Next day parties from the fortress were seen on their own side of the hill, burying numbers slain in the retreat. Altogether, the Russians were estimated to have lost 1000 men, while we had ten killed and sixty wounded; so that this brilliant affair made amends to the army for whatever was unsatisfactory in the combat of the preceding day.

The regiments engaged in this action were—the 30th, 55th, 95th, 41st, 47th, and 49th. The batteries were Turner's, Franklin's (commanded by Captain Yates), and Wodehouse's.

While the Russians were retiring, a French staff-officer came to General Evans, with an offer from General Bosquet of immediate assistance, which Sir de Lacy declined with thanks, requesting him to inform the French general that the enemy were already defeated.

Parties of the attacking force were observed to carry intrenching tools in this enterprise. The design of the enemy probably was, after driving back the troops in front, to throw up cover on the opposite ridge, from behind which they might afterwards attack the same point of our line with sufficient force to follow up any advantage, and meet the Allies on the plains. Had they succeeded in intrenching themselves, we must either have dislodged them at once in a pitched battle, or have allowed them to collect troops and artillery there till it should suit their convenience to attack us with every advantage on their side. The value of the service done in repelling them with so inferior a force (there were 1500 men of the second division engaged against 8000 Russians) was perhaps not quite appreciated. It is scarcely too much to say, that the presence of a strong intrenched force upon that part of the ground would have been a more serious disaster than the loss of Balaklava. However, even had they succeeded in driving back the second division, they would have been encountered by the other divisions coming to its support. But the Russian general probably calculated that the attack on Balaklava of the previous day would have induced us to strengthen that part of the position at the expense of the rest, and that we should be able to oppose but a weak force in an opposite quarter.

All that afternoon waggons were bringing in wounded Russians. Passing the hospital tent of the first division on the way to my own that evening, I saw a neat boot sticking out of the door-way, the wearer's leg being supported by an orderly. I looked in, but quickly withdrew. A young Russian officer, extended on a table, whose thigh-bone had been splintered by a ball, was undergoing amputation of the hip-joint. As I turned away, the booted limb was detached from the bleeding mass and laid on the ground. He died in an hour. Outside the same tent next day, I saw a guardsman making soup in a large camp-kettle, while within a stride of his fire lay the bodies of five Russians, in different postures, who had died of their wounds, and had been laid there for burial. The young officer's body was laid apart, covered with a blanket, and near it, covered also, but not hidden, was a heap of amputated arms and legs.

On the night of the 26th, a body of horse, galloping from the valley through the French outposts, up the Woronzoff road, rushed through the divisional camps on each side, and were supposed to be cavalry on some desperate errand, the darkness preventing it from being discovered that the horses were riderless. About a hundred were captured. They were completely accoutred, some for hussars, some for lancers. Bags of black bread hung at the saddle-bows. All were bridled, but the bits were out of their mouths, as if they had broken from their pickets; and it was surmised that they had been startled by some rockets which the French had fired at troops passing along the valley.

On the 27th, a new parallel was opened as a place of arms in front of our left siege-battery, and a day or two later the French trenches were pushed to within two hundred and fifty yards of the place.

Great anxiety prevailed as to the officers and men missing since the action at Balaklava. It was said that the Cossacks had been seen riding over the field, transfixing the wounded with their lances. On the 28th, Captain Fellowes was sent with a flag of truce to ascertain their fate. He was civilly received—told that the dead were already buried and the wounded cared for—and that, if he would return next day, the names of the survivors should be ascertained and given him, with any messages or letters they might wish to send. On returning the day after, he learnt that only two officers were alive in the enemy's hands, and that but few prisoners had been made. The Russian general is said to have expressed his surprise at the desperate charge of the light brigade; saying, the English cavalry were always reputed brave, but this was mere folly.

I had heard much of the excellent arrangement of the French field-hospitals, and rode one day to see the principal one, near General Canrobert's headquarters. It was a tall wooden building like a barn, very airy, for there was a space between the roof and the walls, yet very warm—the change from the cold air without being most pleasant. The principal surgeon, a man of very fine and intelligent countenance, accompanied us round the beds, courteously indicating the most remarkable cases among the patients. These poor fellows, all wounded men, were arranged in rows, in excellent beds, and seemed as comfortable as such sufferers ever can be. Amputations had been very numerous, and the stumps of arms and legs projecting from the bed-clothes were frequent along the rows. One man lay covered up, face and all; he had undergone amputation of the hip-joint, the surgeon said, four days before, was doing well, and would probably live. I told him of the case of the young Russian officer, which I had witnessed a few days before, as already narrated. There was a little gleam of professional exultation as he repeated the fatal termination of the case to the surgeons in attendance; and then, turning to me, remarked that many similar operations had been successful in their hospitals. He pointed out one man, a Chasseur, who had served in Algiers, as of noted valour. He had lost both arms in the French cavalry charge at Balaklava. The attendants seemed especially tender and assiduous in their treatment of the wounded.

The attacks of the 25th and 26th had shown the necessity of strengthening our position at Balaklava, and opposite Inkermann. A continuous intrenchment was carried in front of the former place, extending from the plateau across the entrance of the valley, up the hills, and round to a mountain path near the sea, which communicates with the Woronzoff road. On the lowest hill on the valley of Kadukoi, a strong fort was erected. Batteries were placed at suitable points of the intrenchment, which was garrisoned by 8000 men, English, French, and Turks. The trees in the meadows and gardens of the valley were cut down, partly to furnish abattis and firewood, partly to prevent the enemy from obtaining cover, if they should succeed in penetrating the outer line of defence. I have already described the appearance of the valley when we entered it. Now it was sadly changed; all traces of cultivation had been stamped out by the multitudes of passing feet and hoofs, and only the stumps of the graceful willows or fruitful apple-trees remained to show where was once a garden or a grove.

The first division was posted about half a mile in rear of the second. On its right an arrow path descended the steep boundary of the plateau to the valley of the Tchernaya, crossing a ford of the stream between the Ruins of Inkermann and the cluster of heights where part of Liprandi's force was posted. About a third of the way down, a shoulder projected from the precipice like a terrace, and on this the French made a small redoubt, into which we put two guns to fire down on the plain, and to sweep the terrace, and which was at first garrisoned by guardsmen, but afterwards made over to the French. The latter had formed an almost continuous intrenchment from their great redoubt on the plateau above the Woronzoff road to this point, and we had begun on the 4th November to carry it onward round the face of the cliff opposite Inkermann, so as to include the front of the second division. But the work proceeded slowly and interruptedly; and up to that time, the ground which had already been the scene of an attack, and was now again to become so, had only two small fragments of insignificant intrenchment, not a hundred yards long in all—and more like ordinary drains than field-works—one on each side of the road, as it crossed the ridge behind which the division was encamped.

Amidst the many loose assertions and incorrect statements which have appeared in the public prints respecting the operations of the campaign, there is one frequently-recurring error which deserves notice, as it is calculated to mislead military readers in forming their estimate of the different actions. Every species of intrenchment which appears on a position is talked of as " a redoubt." At the Alma the English force has been repeatedly described as storming intrenchments, and the battery where the great struggle took place is always mentioned as " the redoubt." The two-gun battery where the Guards fought at Inkermann is also a " redoubt ;" and one writer describes it as equipped with " a breastwork at least seven feet high." A remarkable breastwork certainly, since the defenders, to make use of it as such, must needs be about ten feet in stature.

There were no intrenchments, nor any works intended as obstacles, in the Russian position at the Alma. The only works of any kind were two long low banks of earth, over which the guns fired—intended, not to prevent our advance, but to protect the guns and gunners from our fire. The battery at the Inkermann was a high wall of earth, revetted with gabions and sandbags, sloping at the extremities, and having two embrasures cut in it for the guns to fire through : from end to end it was about twelve paces long.

Now, premising that field-works are said to be enclosed when they afford on all sides a defence against an enemy, and that, when they are so constructed that the defenders behind one face fire along the space in front of them parallel to another face, the one is said to flank the other—a redoubt may be defined as an enclosed work without flank defence. It is either square, circular, or many-sided; and it is evident to the least informed reader, that a continuous parapet and ditch, guarded from behind at all points by musketry, must be a formidable obstacle to assail, and must greatly increase the facilities of defence.

The Ruins of Inkermann, which have often been mentioned in this narrative, and which have given a name to a fierce battle, stand on the edge of a clifflike precipice on the Russian side of the valley, about a mile from the head of the harbour of Sebastopol. They consist of a broken line of grey walls, battlemented in part, with round towers. The yellow cliff they stand on is honeycombed with caverns,—in the valley close beneath runs the Tchernaya, fringed with trees. Behind them the ground slopes upward to plains covered with coppice, and on two high points stand light-houses to guide ships entering the harbour. Masses of grey stone protrude abruptly through the soil around the ruins, of such quaint sharp-cut forms, that in the distance they might be taken for the remains of some very ancient city.

On the 4th of November it was known in our camp that the Russian army, which had been for some days past assembling north of the town, had received an important augmentation, and the arrival of some persons, apparently of distinction, had been witnessed from our outposts. During the night there was a great ringing of bells in the city; but no warning had reached us of the great enterprise in preparation, of which these were the preliminaries.

CHAPTER XIII.

BATTLE OF INKERMANN.

FEW of those who were roused from their sleep by the Russian volleys at daylight on the 5th November, will cease to retain through life a vivid impression of the scene which followed. The alarm passed through the camps; there was mounting in hot haste of men scarce yet half awake, whose late dreams mixed with the stern reality of the summons to battle, many of whom, hastening to the front, were killed before they well knew why they had been so hastily aroused. Breathless servants opened the tents to call their masters; scared grooms held the stirrup; and staff officers, galloping by, called out that the Russians were attacking in force.

It was a dark foggy morning, the plains miry, and the herbage dank. Cold mists rose from the valley, and hung heavily above the plains. During the darkness the enemy had assembled in force in the valley of the Tchernaya, between Inkermann and the harbour. A marsh renders this part of the valley impassable except by the Woronzoff road, which, after winding round the sides of the steep bluffs, stretches, level, straight, and solid, across the low ground. The Russian artillery had probably crossed this in the night, and been brought with muffled wheels to a level point of the road, where, concealed by the jutting of the hill, it waited till the repulse of our outposts should afford it the opportunity of advancing to its destined position.

At dawn they made their rush upon our advanced posts of the second division on the crest looking down into the valley, which fell back fighting upon the camp behind the crest, 1200 yards in rear. The outposts of the division were well accustomed to skirmish with the enemy on the same ground; but Captain Robert Hume of the 55th, whom I met going out in command of a picket the night before, and who was shot through the knee in the action, told me that the Russians had ceased to molest us there since their repulse on the 26th October. A picket of the light division, in the ravine on the left, was captured with its officer.

The outposts driven in, the hill was immediately occupied by the enemy's field artillery and guns of position. These latter are so named, because they are of too large calibre to be moved from point to point with ease, and are generally stationary during a battle in some position which has been previously selected for them. Their range is greater than that of field-artillery; at shorter ranges their aim is more accurate, and the shells they throw are more destructive. The heaviest guns were placed on the highest point, where they remained throughout the day, and the field-guns spread themselves down the slope opposite our right. Our field-batteries, coming up the slope in succession, as they were more or less distant from the second division, found themselves exposed at once to the fire of pieces answering to our 18-pounder guns and 32-pounder howitzers, so placed on the crest of the opposite hill that only their muzzles were visible. Over the brow, and along the face of the gentle acclivity, shot came bounding, dashing up earth and stones, and crashing through the tents left standing lower down the slope, while shells exploded in the misty air with an angry jar. Many men and horses were killed before they saw the enemy. Captain Allix of General Evans's staff was dashed from his saddle, not far from his own tent, by a round shot, and fell dead.

At the first alarm, the crest in front of the tents had been occupied by some troops of the second division. To their left extended the 47th and two companies of the 49th, which were immediately joined by Buller's brigade of the light division. Arriving on the ground, these regiments and companies found themselves close to a Russian column advancing up the ravine, which they at once charged with the bayonet, and drove back. The 41st, with the remainder of the 49th, had been sent to the right with Brigadier Adams, and advanced to the edge of the heights looking upon Inkermann. On arriving at the front, I was sent to this part of the ground with three guns, which opened on a column of the enemy, apparently about 5000 strong, descending the side of a steep hill on the other side of the Woronzoff road, and pursued it with their fire till the side of the ravine hid it from view. Immediately afterwards the enemy swarmed up our side of the ravine in such force that the 41st and 49th fell back; but the Guards, marching up by companies as they could be mustered, came on to that part of the ground in succession, and, passing on each side of our guns, checked the enemy's advance.

Hitherto all that was known had been that there was an attack in force, but the numbers and design of the enemy were now apparent. The plan of the Russians was, after sweeping the ridge clear by their heavy concentrated fire, to launch some of their columns over it, while others, diverging to their left after crossing the marsh, passed round the edge of the cliffs opposite Inkermann, and turned our right. The artillery fire had not continued long before the rush of infantry was made. Crowds of skirmishers, advancing through the coppice (which, as before mentioned, everywhere covered the field), came on in spite of the case shot, which tore many of them to pieces almost at the muzzles of our guns, and passed within our line, forcing the artillery to limber up and retire down the slope, and spiking a half-battery which was posted behind one of the small banks of earth mentioned before as the beginnings of an intrenchment.

Two companies of the 55th, lying down there, retreated as the Russians leapt over it, firing as they went back, and halted on a French regiment that was marching up the hill. The Russians retreated in their turn, and the French, arriving at the crest, were for a moment astonished at the fire of artillery which there met them, while the Russian infantry from the coppice poured in close volleys. They halted, as if about to waver; but General Pennefather riding in front and cheering them on, they went gallantly down the slope under the tremendous fire, driving the enemy before them. It was a critical moment, and the French regiment did good service to the army by its timely advance.

Almost simultaneously with this attack on the centre, and as part of it, a body of Russians had passed round the edge of the cliff, and met the Guards there. There was a two-gun battery, revetted with gabions and sandbags, on the edge of the slope opposite the Ruins of Inkermann, which had been erected for the purpose of driving away some guns which the Russians were placing in battery near the Ruins: this effected, our guns had been removed. Into this the Guards threw themselves, the Grenadiers extending to the right, the Fusiliers to the left of the battery, and the Coldstreams across the slope towards our centre. The Russians came on in great numbers with extraordinary determination. Many were killed in the embrasures of the battery, and the Guards repeatedly attacked them with the bayonet, till, having exhausted their ammunition, and lost nearly half their number, they were forced to retire before the continually increasing force of the enemy. They left one of their officers, Sir Robert Newman, lying there wounded by a bullet. Being reinforced, they returned, drove the enemy out of the battery, and found Newman there dead from bayonet wounds. He, as well as many other disabled men, had been savagely killed by the enemy.

Townsend's battery of the fourth division had arrived at the left of the position during one of the rushes made by the enemy. Four of the guns were taken almost as soon they were unlimbered, the Russians being close to them in the coppice unawares; but some of the 88th and 49th retook them before they had been many seconds in the enemy's hands,—Lieutenant Miller, R.A., taking a leading part in the recapture of one of the guns of his own division of the battery. In all these attacks on our left, the Russians were prevented from turning that flank by Codrington's brigade of the light division, which, posted on the further bank of the ravine, skirmished in and across it with the enemy's infantry throughout the day. Four guns had been detached early in the battle to support this brigade; but they were met, whenever they came into action, by so heavy a fire, that they were compelled to remain inactive, for the most part, under shelter of a large mound of earth.

When the Russian infantry was driven back, a

cannonade recommenced along their whole line, to which our guns replied warmly, though overmatched in metal and numbers. The Russians were computed to have sixty pieces, of which many were guns of position; while we had six 9-pounder batteries of six guns each; but our gunners continued the fire with admirable steadiness.

Soon after the Guards came up on the right, the three guns first sent there had been withdrawn for fresh ammunition, having fired away all in the limbers, and being separated from their waggons. I had then gone to the ridge where the road crossed it. The duel of artillery was at its height,—there was not a moment when shot were not rushing or shells exploding among the guns, men and horses going down before them. Grapeshot, too, occasionally showered past, from which it would appear that the Russians had brought some iron guns into position, as grape fired from brass pieces would destroy the bore from the softness of the metal. The ships in the harbour, and the battery at the Round Tower, also threw shot and shell on to the slope.

This cannonade was the preface to another infantry attack, which now again threatened our right, and a battery was ordered to that flank. While I was delivering the order, a round shot passed through my horse, close to the saddle, and rolled us over. He had shortly before been struck by a musket-ball in the haunch, which did not disable him; and had been wounded by a cannon-ball at the Alma, being one of the few horses that ever survived such an event. This was the poor fellow's last field; while on the ground another cannon-shot passed through him. A sergeant of artillery—a very fine young fellow, named M'Keown—ran to extricate me; he had just lifted me from under the horse, and I was in the act of steadying myself on his shoulder, when a shot carried off his thigh, and he fell back on me, uttering cries as if of amazement at the suddenness of his misfortune. I laid him gently down, resting on a bush, and looked at the wound; the leg was smashed, and almost severed. Calling two men to carry him to the rear, I hastened to the right after the battery.

Advancing in the thick bushes beyond the spot where the battery had come into action, I turned about and saw it retiring. It was already at some distance, and the movement was explained by the appearance of a line of Russian infantry suddenly extending along the upper edge of the slope, between me and our alignment, and at about forty yards' distance. On my left, lower down the slope, as I turned towards our position, men of different regiments, principally guardsmen, were retreating from the two-gun battery. The Duke of Cambridge galloped past me, calling to the men to fire, and ran the gauntlet of the whole Russian line, escaping with a bullet through his sleeve. Being lame from a recent injury, I considered myself lost—the bullets cut the branches and leaves on every side, and all attempts to rally our men were met by the unanswerable reply that their ammunition was spent. At that moment the right of the position was absolutely without defence, and the enemy by advancing resolutely must have turned it. But, from panic or some other cause, they fortunately retired instead of advancing—a friendly dip in the ground afforded a shelter from their last shots, and the men who had retreated rallied and lay down under the low intrenchment already spoken of, while their officers distributed fresh packets of ball-cartridge. On this intrenchment a heavy fire of artillery was directed, which continued for nearly an hour. An officer whom I met here, to whom I was lamenting the death of my horse, told me he had placed his in a hollow close at hand, where he was quite secure—but going to visit him presently afterwards, he found that a shell had penetrated this admirable retreat, and blown him to pieces. I saw a magnificent team of chestnut gun-horses prostrated here by a single destructive shell, and five of the six did not rise again.

Many of the men of the fourth division had but just returned from the trenches when the attack of the Russians commenced. They, as well as those who had not been on duty during the night, were at once marched to the scene of action a mile and a half distant. Arriving at the tents of the second division, they received contradictory orders, and the regiments were separated. Part of the 20th and 68th, and two companies of the 46th, passing to the right of the position, were ordered to support the remnant of the defenders of the two-gun battery. These fresh troops at once charged the enemy, routed them, and pursued them to the verge of the heights, when, returning victorious, they found the battery, as they repassed it, again occupied by Russians, a fresh force of whom had mounted the cliff from the valley. It was while collecting his men to meet this new and unexpected foe that Sir George Cathcart, who had advanced with this part of his division, was shot dead.

At this juncture the remainder of Bosquet's division (except his reserve) came up on the right, and, passing at once over the crest, threw themselves into the combat, and, fighting side by side with our regiments, pressed the Russians back. A *porte drapeau* (ensign bearing the colours) of a French battalion displayed great gallantry in this advance, leaping on the battery and waving the colours, amid a shower of bullets, from which he escaped unhurt. Some French cavalry were moved up at this time; but the ground was unfit for this arm, and they were withdrawn, having lost some men and horses. Shortly after the French regiments came to support ours, we received other efficient aid.

Seeing that our field-artillery was unequally matched with the Russian guns of position, Lord Raglan had despatched an order to the depôt of the siege train, distant about half a mile, for two iron 18-pounders, the only English guns of position landed from the ships which were not already placed in the defensive works at Balaklava and elsewhere. These were at once brought up by Lieut.-Colonel Gambier, the commander of the siege train, who, as he ascended the hill, was wounded by a grape-shot, which contused his chest, and obliged him to leave the field. The guns were then brought up and placed in position among our field-batteries by Lieut.-Colonel Dickson, who directed their fire with admirable coolness and judgment, which he continued to display till the close of the battle, under a cannonade which, at these two guns alone, killed or wounded seventeen men. In a short time the Russian field-pieces, many of them disabled, were compelled to withdraw; and a French field-battery coming up shortly after the 18-pounders opened their fire, posted itself on the right, and did excellent service, though exposed, like our own guns, to a tremendous cannonade, which killed many of their men and horses, and blew up an ammunition-waggon.

Between these two opposing fires of artillery a fierce desultory combat of skirmishers went on in the coppice. Regiments and divisions, French and English, were here mixed, and fought hand to hand with the common enemy, who never again succeeded in advancing, nor in obtaining, in any part of the field, even a partial success.

About noon the fire of the Russian guns slackened, as was surmised from want of ammunition. After a time they reopened, though not with their former fierceness. Their intended surprise, supported by the attack of their full force, had utterly failed; their loss had been enormous, and the Allies had been reinforced. The battle was prolonged only by the efforts of their artillery to cover the retreat of the foiled and broken battalions.

During the battle Sir De Lacy Evans, who had been sick on board ship at Balaklava, rode up to the field with his aide-de-camp, Boyle, and, calling me by name, began to question me about the battle. He looked extremely ill, but was as cool and intrepid as he always is in action. While I was speaking to him, a shell, crashing through some obstacle close by, rose from the ground, passed a foot or two above our heads, and dropping amid a group a few yards behind us, exploded there, wounding some of them,—but Sir De Lacy did not turn his head.

Officers and men fought the battle fasting. About two o'clock a group of us being near General Pennefather's tent, he told his servant to bring out wine and biscuits, which were never more welcome. A shell bursting over the hill sent its flight of bullets through and through the group without touching anybody.

At three o'clock the French and English generals with their staffs passed along the crest of the disputed hill. The enemy's guns, replying to ours, still sent a good many shot over the ridge, but this survey of the field showed it free from the presence of the enemy, whose infantry had withdrawn behind the opposite hill. At half-past three their guns also withdrew, and the whole force of the enemy retired across the Tchernaya, pursued by the fire of a French battery supported by two battalions, which, being pushed forward to a slope of the heights commanding the causeway marsh, converted their retreat into a flight.

At the commencement of the battle, Liprandi's force had moved forward, threatening two distant points of our line,—while a sally was made in force on the French trenches, which was repulsed, with a loss to the enemy of one thousand men, the French pursuing them within their works.

Until the arrival of the fourth division and the French, the ground was held by about 5000 of our troops. In all, 8000 English and 6000 French were engaged. The Russian force was estimated by Lord Raglan at 60,000.

Few great battles require less military knowledge to render them intelligible than this. The plan of the enemy was, after having succeeded in placing their guns unopposed in the required position, to pour on one particular point of our line which they knew to be inadequately guarded, a fire which should at once throw the troops assembling for its defence into disorder, and then to press on at the same point with overwhelming masses of infantry. Our position once penetrated, the plains afforded ample space for the deployment of the columns, which might then attack in succession the different corps of the Allied army scattered on the plateau at intervals too wide for mutual and concerted defence.

The Russians succeeded in posting their artillery,

in sweeping the field selected with a tremendous fire, and in bringing an enormously superior force to a vigorous and close attack. According to all calculation, they were justified in considering the day their own. But the extraordinary valour of the defenders of the position set calculation at defiance. At every point alike the assailants found scanty numbers, but impenetrable ranks. Before them everywhere was but a thin and scattered line opposed to their solid masses and numerous skirmishers, yet beyond it they could not pass. No doubt, to their leaders it must long have appeared incredible they could fail. Again bravely led, they came bravely to the assault, and with the same result; and, unwillingly, they at length perceived that, if the Allied troops could resist successfully when surprised, no hope remained of defeating them, now that they were reinforced, and on their guard.

On our part it was a confused and desperate struggle. Colonels of regiments led on small parties, and fought like subalterns, captains like privates. Once engaged, every man was his own general. The enemy was in front, advancing, and must be beaten back. The tide of battle ebbed and flowed, not in wide waves, but in broken tumultuous billows. At one point the enemy might be repulsed, while, at a little distance, they were making their most determined rush. To stand on the crest and breathe awhile, was to our men no rest, but far more trying than the close combat of infantry, where there were human foes with whom to match, and prove strength, skill, and courage, and to call forth the impulses which blind the soldier to death or peril. But over the crest poured incessantly the resistless cannon-shot, in whose rush there seems something vindictive, as if each were bestridden by some angry demon; crashing through the bodies of men and horses, and darting from the ground on a second course of mischief. The musket-ball, though more deadly, and directed to an individual mark, bears nothing appalling in its sound, and does not mutilate or disfigure where it strikes. But, fronting uncovered and inactive a range of guns which hurl incessantly those iron masses over and around you, while on all sides are seen their terrible traces, it is difficult to stave off the thought that, in the next instant, your arm or leg may be dangling from your body a crushed and bloody mass, or your spirit driven rudely through a hideous wound across the margin of the undiscovered country.

Rarely has such an artillery fire been so concentrated, and for so long, on an equally confined space. The whole front of the battle-field, from the ravine on the left to the two-gun battery on the right, was about three quarters of a mile. Nine hours of such close fighting, with such intervals of cessation, left the victors in no mood for rejoicing. When the enemy finally retired, there was no exultation, as when the field of the Alma was won : it was a gloomy though a glorious triumph.

Neither our loss nor that of the enemy was fully

known that day; but a glance at any part of the ground showed the slaughter to be immense. A few of the enemy were dead within our lines; along the whole front of the position they lay thick in the coppice. Every bush hid a dead man, and in some places small groups lay heaped. In a spot which might have been covered by a common bell-tent, I saw lying four Englishmen and seven Russians. All the field was strewn; but the space in front of the two-gun battery, where the Guards fought, bore terrible pre-eminence in slaughter. The sides of the hill, up to and around the battery, were literally heaped with bodies. It was painful to see the noble Guardsmen, with their large forms and fine faces, lying amidst the dogged, low-browed Russians. One Guardsman lay in advance of the battery on his back, with his arms raised in the very act of thrusting with the bayonet; he had been killed by a bullet entering through his right eye. His coat was open, and I read his name on the Guernsey frock underneath—an odd name—"Mustow." While I was wondering why his arms had not obeyed the laws of gravity, and fallen by his side when he fell dead, a Guardsman came up and told me he had seen Mustow rush out of the battery and charge with the bayonet, with which he was thrusting at two or three of the enemy when he was shot. In their last charges, the Russians must have trodden at every step on the bodies of their comrades. In the bushes all around wounded men were groaning in such numbers, that some lay two days before their turn came to be carried away. I passed a Russian with a broken leg, whom some scoundrel had stript to his shirt, and calling a soldier who was passing, desired him to take a coat from a dead man and put it on the unfortunate creature; at the same time directing the attention of a party of men collecting the wounded to the place where he lay. Passing the same spot next day, I saw the Russian lying motionless with his eyes closed, and told a French soldier who was near to see if he was dead; the Frenchman, strolling up with his hands in his pockets, pushed his foot against the Russian's head; the stiffened body moved altogether like a piece of wood, and the soldier, with a shrug and one word, "*mort*," passed on. Large trenches were dug on the ground for the dead; the Russians lay apart; the French and English were ranged side by side. Few sights can be imagined more strange and sad in their ghastliness than that of dead men lying in ranks, shoulder to shoulder, with upturned faces, and limbs composed, except where some stiffened arm and hand remain pointing upward. The faces and hands of the slain assume, immediately after death, the appearance of wax or clay; the lips parting show the teeth; the hair and mustache become frouzy, and the body of him who, half an hour before, was a smart soldier, wears a soiled and faded aspect.

Down the ravine along which the Woronzoff road runs to the valley, the dead horses were dragged and lay in rows; the English artillery alone lost eighty. The ravine, like all those channelling the plains, is wild and barren; the sides have been cut down steeply for the sake of the limestone, which lies close to the surface, in beds of remarkable thickness. A lime-kiln, about ten feet square, built into the side of the hill, afforded a ready-made sepulchre for the enemy left on this part of the field, and was filled with bodies to the top, on which a layer of earth was then thrown.

While I was on the ground, a day or two after the battle, several shells were thrown from the ships in the harbour, some of which pitched amongst the parties collecting the wounded. General Pennefather, finding I was going to headquarters, desired me to deliver a message stating the fact. Next day a flag of truce was sent into the town to complain of this, and further, to say that, both in this battle and the action at Balaklava, Russian soldiers had been seen killing our wounded on the field; demanding if the war was to be carried on in this manner. The answer of Prince Menschikoff was, that the shells had been directed, not at the parties engaged in clearing the field, but at those intrenching the position; and that, if any of the wounded had been put to death, it could have been only in a few particular instances; in excuse of which he remarked, that the Russian soldiers were much exasperated in consequence of the fire from the French trenches having destroyed one of the churches of Sebastopol.

CHAPTER XIV.

WINTER ON THE PLAINS.

EARLY in November the weather, hitherto mild and sunny as the Indian summer of Canada, began to grow foggy, moist, and raw. The horizon of the Black Sea was blotted with mists, and its surface changed from blue to cold grey, while the sky was either leaden or black with clouds.

About daybreak on the 14th, a strong wind from the south drove before it a flood of rain; the tents, swelling inward beneath the blast, left no slant sufficient to repel the water, which was caught in the hollows, and filtered through. I was awoke by it dripping on my face, which I covered with my cloak, and slept again. Again I was awoke, and this time more rudely. The wind had increased to a hurricane, in which the canvass flapped and fluttered, and the tent-pole quivered like a vibrating harp-string. At the opening of the tent, my servant appeared uttering some words, which were blown away, and never reached me till, putting his head within, he told me I must get up,—adding, that the tents were nearly all blown away. As he spoke, the pegs that held mine to the ground parted—the canvass was driven against the pole, and the whole structure fell with a crash across my bed.

Sitting up and grasping my fluttering blankets, I beheld such of my effects as had not weight enough to keep them stationary, dispersed in the air, and borne on the wings of the wind into a distant valley. Half-written letters clung for a moment, in places, to the muddy ground before pursuing their airy flight, and garments of every description strewed the plain. My servant was in full pursuit of a cocked-hat which was whirled onward at a tremendous pace, till its course was arrested by a low wall ; and on the muddy wheel of a cart hung a scarlet waistcoat grievously bemired. All round me were figures like my own, of half-clad men sitting amid the ruins of their beds, and watching, with intense interest, the dispersion of their property, while those tents which had continued to resist the gale, fell over, one after the other, like inverted parachutes. Horses, turning their scattered tails to the blast, leaned against it with slanting legs, blinded by their clothing, which, retained by the surcingles, was blown over their heads ; and all around were seen men struggling up, with frequent loss of ground, each holding some recovered article. Whatever could be collected in this way was placed beneath the fallen tents, the edges of which were then loaded with heavy stones. In the distance other encampments were seen in similar plight, and everywhere the rows of tents which had dotted the plain had disappeared. Hard as it seemed to be stripped of shelter by the storm, those who had passed the night in the trenches had still greater reason to complain. There they had consoled themselves during the watches of the wet, gusty night, by the promise of warmth and rest in the morning ; and hastening, chilled and weary, to their camp for the comforting hot coffee, and pleasant well-earned sleep, officers and men found their temporary homes level as a row of Persians worshipping the rising sun, and the space they had kept dry in the midst of mire, become a puddle. No fires could be lit, no breakfast warmed, for the blast extinguished the flame and scattered the fuel ; and all that could be done was, to gather the blankets out of the mud, and to try to raise again the fallen tents.

But these were by no means the greatest sufferers. The hospital tents, higher than the rest, were blown down, leaving the patients exposed, almost naked, to the bitter wind and driving rain: and the first efforts of the men in camp were directed to obtain some shelter for these unfortunates. The wooden building already described as so comfortably housing the wounded French, fell over, fortunately without seriously adding to the injuries of the occupants ; but I heard that a Russian prisoner, who lay wounded in another hospital, was killed by its fall.

Towards noon the storm began to abate, though it still blew violently till next morning, when the extent of damage sustained by the ships, towards which many an anxious thought had been cast, was known. Our hardships on shore were as nothing compared with the state of those at sea, who saw instant destruction in the gale,—which bore towards them, on the one side, the most terrific billows, while on the other was a wall of perpendicular rocky cliff.

On the 15th, the narrow harbour of Balaklava was strewed with floating timbers and trusses of hay so thickly, that boats were with difficulty forced through the masses ; while numbers of the drowned were washed about the bases of the cliffs at the entrance. The ships inside, ranged in line close together as in a dock, had been driven towards the head of the harbour, and, pressing in a mass upon the Sanspareil, carried her a hundred yards from her moorings, where she grounded by the stern. One or two vessels went down close to others, who could aid only by saving the crews. Seven English transports were lost at Balaklava, and thirteen at the Katcha. The Resistance, a magazine ship cast away at the former place, contained large quantities of ammunition both for siege guns and infantry ; and the Prince, a very large and magnificent steamer, had just arrived from England with a great supply of warm clothing for the army, all of which went down in her. She had also brought out an apparatus to be employed in our operations against Sebastopol ; and Lieutenant Inglis, an engineer who had gone on board the night before to superintend the disembarkation of the machine, was lost along with the ship and crew. One of our line-of-battle ships was dismasted, and another injured; and the French 80-gun ship, Henri IV., the most beautiful vessel in their navy, went aground in eight feet of water; and it being impossible to float her, she was used as a battery against the shore. The Retribution, an English war-steamer, having the Duke of Cambridge on board, escaped with difficulty, casting her guns overboard.

The army soon felt severely the loss it had sustained when the Prince went down. For the remainder of November it rained almost without cessation, and the plains became one vast quagmire. The soil is remarkably tenacious, and the feet both of men and horses were encumbered at every step with a load of clay. Not only all the interior of the camps was deep in mire, but the floors of the tents themselves grew muddy. It is difficult to imagine a more cheerless scene than that presented wherever you traversed the plains : the landscape, all lead-coloured above, was all mud-coloured below ; the tents themselves, wet and stained with mud, had become dreary spots on a dreary background. Sometimes low walls of stone or mud were thrown up round them, and in part succeeded in keeping out the keen raw gusts. About the tents waded a few shivering men in great-coats, trying to light fires behind small screens of mud or stones, or digging up the roots of the bushes where the coppice had vanished from the surface. Rows of gaunt, rough horses, up to their fetlocks in the soft drab-coloured soil, stood with drooping heads at their picket-ropes, sheltered from wind and rain each by a dirty ragged blanket—in which it would have been difficult for the keenest connoisseur in horse-flesh to recognise the glossy, spirited, splendid teams that had drawn the artillery along the plains of Scutari.

When the Scots Greys, after landing at the Katcha, marched through the camp on the Balbek, the whole army admired their magnificent appearance,—the horses, unsurpassed in any cavalry in the world for shape, size, spirit, and condition, contrasted strongly with those which had been through the campaign, and which, even then, except the strongest and soundest, had begun to look travel-stained and battered. When the winter began, the survivors of the Greys, long-haired, bony, spiritless, and soiled with mire, preserved no trace of their former beauty. Perhaps the most painful feature in the dreary scene was the number of dead and dying horses scattered, not only round the cavalry and artillery camps, but along the various roads which traversed the position. Some had fallen and died from fatigue, some perished from cold, some from starvation. Once down, a horse seldom rose again. After a few faint attempts he lay still, except for a feeble nibbling at the bare ground; then he would fall over on his side, and, stretching out his legs, would so end his career, leaving a smooth space in the mud where his head and neck had moved slowly to and fro, or where his hind-leg had scratched convulsively before he died. Sometimes an ownerless horse, probably too lame and unserviceable to be worth inquiring after, would linger about the neighbourhood of an encampment. Day after day he would be there, waiting patiently, wondering, perhaps, why no hay nor corn came, getting thinner and thinner; nobody could relieve him without robbing his own horse, on whose strength and condition his own efficiency depended—until, after wandering to and fro over the barren spot, if no friendly hand could be found to send a bullet through his head, he would drop and die there a lingering death. It was impossible to traverse the position in any direction without seeing many carcasses—some swollen and bloated, some mere skeletons. Here and there would be seen the curious spectacle of a horse's bones covered only with his loose, collapsed hide, all the flesh, muscles, and even ribs, having disappeared—which would be explained presently, when, on passing the next carcass, a gorged dog would put his head out from the hollow arch of the ribs, and, after looking lazily at the comer, return to his horrible feast. These spectacles never ceased to be painful, though custom diminished their effect; for, a few months before, the sight of a dying horse would have haunted me for days.

The dogs had originally been inhabitants of the farm-houses and villas of the plateau. Driven from their ruined homes, they collected in packs on the untenanted portions of the plain, and fed by night on the dead horses. At first they were, in consideration of their services as scavengers, and their inoffensiveness, left unmolested; but, latterly, I was sorry to see that the French soldiers began to shoot them for the sake of their skins. But very little native animal life was seen after the cold drove the numerous lizards under ground. A hare would sometimes start from a bush; a few crows, magpies, and ravens occasionally held council over some dead horse lying remote from the camp; and, once or twice, I saw large flocks of magnificent eagles swooping so near that their stern searching eyes were visible.

On the setting in of rain, the road from Balaklava to the camp at once became almost impassable. Man and beast plunged along knee-deep, through thick sticky mud in some parts, while in others the mire was sloppy, with slippery stones beneath. Near Balaklava great pools were collected in the low ground: the gardens and vineyards had become swamps, and not a trace of cultivation remained in the desolate and melancholy valley. In a pool, between the posts of the gateway of a field near the town, a camel lay for days, which had fallen from weakness, and was unable to rise; its huge structure of ribs, bald and bare of flesh, was painfully visible; till, dying, it soon almost disappeared in the surrounding filth. Files of cavalry horses, carrying provisions and forage, might be met at all parts of the road, as well as artillery waggons, laden with hay and corn, instead of ammunition, all toiling slowly and painfully through the slough. The

BALACLAVA IN WINTER.

road along the margin of the harbour, more filthy and boggy than the rest, was thronged with arabas drawn by mules, bullocks, and camels, waiting for stores and provisions. These, in their journey to the camp, frequently broke down, or stuck too fast to be extricated; and, once abandoned, a carriage, no matter how serviceable or important might be considered lost, for during the night it was sure to be broken to pieces and carried off for firewood.

Perhaps of all the privations of the army, the want of wood was the severest. Until a supply of charcoal and patent fuel was brought in ships, the necessary quantity for cooking the ration of meat was only procured with much difficulty and labour by those divisions posted on the centre of the plains. About the monastery of St George there was a good deal of thick coppice extending towards Balaklava, and the brushwood was interspersed with oak trees from three to six inches in diameter. These were, for the most part, used for poles by the Turks, who, as soon as the wet set in, quitted their tents and retired underground. Digging a trench about twelve feet long, eight wide, and four deep, they set up along the middle of its length a row of forked poles, and laid ridge-poles across the forks which supported rafters from the bank on each side. These latter were covered thickly with branches, and mud was then plastered over the whole, excluding the air, while the slope of the roof enabled it to resist several hours' rain. A sloping path led down to the door ; no provision was made for admitting light; the smoke escaped through a hole; and when the walls had dried it was much warmer than a tent, which, as may be supposed, is, in wet or windy weather, the dreariest abode in the world.

Now it happened that, in December, some staff-officers, who had built, near the small encampment of which my tent formed an item, a row of huts of the kind just described, only more elaborately finished, were ordered to Balaklava, and three of us, purchasing the fee-simple of the property, entered into possession. The main building, forty feet long by twelve or fourteen wide, was divided in half by a partition wall. The solid roof, perfectly air-tight, was supported by substantial props. To light each apartment there was a square hole in the roof, screened from the rain by a small roof of its own, like a garret window. The fireplace of the outer chamber had a chimney in the partition—that of the inner in the end wall. Near this was another hut, half the size, for a kitchen, and a trench had been already dug and poles erected for a stable, where, with the somewhat desultory and dawdling assistance of a party of Turks, we succeeded in warmly housing all our steeds. About the middle of December we entered our new abode, and were for the next week the envy of all our acquaintance still under canvass. After that it began to rain, and continued to do so for four-and-twenty hours, at the end of which time, the habitation being still dry, we felt more pity than ever for the dwellers in tents, and re-

EXTERIOR OF HUT IN THE CAMP.

tired to rest in a mood at once compassionate and grateful.

While it was yet dark, I was awoke by my companion in this dormitory calling out to ask if I was wet through yet ? and on opening my mouth to make reply, some wet mud dropt from the roof nearly into it. Sluices were established at numerous weak points of the roof, and the murmur of many waters was heard around. In some places the thin cascade poured tinkling into a rill on the floor, while at other points the dull noise of its fall showed some article of wearing apparel to be underneath. My pillow was drenched, my cloak thoroughly soaked, but as yet the water had not penetrated to the blankets ; and after sounding with my hand the puddle on the floor, and satisfying myself that my coat, trousers, and boots could not possibly be any wetter, I became convinced that I might as well for the present lie still, and, drawing the end of my cloak over my head, slept till morning. At daylight, we, the late exulting possessors of the coveted huts, sought shelter in the neighbouring tents. But, having been thus shown the weak point of our position, we took effectual measures to strengthen it ; and procuring from Balaklava enough tarpaulin to cover our roofs, we drained our abode, lit fires on the floor to dry it, and again became its tenants ; and, except when the cold wind forced us to keep the door shut, darkening the place so that we were obliged to breakfast sometimes by candle-light, we really lived in great comparative luxury.

A plan for warming the tents, originating, I think, with the engineers, was very commonly resorted to. The water supply, which the aqueduct passing in front of our camps afforded to Sebastopol, had been cut off, and the pipes conducting it laid bare. One of these, of solid iron, seven or eight feet long, made an excellent chimney, and was enclosed in a trench dug across the floor of the tent, and covered in, except near the door, when the fire was lit in it. The pipe, while conducting the smoke to the open air, became heated, and diffused through the interior a comfortable glow. But the French adopted the most luxurious plan; they elevated their tents on an oval stone wall about four feet high, having a chimney at the back, and opposite a wooden door framed in the opening of the tent : spaces were cut in the canvass, where squares of glass in wooden frames were let in ; and with a good fire blazing in the chimney, the interior was, in the gloomiest day, light, warm, and cheerful.

The soldiers who, poor fellows, could adopt none of these inventions, had only the shelter of the tents, and such articles of clothing as were issued from time to time, to trust to for necessary warmth. Their misery was great, but they met it in an excellent spirit. Crime was rare, insubordination rarer ; there were few murmurs ; and they were as ready as ever to meet the enemy.

From the battle of Inkermann till the end of December but few events occurred to break the monotony of the siege. Day after day, the gunners, at intervals, exchanged shots with the enemy, and the French and English sharpshooters in the advanced trenches fired from their sandbag loop-holes at the Russian riflemen hid in pits or behind screens of stone, without other result than the loss of a few men on either side. Sometimes, shortly after dark, the Russians would commence a sharp cannonade, chiefly directed on the French ; every instant the sky would be reddened by the flashes, visible even in the tents, and the rattle of musketry would be added to the roll of the artillery. Then the turmoil would subside, and the darkness and stillness would remain unbroken, except for the flash and boom of an occasional gun. Very little damage was done on these occasions by the enemy's fire.

Beyond the advanced trench in front of our left attack, the Russians had made some pits, which, screened by small stone walls, were occupied each by a rifleman, and from whence they caused great annoyance to our people in the trench, and to the French across the ravine, whose advanced works they in part saw into. On the night of the 20th November, a party of our rifles was ordered to clear the pits, the men in which were supported from another row of pits behind. Sallying from the right extremity of the trench, they drove the Russians off, after a sharp struggle ; and a working party immediately threw up on the spot cover enough to render the ground tenable. Lieutenant Tryon, who led the attack, was killed by a shot from the pits, and we lost about fifteen men killed and wounded. During the battle of Inkermann, Tryon fought all day armed with a rifle, and, being a good shot, killed an almost fabulous number of the enemy. The service of driving the enemy from the pits was so highly appreciated by the French, that General Canrobert passed a warm encomium on it in general orders; and the enemy's estimate of the advantage they had lost was shown by fierce attacks made to regain the ground, on the two following nights, without success.

We had begun, immediately after the battle of Inkermann, to intrench the front of the second division. The ditch and parapet already there were enlarged, completed, rendered continuous, and armed with batteries. Three redoubts, two French and one English, were constructed on commanding points, ours being on the ridge occupied by the Russian guns of position in the battle. In advance of these, other works and batteries were extended to the verge of the heights looking on the head of the harbour, on the causeway across the marsh, and on the last windings of the Tchernaya. To oppose them the enemy threw up batteries on the heights on their side of the valley, and opened fire from the nearest of them; while, farther back, long lines of intrenchment extended across the hills.

On the 6th December, Liprandi, after setting fire to his huts, quitted his position in front of Balaklava, and retired into Sebastopol, leaving a force of cavalry and infantry, with some guns, in the villages of Kamara and

Tcherzuna, and some field-works to guard the bridge over the Tchernaya. The French reconnoitred the ground in force on the 30th December. Ten battalions of infantry, and six squadrons of horse, with twelve guns, under General d'Espinasse, descended into the plain, and, throwing out skirmishers, supported by a troop of cavalry, advanced towards the hills taken from the Turks on the 25th October. As they went on, the single Cossack sentry always posted on the hill nearest the middle of the plains was joined by a detachment of about a hundred and fifty Russian lancers. These retired in good order, by alternate sections, as the French skirmishers ascended the slope, one section halting as the others went back, and then retiring in its turn while another faced about. The troop of French cavalry supporting the skirmishers, arriving at the summit, charged the section of lancers showing front, and drove it back upon the others; and the French supports appearing, the Russians retired in good order down the defile, across the bridge of the Tchernaya, and into the village on the other bank, leaving about a dozen troopers unhorsed or prisoners. A French officer received a wound from a lance in this affair, of which he died the next day. The whole of the French then advanced towards the river, and followed the bank on their own side till opposite the village, into which they threw some shells, setting fire to some of the houses, and dislodging the cavalry, which retired, covered by eight guns that the enemy withdrew from a field-work on the left bank when the French advanced. In the mean time, Sir Colin Campbell had ordered the 42d to move out of the intrenched hills to the right of Kadukoi, along the face of the mountain to Kamara, of which village they obtained possession without any opposition. Then the French, holding the defile near the bridge, detached two battalions up a mountain path to their right rear to a village in the hills beyond Kamara, where they knew three hundred Cossacks to be posted, and whom they nearly succeeded in surprising, the Cossacks having barely time to escape before the French entered the village : the latter, having destroyed the enemy's huts, and burnt a quantity of forage, rejoined the main body, driving off with them some cattle and sheep ; and the whole of the reconnoitring force, having accomplished their object, which was limited to ascertaining the enemy's actual force and position, returned to the heights.

So ended the year 1854—to nine-tenths of the army beyond measure the most eventful of their lives, and which, in retrospect, wore the air of romance. There were unfolded the departure with tearful friends on the one side, glorious uncertainty on the other—the scenes of the Turkish capital—the pestilence-haunted camps of Bulgaria, whose dreary sites are marked by so many of our comrades' graves—the march across the green sunny plains of the Crimea—our first passage of arms at the Alma— the sight of the prize we aimed at—the bright new-looking city, with its background of blue water—the bombardment—the minor actions of the 25th and 26th October—and the gloomy struggle of Inkermann, leaving us undisturbed possessors of the barren plains, where we had now spent three long months, feeling winter's grasp tightening day by day. Yet that grasp, even-handed to both parties, was not altogether unfriendly to us. Fine weather and good roads would have brought upon us legions of enemies ; day after day we must have renewed, for our bare footing, a struggle against odds sufficient to render it ever doubtful.

But now, while the accessions to the Russian force must, of necessity, be few and scanty, England and France were, to us, prodigal of aid. Our numbers had been inadequate to the task before us, but reinforcements had come, and more were on their way. We had been thinly clad, but comfortable garments were at hand. The state of the roads rendered the necessary transport of stores a work of extreme difficulty, but a railway had arrived, with men to lay it. Tents had for long almost ceased to be a shelter against the wind and driving rain—but now, wooden houses for the army, proposed, as it seemed to us, only the other day, and but half believed in, were actually in the harbour, and, when put together on the heights, would at once place the troops in comparative comfort, and check the progress of disease. Austria was said to have at length joined us in earnest, though the terms of the treaty concluded with her were as yet unannounced. Best of all, we felt how we were thought of and cared for at home, and knew that, for us tattered, bedraggled mortals, shivering on these muddy plains, a regard more anxious, deep, and generous than is often shown, except by the truest and warmest of friends, now formed the one absorbing impulse of the nation.

CHAPTER XV.

CIRCUMSPECTIVE.

During the lull in the operations, a glance at our present situation, and the successive stages which led to it, may not be out of place. We find ourselves, after two great battles and some minor actions, in possession of a position which, itself of great natural strength, has been so fortified as to be almost impregnable, if held by an army sufficiently strong to occupy it throughout its extent. The Allied works are pushed close to those protecting the town, and reinforcements reach us constantly; while the garrison of Sebastopol and the Russian army outside must be suffering great privations, and their expenditure of men and material cannot be replaced. So far the advantage would seem to be with us.

But the sufferings of our troops, exposed to the rigour of winter, without clothing or shelter sufficient to resist it, had, when published from a hundred sources, excited universal sympathy. As soon as the change of temperature checked the ravages of cholera, the wet set in, bringing a new train of diseases. Horrible cramps resembling those of the epidemic, but accompanied by different symptoms and excited by other causes, seized numbers of those exposed, sometimes for nights in succession, to the duty of guarding the trenches. In their ragged garments, and with feet almost bare, they paced the wet mud, or, wrapt in a single blanket, lay in holes which they dug in the reverse of the batteries and lines, shivering the live-long night. When relieved, they crept back, rigid with cold, to the bleak shelter of the tents. On the troops newly arrived from England these unaccustomed hardships fell with double severity, and they died in appalling numbers, while the endurance of those seasoned by the previous campaign was now tried to the uttermost. In the months of December and January the sick in the English camp alone varied from 2000 to 3000; and including those at Balaklava and Scutari, or invalided to England, the sick returns showed the astounding number of 14,000 men ineffective in the British army.

The force thus weakened was by no means replenished by the reinforcements which arrived from England and the Mediterranean garrisons, and, in consequence, the duties of those who remained effective were increased in severity. The trenches must be held at any price, and the same guards sometimes manned them for three successive nights.

To feed the army it was necessary to bring provisions daily from Balaklava; the labour of the siege had been such that up to the end of December our means of transport had never permitted us to accumulate one day's provisions in advance. Day after day accordingly saw men and horses, enfeebled by hardship, traversing the roads, clogged by mire and snow, to and from Balaklava. Strings of soldiers might be met carrying pieces of raw pork, and often these provision-carriers, until late in the afternoon, did not break their fast. The cavalry brought up their forage on their horses, the artillery theirs on stript ammunition-waggons and Flanders waggons. A horse carried a truss of hay weighing from 180 lb. to 200 lb., or a sack of corn—a waggon took five or six trusses, and required ten horses to draw it thus loaded; and these, starting from the camp soon after daylight, seldom returned till late in the afternoon. Rows of waggons and of cavalry horses waited (men and animals up to their knees in mud) till their turn for loading came—the rule being that only one boat-load of forage should be disembarked at a time, as very few commissariat clerks could be spared to superintend the issue. It occasionally happened that the men of some of the divisions were for a day, sometimes two, without the ration of meat and rum, having only biscuit and unroasted coffee; while half allowance was by no means uncommon. Now, if the reader will visit, in the coldest days of English winter, the poorest family in his neighbourhood, whose food is just sufficient to sustain existence; who, never getting coals except in charity, search the neighbouring commons and hedges for furze and sticks wherewith to cook their meagre meals; who lie down hungry and cold at night on a miserable pallet, to shiver till cheerless morning,—and will then remember that to all these privations were added want of shelter from drenching rain, and sleet, and frost, he will be able to realise the condition of the troops in front of Sebastopol after the end of October.

These facts, once known in England, excited sympathy entirely unbounded, and, with the supplies sent to our relief, the public poured forth indignant questions as to how our straits had arisen. Why had the expedition been delayed till so late in the season? When so long delayed, why was it attempted? Why had provision not been made for a winter campaign? Why was our force not more commensurate with the difficulty of the proposed achievement?

It is evident that so long as Silistria was likely to fall—that is, till July—the most important object was to check the progress of the hitherto successful invader towards the Turkish capital. Soon after the Russians had retired across the Danube, and before the preparations necessary for assuming the offensive in this new aspect of affairs could possibly be completed, the cholera broke out.

But the English public, through the press, were clamorous for immediate action. Taunts on the inactivity of the forces, pictures of the success which awaited bold and sudden measures, invidious comparisons between such generals as were supposed to be in favour of delay and those eager for enterprise, depreciating estimates of the enemy's resources, and exaggerated statements of our own,—these formed the staple of the articles of the public journals, and to these were added frequent false reports that the enterprise so insisted on was already commenced. Seldom has the British public been more clamorous for any one thing than for the expedition to the Crimea.

Thus urged, the Allied army, enfeebled by sickness which continued to pursue it, completed in all haste the most necessary preparations, and sailed to invade a country concerning which, for all purposes of war, a remarkable degree of ignorance prevailed. Travellers who had hastily traversed these regions suddenly found the notes and observations made for their own amusement or profit become information of the first importance. A reconnaissance of the coast had enabled us to select a suitable spot for the landing, but had left us as completely in the dark as to the obstacles interposed between us and our object as were Jason and his companions when they sailed in search of the Golden Fleece. The maps showed us three rivers between the point selected for landing and the city aimed at, any or all of which might be strongly guarded; the numbers and resources of the defenders of the soil could be only guessed at; and the city was surrounded by fortifications, of the nature and strength of which no certain intelligence existed.

Landing unopposed, we overthrew the enemy at the Alma, when such a shout of triumph arose in France and England that the mere reverberations were mistaken for fresh pæans of victory, and on the 18th of October the men in front of Sebastopol read what seemed to them the bitter mockery of its reported fall. It is not easy to suppose that the confident anticipations, thus rife at home, of the speedy accomplishment of the enterprise, should have been without effect on the efforts made to provide for the contingency of a protracted siege. Nevertheless, before the middle of November, a supply of warm clothing arrived, which unfortunately was lost with the steamer Prince. Other supplies following were landed and distributed as soon as possible to the troops, the greater part of whom, however, remained without drawers, flannel shirts, or new clothes till January, when these articles began to arrive in a profusion quite beyond our means of transport, which, at first inadequate to the wants of the army, had diminished every day.

Offering the foregoing remarks as in some degree explanatory of why the enterprise had been delayed, why it had taken place, and why better provision was not made for a winter campaign, I now come to the other question, as to the inadequacy of the expedition to accomplish its ends.

Experience daily strengthened the conviction that

the radical deficiency to be lamented in the British army was in the means of transport. It was in vain that supplies were landed at Balaklava, while no medium of conveyance existed from thence to the already over-taxed troops in camp. The baggage animals originally left behind at Varna had been brought to Balaklava, but the losses among them were so numerous and constant, that sufficient horses, ponies, and mules did not remain to bring up the necessary provisions and supplies of ammunition. Thus it happened that we had the mortification of seeing ships lying in the harbour at Balaklava, containing clothing to warm and huts to shelter the suffering troops, yet of no more avail, for want of means to transport them, than if they had been a thousand miles off. It is an old complaint that British troops in the field, in Europe, have been always deficient in means of transport, and never was the fault more apparent, or more severely felt, than in the campaign in the Crimea. Light capacious carriages, drawn by strong, well-fed animals, and driven by persons in whom there was no necessity for demanding the same physical requisites as in soldiers, would have been invaluable. The troops would have been regularly supplied, clothed, and housed, and a great number set free to lighten the military labours of the siege; guns would have replaced those disabled in the batteries, and ammunition would have been accumulated in sufficient quantity for a sustained attack.

The efforts made to supply the constant drain of the English army left Gibraltar, Malta, Corfu, and the British Isles denuded of troops. As efficient soldiers cannot be raised at short notice, it seems that the want of men now felt was altogether owing to the small number of troops which the national jealousy of a military force allowed to be kept on a peace establishment. The army in all its branches of cavalry, infantry, artillery, and medical staff, being systematically kept down to the very lowest point consistent with affording the appearance of garrisons to our colonies and fortified places at home and abroad, while baggage and hospital trains are absolutely unknown, must of course be always found insufficient, and its arrangements defective, in a first campaign against a powerful enemy. Doubtless, to the British people, proud of the achievements, and deeply moved by the privations of their army, it appeared impossible that they were themselves the authors of the disasters they deplored. Yet how long is it since oracles who proclaimed the impossibility of future European wars, and denounced our army as a useless and expensive encumbrance, commanded attention and applause? How long is it since the officers now held up to the world as heroes were considered fair targets for daily slanders and abuse, while the public looked on, applauding and amused? And when did any minister, charged with the office of seeing that the nation got present substantial returns for its expenditure, venture to propose an augmentation of the forces now proved to be inadequate in all except what the public cannot bestow, to maintain those interests which have so long engrossed the energies of our thriving people?

The naval portion of our armament was splendid. Our ships of war, our fleets of powerful steamers and huge transports, commanded the admiration and respect of the French. No signs of national frugality or shortcoming were visible there. But a very cursory glance at the condition of our military force, when the war began, will show its utter inadequacy to our rank and pretensions in the scale of nations. In all our garrisons at home and abroad the troops were barely sufficient to supply the necessary guards. At Gibraltar we had 800 guns, and 500 artillerymen to work them. At Chobham we thought we had done great things when we assembled 10,000 men to play at soldiers, while foreign potentates laughed in their sleeves at the display. Our cavalry force was absolutely ridiculous in its weakness, fitter numerically for some petty principality than for a mighty monarchy. Regiments appeared in Turkey, admirably equipped, but inferior in numbers to a respectable squadron. The artillery, that complex arm, involving duties so various, and which demand so much time in acquiring, has been always kept at a strength below its due proportion in an army such as is now in the field. Batteries at Woolwich for years consisted of four guns and four waggons, each drawn by four horses, with gunners and drivers in proportion; whereas, in the field, each battery has six guns, drawn each by eight horses, and seventeen waggons of various kinds, ammunition, store and forge waggons, with three times the number of horses considered necessary on the peace footing. The horses, both of artillery and cavalry, always accustomed to be separated by stalls, at the beginning of the campaign perpetually kicked each other as they stood at their picket-ropes, and numbers of them were thus crippled for weeks, and some permanently injured. The train of carriages with the supply of small-arm ammunition for the infantry was devised at Woolwich when the war broke out, and the vehicles were constructed in such a fashion that the animals of the country we were employed in could not draw them, and they were left useless at Varna; which could not have happened had our field equipments been systematically kept as efficient as those of Continental armies. And, in mentioning Continental armies, I do not mean to draw any comparison unfavourable to our own troops and our own system, so far as they go. We have little to learn in war from any nation, and the superiority in the internal management of the French army is principally due, in my judgment, wherever it really exists, to the ample supplies of men and material which, maintained and practised in time of peace, respond with ease and efficiency to the requirements of war.

Probably all this will now be remedied. Soldiers will be enlisted, transport procured, surgeons commissioned, and the glory of England maintained in a fashion worthy of her unrivalled resources—and then will come peace. And with peace will return our habit of considering that alone valuable, the value of which can be measured by the commercial standard: the army will shrivel to a skeleton—its members will be again the object of jealousy and taunts—until, in a new war, we shall again learn our deficiencies from our misfortunes. In our first campaigns, our victories will remain unimproved for want of cavalry; our supplies of all kinds will fail for want of transport; and our troops, suddenly transformed from popinjays to heroes, will be called on to make good with blood and sweat the parsimony of the repentant nation.

Lastly, to consider what course of action, having for its object the capture of Sebastopol, would have been preferable to that we had adopted, or rather, into which we had been urged.

If, landing in July, we had been conducted by the same sequence of events to our present position, where should we have been in September? The garrison would still have fortified the south side as fast as we could erect batteries to assail it. Our reinforcements could arrive no more quickly in summer than in winter—the command of the sea made the seasons equally available to us. But with the enemy the case was different. Myriads of troops, marching from the interior, would have thronged the roads of the Crimea. Supplies, not merely sufficient for the present, but for any future emergency, would have been accumulated in Sebastopol, and the neighbouring towns. The garrison, secure of help, would have been encouraged to double efforts; and when that help arrived, it would have been so effectual as, eventually, no matter how gallant and desperate our resistance, to penetrate by force of numbers our position, and drive us into the sea.

If the enterprise had been delayed till the spring of 1855, it is quite possible that our landing would have been no longer unopposed or cheaply effected. The Russians, alive to the danger, would have intrenched their coast line, reinforced the garrison, and augmented their forces in the Crimea. It may be said that we, too, would have been better prepared to sustain the enterprise. It might have been so—but, to learn wisdom or precaution in the conduct of a war, from anything but disaster, would have been contrary to our national custom. It is more likely that the army, inactive for a year in Turkey, would have been the fertile theme of leading articles, sarcastic, indignant, or abusive; that public zeal, exhausting itself in invective, would have left us little better provided for the enterprise in 1855 than in 1854; and that, if not baffled by the obstacles interposed by the forewarned enemy, our successes would have been purchased at a cost of life still greater than that we deplore. Therefore it seemed to some that, though our losses and sufferings had been great, we had not paid too dearly for our foot-hold on the enemy's soil, if the capture of Sebastopol should produce effects permanently crippling to Russian power. Those losses and those sufferings were due to the time-honoured policy of our nation. Our troops were paying the drawback on the pride of being Englishmen. They were brave and indomitable, therefore victorious ; but few, and ill provided for war, therefore sorely distressed. But the nation was aroused, and relief was, it was trusted, at hand. A little more endurance, a little more misery borne with cheerfulness, and we should see the prize in our grasp,—while the Czar, impotent to succour, would witness, with fruitless rage, the fall of the illustrious city.

CHAPTER XVI.

THE HOSPITALS ON THE BOSPHORUS.

The sick forming so large a portion of the army, as stated in the last chapter, it becomes a matter of interest to see how they were disposed of.

A soldier seized with illness generally lay a short time in the hospital tents, large and lofty marquees, round the sides of which the patients were ranged on wooden stretchers; while sick officers remained in their own tents, which were in nowise superior, except in privacy, to those tenanted by the men. Nothing could well be more desolate than the interior of the tent of an officer who had landed with the army, and whose baggage might be on board a transport not yet arrived in Balaklava. A pallet of cloaks and blankets in one corner—a couple of bullock trunks or portmanteaus serving as tables on which to arrange the tin platter and cup which constituted a Crimean service of plate—or two huge bags of Russian leather, purchased in the bazaar of Constantinople, as more portable and more easily packed than trunks,—these formed the only spots of furniture on the grassy or mud-spread floor. Those officers who joined subsequently from England were better provided, bringing portable beds and chairs, and other conveniences of camp life, as well as plenty of warm clothing. The men of the companies of artillery which arrived from England in December had strong serviceable long boots, and warm great-coats and under-clothing, which rendered them the envy of their half-clad comrades.

But the generality of tents, both of officers and men, were very comfortless, and afforded little chance of recovery to the sick, who were therefore sent, the slighter cases to Balaklava, where they were placed under roofs or on shipboard—the more serious to the great hospitals at Scutari, where they remained till either fit to return to the camp, or invalided to England. The ambulance waggons, long omnibus-shaped vehicles, containing brackets on which those unable to sit up could be laid, stretchers and all, as on shelves, and seats *dos-à-dos* with supports for the arms and feet, the whole eased by high springs, were much more comfortable and better adapted for invalids than the French ambulance mules, with a seat for a man on each side, but were far too few to accommodate the host of sufferers daily requiring removal. Most of them were, accordingly, sent down mounted on cavalry horses (another heavy, though most necessary, tax on our feeble means of transport,) and few sights can be imagined more melancholy than that of a troop of cadaverous, feeble, suffering beings, wrapt up in their blankets, swaying to and fro on the saddle, or crouching on the necks of the horses which bore them slowly towards the longed-for haven, where they might hope for some remission of their misery. Too often it happened that, on reaching the beach, no sufficient measures had been taken for conveying them on board, or accommodating them in the ships. Many died before being laid in the boats, and many more on their passage to Scutari; while a voyage across the stormy Euxine must, to a great number, have been more terrible torture than all they had previously undergone.

In the middle of January I was despatched to Constantinople in the Sphinx, a war-steamer, to send up a number of transport animals, equipped with waggons, clothing, and drivers, for the service of the army. Riding down to Kamiesch in a thick blinding snow-storm, through which the track was hardly discernible, I embarked; the ship started at once, as she waited only for the despatches which I had charge of, to deliver to the Queen's messenger at Constantinople; and, after a stormy passage with a head wind, we reached the mouth of the Bosphorus in thirty hours. The next morning saw us anchored off the Tophana.

I had last seen the city and the banks of the sea-river clad in all the warmth and brilliancy of summer. The white walls would then have been too dazzling in the hot sunlight, but for the lavish relief of trees, whose cool foliage or gay blossoms everywhere spotted the glare : while the light blue water, unrippled as a lake, was so transparent that the caïques hung as if balanced in air on their own reflections, " floating, a double light, in air and wave." On each side jutted, farther and farther off, and still becoming more fairy-like in their indistinctness, the green and flowery banks of the Bosphorus, till a low line, purpled by distance, closed the view; and everywhere the white birds, the white sails, or the white tunics of the boatmen, specked brightly the blue or the green.

Going on deck on a bitter cold morning (the 15th of January), I saw close before me the city, dreamlike as ever, but of a character altogether changed. Every dome and roof was covered with snow, the grey shadows melting into the grey background of sky. An icy purity had taken the place of the brilliant glow,—the minaret points sparkled with a cold glitter, the mosques rose like huge twelfth-cakes, frosted and fretted, above the snow-clad roofs, and the buildings on the Stamboul side of the Golden Horn looked faint and sketchy against the sky. Keen squalls whistled down the Bosphorus, casting shadows like stains on the slaty water, and making the caïques reel and dance, while the whitened waves marked the hasty footsteps of the blast. Upward and downward cold shores stretched whitely and mistily out between the dull sky and dark water, the black stripes of cypresses giving solidity to the else vapoury landscape. The boatmen had exchanged their white tunics for warm brown jackets, and had wound shawls round their skull-caps; the caïques, faded and dim in colour, seemed to think it no longer worth while to look at themselves in the water, and floated shadowless.

Going on shore, the change from poetry to prose was sudden as ever. Constantinople is like the well-painted drop-scene of a theatre. Beautiful and imposing at the right distance, a closer view reveals the coarse texture of the canvass, and the rudeness of the daubing which has produced so excellent an effect. The sun, struggling forth at noonday, sent the dissolving snow in flood from the spouts of the houses, which, mingling with that already blackened by the tread of the passing throng, poured down the steeper streets and settled in pools along the level ones; and every projecting stone that offered a friendly means of transit was disputed by elbowing Turks, Greeks, Armenians, Jews, and English and French soldiers and sailors. These latter had become somewhat noisy and troublesome in their visits ashore, and some frays had ensued, in which lives were lost, between them and the inhabitants. I saw a drunken English merchant seaman persist in an attempt to fight a French officer, because the latter had declined to join him in singing "Cheer, boys, cheer." The Frenchman showed much dignified good-nature, and the rascal was dragged away by his comrades. The same day I saw a French soldier, very drunk, holding in his left hand a drawn sword, which he flourished in the faces of the passengers, proclaiming vociferously his devoted friendship for the English and his disapprobation of the Russians. This respectable ally also was disarmed and quieted by his comrades.

The hotels were filled, for the most part, with military men, some come down sick from the Crimea, some arriving from England and France on their way to the war, some amateurs of the English or Anglo-Indian army desirous of seeing the nature of the service which afforded a theme of interest for all Europe. The conversation at the *table d'hôte* consisted entirely of criticisms on the conduct of the war, anecdotes from the camp, and debates on the chances of peace ; and, occasionally, some of us had the advantage of hearing portions of the actions we had been engaged in, or the manœuvres we had witnessed, placed in an entirely novel light, by critics who had been distant some thousand miles from the scene of action.

The Golden Horn contained almost a fleet of French and English men-of-war undergoing repair, and was thronged with transports lying off the arsenal, or between the bridges which connect Pera with Stamboul. Whenever a ship moved out, a portion of the bridge was swung back to leave the passage open, and the tide of passengers pressing across suddenly found a yawning gulf between them and their goal. The operation of opening and reclosing the bridge being conducted with all the deliberation which characterises Turkish proceedings, the throng of passengers on foot, on horseback, and in carriages, sometimes increased till it filled the bridge and threatened to overflow into the space between, where caïques were hovering to convey across the more impatient. The bridge itself, flooded in the level portion with some inches of water, and having holes broken through at the sides in many places, through which the unwary might well slip, reminded me of that which Mirza saw in his vision in Addison's tale.

The first day I tried to cross the strait to Scutari, it blew so hard that the caïque was obliged to put back ; but on the following day the water was comparatively calm. The barrack occupied by the English in the spring—a large, quadrangular, white building, with a tower at each corner, standing on the edge of the bank—was now the principal English hospital. A boat was alongside the wooden pier, with sick and wounded men just landing from a ship, the Shooting Star, which had been detained by some accident from rough weather in the Black Sea for a great many days. These men, laid on stretchers, each borne by four Turks, were carried up the steep hill to the hospital, moaning as they went, and received within the portal where rest and comfort awaited them.

There are several storeys in this huge building ; and on the inside, looking into the square, a corridor opening from the rooms, paved with stone, and four or five yards wide, goes quite round the whole extent. All the corridors, as well as the rooms, were filled with patients, and the visitor walked between a double row of beds. At the points where the stairs connected the different flights, wooden partitions were erected to repel the cutting draughts, and stoves kept the temperature pleasant; and thus the corridors were as habitable as the wards.

There was one room in which I took peculiar interest—for, having my leg broken in June by the kick of a horse, I lay there, fixed to one particular spot, for six long weeks before I rejoined the army at Varna — and this was the first I visited. It was occupied by three officers, all strangers to me, and I therefore took but a hasty glance—but that included each well-remembered crack and crevice in the wall and nail in the wood-work, and the large cupboard-door which, laid on two arm-chests to raise me to the level of the window, had, with a mattress on it, served me as a bed. On the level of that window, just opposite, at a hundred yards' distance, rose a tall white minaret, with a low arch opening into its balcony, from which I had seen the muezzin emerge at regular intervals each day to call aloud to the faithful, till I was intimately acquainted with his appearance and the inflections of his voice, in the sweet, sad tones of which he used, after nightfall, to chant a monotonous prayer. While I had lain there, the army was in Bulgaria, preparing, as was supposed, for an active campaign on the Danube, and each friend who bade me good-by expressed by looks, if not by words, that he thought me shut out from all chance of participating in the adventurous future opening for him. Some of those who went forth so buoyantly are now laid for ever beneath the soil of the Crimea, in spots where the hopes of others, as well as their own, are buried. Many such recollections arose during that hasty glance round the well-known chamber. These revisitings of a marked spot sometimes round off and include a phase of existence. I had seen much of stirring life since I quitted that room on crutches.

Entering any of the corridors or wards, the same scene presented itself. The occupants of some of the beds sat strongly up, eating heartily their soup and meat; others, emaciated to skeletons, more like corpses than living beings, except for the large, hollow, anxious eyes, lay back on their pillows, or tried with difficulty to swallow the spoonfuls of arrowroot or sago offered to them by the attendants. There seemed no doubtful class—all were broadly marked either for life or death. The patients appeared comfortable—had good beds and plenty of bed-clothes—and the temperature of the chambers was, as before said, regulated to a very pleasant warmth. At some beds, a woman, the wife of the patient, sat chatting with him; beside others stood the somewhat ghostly appearance of a Catholic sister of charity, upright, rigid, veiled, and draped in black;—the veil projecting far beyond her face, threw it, as well as the white linen folded across her bosom, into deep shadow. The thinness of some of the forms propped up against their pillows, their chests exposed by the open shirts, was absolutely frightful; the bony hands wandered vaguely about the hair and sunken temples, and the eyes were fixed on vacancy. Some lay already in the shadow of death, their eyes reverted, showing only the whites beneath the drooping lids; and others had passed this last stage, and waited only for the grave.

At the end of a corridor in a tower were quarters once held by General Sir George Brown, but then occupied by gentler tenants. There dwelt the sisterhood that had come from England to tend the sick— the Rebeccas to the Ivanhoes of the Crimea. That quarter of the building threw a softening and romantic tinge over the rest;—in its neighbourhood pain and misery seemed less forlorn. The corridor opened on a kitchen where some good sisters were preparing soup, sago and wine, and other comforting compounds. Doorways opening from the kitchen were screened by long folds of black cloth or tapestry, behind which dwelt the lady sisters; and high up the wall of the kitchen were windows, across which flitted nun-like forms, heard presently to descend the stair to our level. It was while one of two or three who accompanied me, a man of sedate and respectable aspect, such as might without presumption engage the attention of a sister of charity, extracted from a motherly benevolent lady some statistical details of the sisterhood, that the chief of them herself, Miss Nightingale, lifting the piece of tapestry before her door for a parting visitor, stood for a moment revealed. During that short interval the statistics of the motherly lady were unheeded—we steadily regarded the chief as she bid her visitor adieu—then the tapestry fell and she vanished.

There were eight Protestant ladies, and a rather larger number of Catholic sisters: in all, with their attendants who officiated as nurses, there were about forty in the sisterhood.

In the great kitchen, close by their quarter, rice-pudding, manufactured on a grand scale, was transferred, smoking, by an enormous ladle to the destined platters; beef-tea and mutton-broth were being cooked in huge caldrons, such as the witches danced around; and flocks of poultry were simmering into boiled fowls or chicken-broth.

There were three English hospitals besides this. One at a little distance, a large red-brick building, was originally built and used for the purpose by the Turks: it was the most comfortable and best suited to its object of all. Another is known as the Kiosk, or Palace Hospital; and the third was at Coolali, a place some miles up the Bosphorus, on the Scutari side, where there is a large barrack which was occupied by the English cavalry and artillery before the army left for Varna. All these buildings were clean, cheerful, airy, and comfortable. They contained in all, at the time of my first visit, 4700 sick, increased to 5000 at the end of January; and from first to last 10,000 men had passed through,—some back to the Crimea, where in many cases they had relapsed into sickness and died—some to England—and some to their final resting-place.

On the edge of the bank of the Sea of Marmora, a few hundred yards to the left of the mouth of the Bosphorus, is a level space of greensward, used by the English, from the time of their arrival in Turkey, as a burying-ground. The placid sea, the distant isles, the cape of Broussa on the left, and Seraglio Point on the right, make up a lovely view from the melancholy spot. At the southern extremity of the ground are single graves, neatly defined and turfed, where those who died while the army halted here in the spring are laid. But the press of mortality no longer admitted of such decent burial. To those accustomed to see the departed treated with reverence, and attended solemnly to their last habitation, there was something horribly repulsive in a wholesale interment, where the dead far outnumbered those who stood round the grave. A pit, about ten feet deep and fourteen square, received every afternoon those who had died during the last twenty-four hours. A rickety araba, or country cart, drawn by two oxen, was the hearse which conveyed them from the neighbouring hospital to the place of sepulture. In the yard of the hospital is a small dismal house, without windows; for its tenants no longer needed the light. Thither those who have died in this and the neighbouring hospitals were brought on stretchers, and packed like sacks in a granary till the araba came for them. Sewed, each in a blanket, with sufficient tightness to leave a caricature, mummy-like resemblance of humanity, a score of bodies were laid on the vehicle, and travelled slowly, dangling and jostling as they went, to the mouth of the yawning pit, where the party who dug it awaited the coming of the cart. There was no time for ceremony; each poor corpse was hastily lifted off, and, doubled up limply in cases of recent death, or stiff and stake-like where it had been longer cold, was handed down, nameless, unknown, and void of all the dignity of death, to its appointed station in the crowd. One row laid, the next covered it, and the feet of those who deposited them necessarily trampled on the forms below, leaving muddy foot-prints on the blanket-shrouds. Sixty-one (about the daily average number at the time) were buried together on the day I visited the spot. Noticing one corpse in which the lower part of the outline seemed unusually thin, I remarked to the corporal in charge that the deceased must have been long ill, to be so wasted; but he pointed out to me that one limb had been amputated. A clergyman waited till all were deposited to read the funeral service; close by, another pit was being dug for the requirements of next day, and we had seen in the hospital many of those unmistakably destined to fill it. Altogether the scene reminded one of Defoe's account of the burials about London in the time of the Great Plague.

I have mentioned elsewhere the trenches dug on a battle-field to contain rows of dead. But there they lie like soldiers, with an awe and glory on their blood-stained uniforms and upturned faces, which no pall nor coffin could bestow. In the pits of Scutari, Death was deprived of his sanctity, majesty, and mystery, and retained only those elements which constitute the grotesque.

Officers were buried singly in graves close to the edge of the bank, where cross-headed slips of wood, like those which mark the plants in a greenhouse, and not much larger, were labelled, sometimes with the name of the occupant below, sometimes less specifically—as " A Woman," " A Russian Officer."

Wishing to see the French hospital in Pera, I applied to M. Lévy, the Inspector-General, who very kindly gave me a note to M. Morgue, the principal medical officer, in which he prayed him to receive some other Englishmen and myself " avec la courtoisie que meritent si bien nos dignes alliés."

The building, standing on a high point of ground above the new palace of the Sultan, and conspicuous from the Bosphorus, was originally intended as a school of medicine. It is very large, newer and fresher, and the wards and apartments loftier than those of our hospitals. At the door was a covered cart, with a cross in front, filled with coffins, and drawn by oxen. In the first room we entered, besides some French officers, there were a Russian captain and two subalterns, wounded at Inkermann, playing at some game like draughts. In the next room, a very spacious one, with a painted ceiling, and windows opening to the floor, looking on the Bosphorus, were five or six French officers, apparently very comfortable. The corridors, like those of our hospitals, were filled with patients; in the wards, the beds on each side were raised on a platform above the floor: there was a very thick paillasse under each man; across the rail at the head of the bed was a shelf with his medicine-bottles; and on a card at the foot was a description of his case. The surgeon who accompanied us round pointed out a remarkable case, that of a man who had received a bullet in the head, which entering on one side had gone out near the opposite ear, passing close to the lobe of the brain; he was sensible, apparently suffering but little pain, and would, the surgeon thought, live. Opposite him was another with his skull fractured by a sabre-cut from a Russian officer; the surgeon, removing the dressing with tweezers, tapped them audibly, without paining the man, on the bare skull-bone, which was cleft for about an inch, and surrounded by a gaping wound in the scalp. The poor fellow whined dolefully as the instrument-case was unfolded; but the surgeon reassured him, saying he was only going to move the dressing; he told us afterwards, he thought it would be necessary to trepan him. Sisters of charity, with the freshest of complexions and the snowiest of caps, moved to and fro among the beds; one of them was an Irishwoman from Meath, who had left Ireland, as she told us, five years before to join the sisterhood. One corridor was filled with convalescent Russians in their uniforms of grey or blue, surmounted, in many instances, by a French cap; they stood up respectfully and grinned approval when the good doctor patronised them by a tap on the back or a pull of the ear. The chief distinction between this hospital and ours seemed to be that here the patients were classified according to the nature of their ailments; one ward was filled with cases of frost-bites, another of wounds, another of fever,—a plan tried at first in our hospitals, but broken in upon by the throng of sick arriving. It is probable that the worst cases are kept apart in the French hospitals, as none of the men we saw seemed in extremity; and it is certain that *nos dignes alliés* like to exhibit, on all occasions, the best side of their management. The doctor said the deaths averaged seven or eight a-day out of fourteen hundred—about half the proportion of those in our hospitals; a variation somewhat puzzling, since there seems nothing in the difference of accommodation, care, nourishment, or treatment sufficient to account for it.

Our hospitals, with their staff and orderlies, were under the commandant of Scutari, Brigadier-General Lord W. Paulet. The duties of the staff were extremely, almost hopelessly perplexing, from the confusion of the accounts of pay, necessaries, stoppages, &c., of such a number of men of different regiments. To the commandant, all officers halting on their way to and from the Crimea reported themselves, and he applied for a passage for them, and also for the patients rejoining the army, or invalided to England, to the admiral, who had control over all the transports and men-of-war. These two form, with the chief commissary, a trio supposed to work in unity—as Mrs Malaprop says, " like Cerberus, three gentlemen in one." It is most necessary they should act in concert, for many services to be performed here demand a combined exertion of the authority of the three, as absolutely as a bill requires the consent of the Three Estates to become law.

The dealings of the commissariat were very various and extensive, comprising contracts for all the supplies of provisions, clothing, and forage for the army, besides what came from England. The constantly-varying rate of exchange must have greatly increased the complication of their duties. Several large steamers were appropriated exclusively to the commissariat as cattle-ships, which, at certain points of the coast, embarked bullocks, already collected by their agents in the surrounding district, and conveyed them straight to Balaklava.

CHAPTER XVII.

EXCULPATORY.

IN the earlier chapters I have rather avoided comment, confining myself to a plain narrative of the course of events as they flowed one into another. The public had been more than content with the campaign, and demanded only an intelligible and detailed account of the occurrences which had led to such pleasing results. But opinion had begun to exercise so large an influence on the war, that a record of its progress would be defective in which this new element should be left unrecognised.

The dull expanse of the siege, unrelieved, after Inkermann, by any bright red spots of victory in the foreground, was kept incessantly before the eyes of the public in its most dismal and lurid colours. Inflamed by the letters from the camp, and leading articles, with which every newspaper teemed, descriptive of the sufferings and losses of the army, and charging the authorities, military and ministerial, as the chief sources of disaster, the nation joined in one indignant outcry against the Government and the

General. The plaudits of anticipated victory were changed to threats, forebodings, and despondency. Where a speedy triumph had been expected, there had been comparative failure ; where national glory was to have been cheaply obtained, there had been losses and misery amounting to national disaster : therefore there must be blame. Such was the process of reasoning conducting to a conclusion almost unanimously assented to ; the clamour swelled daily ;—Mr Roebuck gave notice of his motion of inquiry into the conduct of the war ;—Lord John Russell suddenly quitted the Government ; and the Ministry, defeated on Roebuck's motion by a majority of two to one, went out amidst such a clamour as greets the last moments of a criminal on the scaffold.

Amid the din of invective, those who read the parliamentary debates and leading articles of the time, will be puzzled to detect the true ground of censure. They will see that the nation was dissatisfied, and with whom, but will have some difficulty in knowing why. Everybody has been ready to indicate the culprits, but none to specify the crime, except in the general terms of neglect, ignorance, and apathy. But though the accusers were confessedly in want of specific charges, yet the causes of our failure, in those points where we had failed, having been divined, or imagined to be divined, it was easy to ask why those causes had been allowed to exist.

For instance, it was known that the severest hardships of the army had arisen from the want of a communication between Balaklava and the camp ; and it was asked why a road had not been made ? It should have been made, it was urged, at the commencement of the siege, and should have been the first thing thought of.

Now, at the commencement of the siege, and for six weeks afterwards, the roads were hard and good. Before us was a place which we hoped to take after a short cannonade, and, notwithstanding that all the men available were employed in the trenches and batteries, and transporting armament and material for the works, the delay still seemed very tedious to the impatient troops. The trenches, once constructed, must be manned ; and, thinned as the army was by sickness, to do this adequately absorbed all our available men. To make a road seven miles long was no light task, even if men and time could have been spared for it.

After a time, it began to be seen and admitted by the press, that the army once landed in the Crimea, the events, up to the end of October, followed in a sequence easily accounted for, without fixing culpability on the chief actors. It was seen that to have occupied the first period of the investment in making a road, would have called forth deservedly a charge of deferring the completion of the enterprise, in order to carry on an extensive work which might never be wanted. As the season wore on, the days between us and winter, like the Sibylline books, grew in value with each diminution of their number, and not one could be spared from the business of the siege. The enemy were seen throwing up their defensive works, and unless we kept pace with them, we must expect to break ground under an overwhelming fire. On the other hand, to have pushed the enterprise to a rash termination, by assaulting the town without waiting for the battering-train to do its work, would have entailed, even with success, the yet more serious charge of incurring an unnecessary waste of life, when a little patience and trouble spent in availing ourselves of the means we possessed, might secure a comparatively bloodless victory,—a charge which all but men of surpassing self-reliance would shrink from the risk of. Viewed in retrospect, it is easy to detect our errors, and to point to a better course of action; and the least sagacious and resolute general of the Allied army would, if the problem were again set before him, apply the lesson of experience in the alternative of a speedy assault or deliberate provision for wintering on the heights. It is a cheap sagacity, and pleasant to exercise, which points out the faults of the past. In fighting our battles o'er again, mediocrity becomes infallible, and doubt and difficulty are no longer elements of warfare.

If, then, it is granted that, up to the end of October, things had gone as well with us as could fairly be expected, let us take that as the starting-point of imputed error. It is said that, it being then clear that no prospect remained of a speedy capture of the place, measures should at once have been taken to provide against winter. A road should have been made, provisions stored, and huts and stables constructed,—all very desirable measures, but unfortunately not practicable. As already mentioned, the duty of the trenches exceeded our means, when guards, pickets, and the covering force were provided for, and our men were already dying of fatigue. Therefore, in order to begin other works, men must be taken from the trenches. But to guard the trenches insufficiently would be worse than not to guard them at all : it would be adding the slaughter of men to the loss of guns, therefore they must be abandoned ; and to withdraw the guns and ammunition, and dismantle the batteries, would have been of itself a considerable labour. But our lines once abandoned, the French could no longer hold theirs, as they would have been liable at any time to be taken in reverse ; therefore the whole siege-works must have been given up, to be reconstructed at a more convenient season, while the Russians augmented their defences without interruption. Would this have suited either army or either nation ? Or would it have been considered preferable to the severe losses we have suffered ? Besides, our attention was no longer confined to the siege. The army in the field against us was daily increasing, and had already attacked our position twice. Such were the circumstances under which it is said roads ought to have been made, provisions stored, and the troops sheltered.

The asserted superiority in the condition of the French army was cited as proof that we were in much worse state than we need be. It is by no means certain that our allies were much better provided than ourselves; at the same time, it is difficult to compare with accuracy the condition of the two armies, because the French systematically represent their own affairs in the most favourable light. And without presuming to doubt the advantages of a free discussion by the public press of our military system and operations, yet we must admit it to be, if a weakness, yet a natural one, on the part of our allies, to veil their own proceedings as much as possible from an equally severe scrutiny. Assuming, therefore, that inquiries made from the French as to the progress, reinforcements, and general state of their army, did not always elicit unadultered facts, we may still find indulgence for the motives which tinged those facts with a roseate hue. To hear that its army was disorganised, famished, and dying of disease, and to be held up to the world as an example of disastrous military policy, might, however interesting to the public, be somewhat obnoxious to the vanity of a warlike nation, proud of its achievements, and fond to excess of glory.

There is no doubt that, during the early part of the campaign, the French suffered more from disease than we did. If, during the winter, the case was reversed, the change is easily accounted for. Large and constant reinforcements from France lightened the labours of the siege, and left plenty of men for the construction of the road from Kamiesch to their camp. While our men, from the fewness of their numbers, were often two, even three, nights in succession in the trenches, the French spent four nights out of five in their tents. Six days enabled them to communicate with Marseilles, and six or eight more to procure from thence any supplies which might be suddenly found needful.

It was said we ought to have insisted on the labours of the siege being proportioned to the strength of the two armies respectively. But at the commencement of the siege we rather outnumbered the French, who offered us our choice of the right of the attack, with Balaklava as a port, or the left, with Kamiesch. We chose the right, principally for the sake of holding Balaklava, which was altogether in our hands, and its harbour filled with our vessels. When reinforcements arrived to the French, they had a greater extent of trenches to occupy than we, owing to the nature of the ground in their front permitting a nearer approach to the place. The whole of the French troops, with the exception of Bosquet's division, which was posted near the Woronzoff road, encamped in rear of their own lines, where, however convenient for the relief of their trenches, and for supplies from Kamiesch, they were at a great distance from any point of the position liable to be attacked. It would certainly appear to have been more desirable that they should have contributed a larger proportion to the covering force ; and, after the battle of Inkermann, they sent troops of all arms to reinforce our first and second divisions, and placed a brigade of infantry in the lines of Balaklava. At the beginning of February, the French, numbering more than 70,000, which was five times our effective force, took the whole of the lines and field-works on the hills around Inkermann, while we armed the batteries with guns, and furnished artillerymen to work them. Had the army been all French or all English, of course every reinforcement would have lightened the burdens of the whole ; but, in the absence of any express stipulation for such a contingency, it was natural that the French should avail themselves of their superior numbers to relieve our men and forward our works only so far as was feasible without detriment to their own.

The commissariat of our army has received a good deal of censure. The only school in which its officers can learn any part of their duties is in our foreign garrisons and colonies, where their business is to issue pay to the troops, to make contracts for provisions, and to see that these are of good quality. This is obviously a somewhat slender preparation for the duty of supplying an army in the field ; and many among the juniors had not even this advantage. Those members of the service with whom I am personally acquainted, certainly cannot be charged either with indolence or incapacity.

In offering the foregoing remarks, I by no means

intend to say that every possible measure was taken to alleviate the distresses of our troops. Better order might probably have been established, and the insufficient means at their disposal turned to better account. But I do intend to say, that, in the absence of large reserves of good troops, and an efficient transport corps, no sagacity or foresight could have obviated, to any extent, the evils which have befallen us. The Government may, or may not, have exerted itself to the utmost in carrying on the war: if it possessed the means of remedying the deficiencies I speak of, it ought to have been called to account long ago for neglecting to do so. But let the condemnation be on just grounds:—the protraction of the siege amid suffering and loss is, in itself, no fair proof of incompetence. The British people, hardest of taskmasters, demanding bricks where they have denied straw, look only to results; and the ministry and the general who commence a war must always, unless aided by fortune to an extraordinary extent, incur the national displeasure at the first arduous undertaking of the campaign; and it will be well for the country if it possesses men capable of efficiently replacing them. Such has been the fortune of the first actors on the present stage; censure has been loud and general, and the difficulties encountered never fairly taken into account. In front, a city of great and daily-increasing strength, with a numerous garrison, and offering unusual natural obstacles to a regular attack—an army in the field threatening us

—our forces thinned by sickness, and clad in worn-out summer uniforms, while winter was pressing so close that we felt his breath on our cheeks—supplies daily less attainable, men and horses daily dying—and no retreat. What a problem to set before a General, an Army, and a Government, trained amid the experiences of a forty years' peace! The genius of Napoleon, combined with that of Chatham, might have gained lustre by a triumphant solution. It will be said that the conditions enumerated ought never to have been allowed to exist; but I have in some measure anticipated the objection in a former Chapter (XV.)

It is very natural that those who saw our gallant army quit England, splendidly equipped, elate, and eager for battle, should feel sorrow and indignation at the miserable end which so many of these noble troops have met. It is natural that, when men of talent have exerted all their descriptive power to set the sufferings of the army in the strongest possible light, their readers should be excited to a pitch of sympathy even beyond that which an actual sight of the horrors so vividly depicted would produce. With advancing civilisation, human life has risen in value and consideration to an unprecedented extent; our soldiers, no longer accounted as food for powder, are thought of as equal in all respects, superior in some, to those citizens of ancient states who have made famous the names of Thermopylæ, Platæa, and Marathon; and those who would scruple to deprive the worst criminal of existence, cannot hear of so many brave men perishing without horror. The expression of these feelings, under the circumstances, is natural and inevitable. Not so the contrast, so frequently drawn and so strongly dwelt on, between our army and that of the French, and which, coming from ourselves, cannot have failed to efface some of the respect which the sight of the battery at the Alma, where three Russians lay dead for every Englishman —of the charge at Balaklava, where our heavy brigade of cavalry met and put to flight three times their number of horsemen—and of the bloody resistance at Inkermann, so signally produced. Is it politic to insist so strongly on our inferiority?—or, if politic, is it just? I have heard of letters from Paris alluding to others received from the French camp, in which the French army is described as being entirely occupied with taking care of the English. The Continental states, taking us at our word, begin to affect compassion for the military system of the nation which is stronger in resources now than when it saved Europe. Cannot necessary reforms be effected without such depreciatory outcry? Might not the comparisons I speak of be drawn with greater fairness? Legions of fresh troops were always ready to cover, and more than cover, the losses of the French. England and France are friends—long may they continue so—nor should any subject be hinted at which is likely to excite jealousy between them; but let us be just to ourselves. Nothing has yet occurred to prove that our ancient reputation in arms is endangered.

CHAPTER XVIII.

PROGRESS OF THE SIEGE.

BEFORE leaving Constantinople, when the object of my mission was accomplished, I visited again the hospitals at Scutari, and noticed a remarkable improvement in the appearance of the patients. Formerly a large proportion were evidently past recovery; but now, although the hospital was fuller than ever, the *facies Hippocratica* lent its ghastliness to a far less number of pillows. The most appalling cases were those of frostbite, and I saw one dreadful instance where the bones of the toes stuck out white and naked from the black and swollen feet.

On the 17th of February I sailed for the Crimea, and thus terminated the cheerful glimpse of civilised life which I had enjoyed doubly from contrast with the stern scenes which bordered it. From a smoky hut in a quagmire, to a pleasant room looking on the Bosphorus—from the *Barber of Seville* at the opera of Pera, to the grim drama of the siege with the snowy waste for a drop-scene — the change was indeed "from grave to gay, from lively to severe."

The ship had been ordered to start a day before her time, and I had hurried down to the Golden Horn, followed by a porter bearing a huge pie, made under the special directions of my hostess, and so stuffed with every available bird of the air as to be a sort of aviary in paste. Woodcock, red-leg, pheasant, and the domestic fowl, nestled in harmonious and sweet companionship on layers of veal and ham, their union being cemented by truffles. It was smoking hot, being drawn from the oven barely in time for my departure. Placing it carefully in a caïque, I seated myself therein, and directed the boatman to row to the vessel, which was hissing with steam as if about to start. On reaching the accommodation-ladder my first care was for the pie, which I well knew would be warmly welcomed " before Sebastopol;" and, lifting it from the caïque, I placed it on the step of the ladder, and was about to follow when the boatman let the caïque fall off from the ship's side, and I was obliged to quit my hold of the ladder. The pie, left unsupported, was too broad for the step, and toppled over. For one agonising moment it seemed about to fall into the water; it remained resting on its side, and forth gushed a flood of gravy, filling the air with such odours as saluted the nose of Sancho when he lifted the lids of the fleshpots in Camacho's kitchen; or Mr Codlin's, when the host of the Jolly Sandboys took the cover off the stew. Attracted by the steam of rich distilled perfumes which rose upward, about four hundred Croats, who were shipped on board for the Crimea for the purpose of making roads, flocked to the side of the vessel, and the pie was conveyed across the deck through a crowd of picturesque savages, who hovered fondly around it, snuffing up the fragrance, and who could with difficulty prevail on themselves to quit its neighbourhood. However, it turned out eventually but little the worse, and had, moreover, the advantage of being discussed in a most uncritical spirit.

The harbour of Balaklava was so thronged that the steamer could not enter, and I went in a boat. The place was greatly improved since I had last seen it. The streets were cleaner, the frost had dried the roads, and there were more conveniences for landing. The railway ran from the heart of the town, through the meadows which last autumn teemed with vegetables, fruit, and vines, to the side of the hill beyond Kadukoi at the head of the valley; and huge fat dray-horses, suggestive of ale and stout, stalked ponderously by. Ascending the heights to the plateau, too, circumstances were changed greatly for the better. Many huts had been brought up, forming in some spots small villages. The dead horses had been buried, and the live ones sheltered, either in stables of plank, or in trenches covered in with boards or tarpaulin; while the troops had been for some weeks enjoying the comfort of plenty of warm clothing, and wore the appearance of health.

So many stories of desperate sorties, threatened

attacks by the Russians on Balaklava, and combats more or less disastrous to the Allies, were always floating about the *table d'hôte* at Pera, generally supported by plausible authority, that I hastened to inquire into the truth of some which had appeared better authenticated than the rest. With the exception of one or two sorties, however, nothing had occurred to break the monotony of the siege. But the night of the 19th February (the day I landed) had been fixed on for an expedition into the valley of the Tchernaya, to surprise the Russian force there, and to effect a reconnaissance of the surrounding country. General Bosquet was to command a considerable French force ; and the Highland brigade, with two batteries of artillery, and about three hundred cavalry, was to co-operate with him.

Though the day had been fine, a bitter north wind, with snow, blew all night, and the cold was so intense that the order for Bosquet's division to march was countermanded. The staff-officer, who was sent to apprise Sir C. Campbell of the postponement of the enterprise, lost his way in the snow-storm, and at two in the morning the English force marched out of Kadukoi, proceeding across the plain towards Tchergoum, where, according to the original plan, they were to have engaged the attention of the Russian force, while the French, crossing the bridge, turned their flank. There seems good reason to believe that, had the design been carried out, it would have been attended with success ; the Russians had neglected their outposts, and nothing occurred to interrupt the march. Daylight showed the Russian force across the Tchernaya, two miles off, ill prepared for an attack, and it was nearly half an hour before they got under arms. When it was seen from the plateau that the English had advanced, a body of French was despatched to support them; and nearly at the same time came the order countermanding the enterprise. In marching back, the ammunition-mules were separated from the troops, and, a body of Cossacks appearing behind a neighbouring hill, two of them, with levelled lances, galloped down to intercept the rearmost animal; but a sergeant and private of the infantry escort, running out, fired at them, and they turned and retreated, while a detachment of our cavalry came back to protect the ammunition. Some of our men were frost-bitten; and another misfortune arising from the abortive attempt was, that the enemy were thus placed on their guard against a repetition of the enterprise.

Before this, intelligence had arrived of an attack made on Eupatoria by the Russians, who had been observed on the 15th to receive large convoys and reinforcements from the eastward.

At daylight on the 17th they came on in numbers estimated at 40,000 of all arms, with from sixty to one hundred guns, and opened with their artillery on the intrenchments surrounding the town. Skirmishers covered the guns, the battalions were in rear, and the cavalry on the flanks; subsequently the guns advanced, and under cover of their fire the infantry, forming behind a wall 600 yards distant from the right of the town, made their attack, and were repulsed; at other points also they were driven back; and at ten in the morning they retired, covered by the artillery and cavalry. Liprandi's division (the 12th), formerly posted in front of Balaklava, was present in this action.

A battery of Turkish artillery was disabled in the attack, every gun being struck, and a third of the horses killed, with nineteen gunners. There were ninety-seven Turks killed, and 277 wounded in all; a French detachment acting with them lost four killed and nine wounded; and of the Tartar population thirteen were killed and eleven wounded. Selim Pasha, an Egyptian, commanding a brigade, was among the slain. The Russians left 460 dead; and if the snow-storm on the night of the 19th found them on the march, or unsheltered, they must have suffered severe loss.

For some time a cordon of Russian cavalry had surrounded Eupatoria. A depôt of provisions and military stores had been collected there, and a garrison from the Turkish army on the Danube under Omer Pasha; but their great deficiency was in cavalry, the scanty number of which barely enabled them to furnish the necessary videttes. While in Constantinople, I was glad to hear that 4000 cavalry were soon to be despatched to Eupatoria; in an action taking place on the plains between that town and Sebastopol, victory would almost certainly remain with the side which was strongest in that arm.

During the early part of the siege the garrison of Sebastopol had never displayed any great degree of enterprise, though they had stood well to their guns, and worked diligently at their defences. But on the night of the 22d of February they seized on a hill about 400 yards from the advanced trench held by the French in front of Inkermann, and began to construct a battery there. All the redoubts now erected on the battle-field of the 5th of November were garrisoned by the French, who had also constructed some very well-finished lines extending from the batteries opposite the Inkermann Lights, around the face of the slopes looking towards the Round Tower, in which direction approaches had been pushed to the advanced trench in question, which was at a considerable distance from the redoubts.

Being in the trenches of our right attack on the 23d, I had a good view of this new Russian work. A row of gabions had been filled, and a second placed on the top of a small hill between Careening Bay and the French trenches before Inkermann; and a few men were employed in working behind the hill, which hid them from the French. It was evident that the latter could not permit the work to proceed unmolested, and an attack was ordered for the same night.

At an hour after midnight, 2500 French infantry,

REPULSE OF THE FRENCH.

consisting of a battalion of Zouaves, and one each of the line and of marines, sallied from the trenches; and the two latter remaining in support, the Zouaves advanced without firing, to the foot of the eminence on which the battery was posted. The Russians were prepared, and received them with a volley from the work in front, and from a line of infantry extended on each side to flank the approach. The Zouaves returned the fire, and pressed on, and a combat of musketry and bayonets ensued, which lasted for an hour. During this time the Russian batteries opened against the hill, firing shot, shell, and rockets, without intermission. The French succeeded at one time in entering the work, and driving out its defenders, but were checked by the Russian supports, which were posted behind the hill in great strength, evidently in expectation of an attack; and the Zouaves, after suffering severely, retreated, bringing with them General Monet desperately wounded. They had fifteen officers killed and wounded, out of the nineteen lost in all by the French, whose loss in men was variously stated at from 300 to 500.

It was rumoured and expected for some days afterwards, that the French would make another effort to take the hill. The Russians placed riflemen behind the work they had thrown up, and in a small enclosure of loose stones near it, who exchanged a brisk fire with the French tirailleurs in the advanced trench, but without much damage to either side. The attack was not renewed by the French, and the enemy proceeded to complete the work unmolested. The French, however, sallied from their lines on two or three successive nights upon the rifle-pits occupied by the Russians towards Inkermann, and on one occasion drove out the occupants of the pits and repulsed the troops supporting them ; but neglecting to destroy or occupy the pits themselves, the Russians returned to them when the French withdrew.

At the beginning of March the winter seemed to have departed, leaving only a few cold days lingering in scattered order in its rear. The health of the troops was steadily improving ; they were in comparative comfort, and their labours were lightened. New batteries, admirably constructed, were in course of completion, far in advance of those used in the first attack, and connected with them by long lines of trenches. Guns for arming them were in our siege depôts, those damaged by the long-continued fire were replaced by others, and we had lent a number to the French. Inkermann was not only defended against a second assault like that of the 5th of November, but was now the most strongly intrenched point of our position. Finally, the supply of ammunition necessary for reopening a general and sustained cannonade was being fast accumulated, while the fire of the enemy, who but lately had returned ten shots for one, was materially slackened.

A Russian steamer, armed with two heavy guns, had for a long time been anchored near the head of the harbour, at a point from whence she could fire towards Inkermann, and had frequently annoyed our working parties there. On the night of the 6th, the embrasures of three guns in our battery facing Inkermann Lights, 1800 yards from the ship, were unmasked, and shot heated. At daybreak the guns opened; the first shot passed over the vessel, and did not attract the notice of the sentry who was pacing the deck—the second struck the water near, when he jumped on the paddle-box and alarmed the crew. Seven or eight shot struck her, and damaged her machinery so much that, though the steam was got up, the paddles did not revolve, and she was warped round into the shelter of a neighbouring point. Her crew immediately left her, and she was careened over for repair. A deserter told us that three men were killed and three wounded on board.

On the 9th a telegraphic despatch was received at the British headquarters, stating that the Emperor of Russia had died on the 2d, with the words appended, "This may be relied on as authentic." The news spread rapidly through the camp, and, notwithstanding its surprising nature, it was at once believed. Next day the French General received a despatch to the same effect from a different source.

By the construction of the lines and batteries at Inkermann the Allies had to a great extent effected the object of enclosing the defensive works south of the Great Harbour. In front of the Round Tower (called by the Russians Malakhoff), and to the right of our right attack, was a hill of the form of a truncated cone, nearly as elevated as that on which the Round Tower stands, known by us as Gordon's Hill, and by the French as the Mamelon. It had been intended that the French should obtain possession of this hill under cover of a cross-fire, from our right attack and the left Inkermann batteries, upon the ground behind it; and that works should be constructed on it, which, at about 500 yards, would bear on the works of the Malakhoff and the Redan. This design was anticipated by the enemy, who, on the morning of the 11th, were found to have seized on the hill during the night, and commenced a battery there. A fire of shells from our right attack drove their working parties out, and prevented them from making much progress by day; but though the fire was continued at night, its effect was too uncertain to prevent the enemy from working there during the darkness.

At seven o'clock on the evening of the 14th, Captain Craigie, R.E., was returning up a ravine from the trenches with a party of sappers, and was already at a great distance, when a stray missile came through the air towards them. He remarked, " here comes a shell," and at the moment it burst above them. All put up their arms to shield their heads from falling splinters; when they looked round, Craigie was lying dead—a piece of the shell had gone through his side into his heart. The sappers bore him to his tent, many of them strongly affected, for he was a great favourite with his men.

In the middle of March the French connected their

lines at Inkermann with those of our right attack by parallels, the advanced one passing in front of the Mamelon at less than 500 yards from it; thus rendering the line of intrenchment continuous (except where the great ravine interrupted it), from the battery opposite Inkermann Lights, on our extreme right, to the French works on the left, which enclose the salients defending the town. Facing the advanced parallel between it and the Mamelon was a row of Russian rifle-pits, distant from the French less than 100 yards, which caused great annoyance to the guards of the trench. At the request of our allies, a 24-pounder in our right attack was directed on the pits, and the second shot piercing a small work erected to shelter several riflemen, called by the French a *gabionade*, its occupants, to the number of eight, ran away, escaping uninjured through the fire of musketry poured on them from the French parallel; but they came back in the night. Next day I was in a new mortar-battery we had erected in front of the light division, watching the practice from our right attack against the Mamelon, when the colonel of the 5th regiment of French infantry, leaving his horse in the battery, walked down to the trenches, not by the ordinary path of the ravine, which affords shelter all the way, but over the hill; as he approached the lines he was shot dead by a rifleman from the pits. On the night of the 17th, about nine o'clock, it being very dark, a furious fire of musketry was opened from the French lines, and for upwards of an hour incessant volleys showed several thousand men to be engaged. The whole camp was on the alert, and the staff-officers despatched from the French and English headquarters to ascertain the cause, brought word that it was a renewed attack by the French on the Russian rifle-pits; and in the morning we heard that the French had taken them; nevertheless, at daylight the Russian sharpshooters were at their old post. The French were said to have lost upwards of a hundred men; next night they bombarded the town from eight o'clock till midnight, inflicting great loss on the garrison, according to the report of a deserter.

On the 19th, a deserter brought intelligence that Menschikoff was dead. Next day another corroborated the intelligence, and added that Admiral Istamin had been killed in the Mamelon by a shell. He also told us that the Russian batteries had been forbidden to fire, and, in fact, they did not fire for two days.

On the 20th, Sir John Burgoyne, who had hitherto been charged with the chief conduct of the siege-works, left the army, for the purpose of resuming his duties in England as Inspector-general of Fortifications. His successor, General Jones, had arrived some time before. On this day we received the English papers up to the 5th, containing the original despatches announcing the Czar's death, the remarks thereon in Parliament, and the leading articles speculating on the new aspect which the war and the pending negotiations might assume when so important an actor had been suddenly removed.

CHAPTER XIX.

THE BURIAL TRUCE.

THE advanced trenches of our right attack met the advanced parallel of the French in front of the Mamelon in the ravine, which at this point is broken by numerous small quarries, or rather commencements of quarries. The ravine, passing on through the intrenchment, sweeps round to the left between our attacks and the Malakhoff, and runs into the basin of Sebastopol.

A night attack in great force was made by the Russians on the 22d, caused, as was afterwards reported, by the return of the Grand-duke Michael to the fortress. The principal body of the assailants advanced up the ravine aforesaid, and along the ground in front of the Mamelon, occupied during the day by their riflemen; while others, crossing the ravine, entered the advanced trenches of our right and left attacks. An Albanian, who had frequently headed sorties from the garrison, led the enemy assailing our right. The night was extremely dark, with a strong southerly wind blowing towards the enemy, and assisting to conceal their approach. Leaping into the trench, they were at first taken for Frenchmen, and greeted as such ; but the nearest man of ours being bayoneted, the working party occupying the trench perceived their error, and, seizing their arms, at once met the assailants. The Greek leader of the Russians shot Captain Browne, of the 7th Fusiliers, with his pistol, and was immediately killed himself. Captain Vicars, 97th, forming his men, called on them to charge, and they leaped over the parapet, drove back the enemy, and pursued them down the slope, where Vicars fell mortally wounded. The Russians took with them our men's intrenching tools and fifteen prisoners, among whom were Lieutenant - Colonel Kelly, 34th, and Captain Montague, R.E. The latter was captured on our left attack, where also the enemy was repelled at once. Major Gordon, R.E., who had been charged throughout the siege with the conduct of the right attack, and who was always conspicuously careless in exposing himself to fire, received, while standing on the outside of the trench, two bullets, one in his hand, the other in his arm.

Meantime the attack on the French had been, after an obstinate resistance from a party of Zouaves, partially successful, and the guards of the trenches were driven out of the advanced parallels into one of the *boyaux* communicating with it, while the enemy occupied, and began to destroy, an advanced *boyau* which the French were pushing towards the most troublesome rifle-pits, as well as part of the parapet of the parallel. The struggle, in which several thousand men were engaged on each side, was very close and desperate. Eventually the Russians retired, leaving a great number of dead, and having inflicted severe loss on their opponents, whose killed and wounded were reported to amount to 450.

A truce was agreed on for the purpose of burying the dead, to commence at half an hour after noon on the 24th. At that time a number of officers had collected at different points commanding a view of the Russian works, awaiting the concerted signal of the pause in hostilities. At noon the firing had almost ceased, and, at the appointed hour, a white flag was elevated over the Mamelon, while one appeared simultaneously in each of the French and English works, when those who had been watching for it at once streamed down the hill to the scene of contest. The spectacle that followed was one of the strangest that had occurred during the campaign.

While we went down the slope to the ravine, the French burial-parties advanced from their trenches, and hundreds of Russians came out from behind the Mamelon and approached our works, some of them bearing stretchers. Passing through the interval in our rearmost intrenchment where it crosses the ravine, we first saw a small heap of bodies, six Russians and two Frenchmen, lying on the side of the hill, having probably fallen within the French lines, and been collected there during the preceding night. At the point where the advanced trench meets ours, the ravine is, as I have before said, very rugged and broken, and those who had ridden down left their horses there. The first object I saw there was the body of the Albanian leader, who had fallen in our trenches, borne by four of our men on a stretcher to the outside of the parapet, where it was received by Russian soldiers. It had been partially stripped, and covered again with his white kilt and other drapery, leaving his feet bare, as also his breast, on which, as on Count Lara's, appeared the scars of several old wounds. In a deep gully, below the verge of our slope of the hill, lay a Russian on his back. He had been wounded in the neck, and had lain there since the night before last, suffering and alone, on a bed of loose stones, with his head, which he had pillowed on his forage-cap, lower than his body. Judging from his aspect, his case was by no means desperate. His comrades, at the call of our men, who discovered him, flocked round and carried him off. I crossed the broken ground, which was sprinkled with dead, to the opposite side of the ravine, in front of the French parallel, where a crowd of Russian and French officers and soldiers were intermixed, with a good many English officers as spectators. The French had drawn all the Russian bodies outside their lines, where they were collected in one heap, in a spot between the French trenches and the Russian rifle-pits. Some of these latter were semicircular trenches, five or six yards in extent, with the earth thrown up in front, surmounted by a row of sandbags, and capable of holding nine or ten men;—some of them small screens of stone, or of a couple of gabions filled with earth, behind which a single rifleman was hid. The nearest French and Russian sharpshooters were about seventy yards asunder. The French seemed to think it necessary to guard against surprise or breach of faith on the part of the Russians, and kept their trenches strongly manned, while armed parties were drawn up outside.

The Russian officers not employed in the burial duty mixed with the French, chatting, and exchanging cigars. The soldiers of the enemy looked dirty and shabby, but healthy and well fed. Most of them were of larger frame than the French, while the English surpassed both in size and stature; the countenances of the Russians, short and broad, with thick projecting lips, pug-noses, and small eyes, betokened a low order of intellect, cunning and obstinate. Many, both officers and men, wore orders and medals. Between these groups passed and re-passed the burial-parties, lifting each grim gory figure from its face or back, placing it on a stretcher, and bearing it, with the dead legs swinging and dragging, and the arms vibrating stiffly to the steps of the bearers, to be added to the dreadful assembly. Not one of those looking on could feel secure that in the next twenty-four hours he would not be as one of these. About half-way between the Mamelon and the French lines was a large rifle-pit like a small field-work, and near this lay another heap of bodies, probably collected by the Russians during the night. Behind, at 450 yards' distance from us, rose the Mamelon, its battery surmounted by the white flag, and the parapet lined with spectators. Next, on the left, as we looked, separated by a level space of 500 yards across, stood the Malakhoff hill, with its ruined tower surrounded by earthen batteries; and to our left of that, between it and the Redan, appeared the best built portion of the city, jutting out into the harbour. These were seen so close that the main features of the streets and buildings were distinguishable—large barracks and other public buildings, with their long regular rows of windows arched or square; the green cupola of a large church; and, on a high point, amidst well-built houses, a handsome edifice surrounded by a colonnade like a Greek temple. In front of the large barrack was a dark line, seen through a glass to be a body of troops; and the telescope also revealed people walking about the streets, the arrangement of the gardens, and the effect of our fire upon the town, the roofs of the houses being broken through, and the walls thickly dotted with marks of shot. The masts of the inner line of ships sunk across the large harbour were plainly visible; one or two small boats were sailing about inside the obstacle.

Crossing the ravine to the front of our right attack, I found the Russian dead, to the number (as one of the men employed in conveying them told me) of about forty, already removed. Altogether, judging from those who had fallen in our lines, and the bodies

I had seen in front of the French, the Russians must have had four hundred killed in this attack. As soon as the bodies were all conveyed within the Russian line of rifle-pits, cordons of sentries were drawn across the space between; nevertheless several Russian soldiers remained for some time amongst our men, who seemed to regard them with a sort of good-humoured patronage, calling them " Rooskies," and presenting them with pipes and tobacco. One of them, who, besides tobacco, got a brass tobacco-box, absolutely grinned with delight. From this point of view (the ground in front of the advanced batteries of our right attack) the whole plain undulated in every direction into bluffs and knolls; everywhere it was bare and covered with short grass, plentifully dotted with grey stones. In front was the Redan, and nearer to us a line of screens, of grey stone, like rude sentry-boxes, each holding a rifleman.

According to arrangement, the white flag was to be kept flying in our batteries till that in the Mamelon was lowered. At a quarter past three, the bodies being all removed, and the Russians having withdrawn within their defences, it disappeared, and presently the puffs from the Russian rifle-pits and French lines showed that the ground lately crowded with soldiers of both armies working in unison was again the scene of strife. A gun and mortar from Gordon's battery threw shells into the work on the Mamelon; the nearest French battery at Inkermann did the same; the guns on the Mamelon, opposed to the latter, replied; the Malakhoff guns fired on the French lines and on our right battery; and two nine-pounders in our right advanced work sent their shot bounding among the Russian rifle-pits.

In the night the Russians connected the pits by a trench, which they extended to the verge of the ravine. Thus an intrenched line was formed and occupied within eighty yards of the French, supported by, while it covered, the Mamelon.

During March, the railway advanced steadily towards the heights. Since Admiral Boxer had taken charge of the port of Balaklava, convenient wharves had been built on both sides of the harbour. On the side opposite the town, at the Diamond Wharf, great quantities of stores were landed; a branch of the railway ran to the wharf on each side, where an artillery officer superintended the transmission of the guns and ammunition towards the camp. About the middle of the month the railway had advanced three-quarters of a mile up the hill beyond Kadukoi, where an engine was set up, and trains began to run; and a week later, all the powder landed at Balaklava was conveyed to a depôt still nearer the camp. At the end of the month the rails reached the top of the plateau, and conveyed seventy tons of stores per day. An electric telegraph was also established at headquarters, communicating with Balaklava, with different parts of the camp, and with the right and left attacks.

We had now been half a year before Sebastopol. Coming in the middle of autumn, we had seen the season fade while we expected to enter the city. At that time there had been no thought of wintering on the heights ; our speculations were directed to the chances of occupying the place, or returning to Constantinople, and to our own possessions in the Mediterranean, to await the next campaign. Rumour had already named the divisions which were respectively to occupy Scutari, Corfu, and Malta. Then, unawares, came the dreary winter, and the daily struggle to maintain ourselves, amid snow, choked roads, filth, and death. The warm days of March had begun to dissipate the impressions of that time of misery, and it was now looked back on as a dismal dream filled with gloom, carcasses, and a nameless horror. Our present prospects, though much brighter, were no less dubious. Negotiations for peace were pending, while we were preparing for another attack with increased means, but with confidence diminished by former disappointment. A few days would see commenced, either the armistice as the preliminary of peace, or a bloody struggle with doubt beyond. Before our eyes was the great If, Sebastopol ;—that once taken, we could venture to look forward either to a glorious return, or to a brilliant campaign.

Though the English public, and many in the army, were inclined to take a gloomy view of affairs, yet to the Russians they must have worn a far less promising aspect than to us. The great provoker and conductor of the war was gone—he who alone knew the intricacies of Russian policy, and could set in motion the cumbrous machinery of his monarchy. There was no great name now for the Russian soldiers to invoke, no great reputation to look to for shelter. The garrison of Sebastopol had resisted thus far successfully, it is true, though their constancy had never been proved by an assault, and the north side was still open. But the force at Eupatoria was now increased to 45,000, with 4000 cavalry, and might soon threaten their communications with Simferopol. Day and night our guns broke the silence, and our shot whistled among them; in the Malakhoff and Mamelon alone they were said to lose a hundred men a-day. Each day saw our works advancing, and they knew that we were accumulating the means for a second attack, which, successful or not, must cause them terrible loss. A great part of their large fleet had been sunk; a war steamer, French or English, watched the harbour incessantly; and our vessels passed to and fro, at all hours, in full view of the place, bringing supplies, troops, and regular intelligence, from England and France.

The remarkable event of the month was the death of the Czar. Happening, as it did, beyond all calculation, it seemed at first to cut the Gordian knot which complicated the affairs of Europe. Everywhere it was felt that a great constraining power had ceased; but the relief thus brought left something for the imagination to regret. In a dearth of great men he had risen tall and massive above the northern horizon. While in the cabinets of Europe his subtlety and force were felt and acknowledged, in his own vast dominions he commanded not merely unquestioning obedience, but universal veneration. With far more truth than the Grande Monarque he might have said, "*L'état c'est moi;*" he was indeed embodied Russia. The enormous power wielded by a single man was heightened by the mystery which surrounded it, and in the dissolution of the cloud-capt fabric, this everyday world lost something of romance.

CHAPTER XX.

VIEW OF THE WORKS.

THE works of the besiegers, though extraordinarily diffuse and extensive, had now assumed the appearance of regular scientific attacks. The batteries, no longer isolated, nor confined to one line, were connected by parallels; and those in advance were approached by regularly constructed *boyaux* or zigzag trenches. If the reader will accompany me to a commanding point, I will endeavour to set before him a view of the siege operations.

In front of the Light Division camp, near the Woronzoff road, is a building marked on the plans as the picket-house. Down the slope beyond, and a little to the right of it, is a mortar-battery, and 100 yards beyond the battery is a small breastwork of stone, covered with earth from a ditch in front, and of sufficient thickness to resist a shot. A few spectators with telescopes were generally stationed here, watching the desultory fire of the opposing batteries; and from hence a more compendious view of the siege could be obtained than from any other point.

SEBASTOPOL FROM THE PIQUET HOUSE, NEAR THE WORONZOW ROAD, AUGST 1855.

ASPECT OF THE TOWN.

The town of Sebastopol is naturally the first object that attracts attention in the view, of which it occupies the left centre. First, in a basin of the slopes below you, appear three long white lines of building, nearly two miles and a half distant, dotted with numerous windows regularly placed. The two nearest are a great barrack and dockyard, both on our side of the inner harbour,—the third, separated from them by the inner harbour, the entrance of which is just visible, contains arched windows, and terminates in Fort Nicholas, a low, solid-looking round tower. The outer harbour rises blue and clear above the third line of building to where the low north shore juts out, terminating in Fort Constantine, a round tower of much larger circumference than Fort Nicholas. The horizon of the now blue and bright-looking Euxine rises high into the picture above the landscape. To return to the town. Behind the great barrack rises a tall building with a turret surmounted by a lead-roofed dome and spire, and close by it a short column, like a piece of the Monument, with a balcony round the top. Beyond, near the sea, in a garden, is another low white column. To the left is the town, built on a rounded eminence, half-way up the slope of which is a wall fencing a road which passes above the inner harbour. A large solid building faces the road; to the left of it are large gardens and well-built streets and houses. Conspicuous among the latter is a white building covered with sharp white pinnacles. All the roofs and walls are clearly relieved against the sea. Again, as you turn to the left, separated by a dip in the ground, is another eminence, with houses of a meaner and more suburban description. To the left, again, are earthen batteries surrounding the town, and parallel to these run the French lines, furrowing yellowly a greenish barren-looking plain, which in the distance seems more level than it is. In the light blue water rising beyond are a few line-of-battle ships. In the middle distance, on our left, the first parallel of our left attack runs towards the French lines, from which it is separated by the great ravine. In the continuation of the parallel the right extremity of Chapman's Battery is visible descending the side of a knoll, with its men, guns, and embrasures dotting darkly the earth-coloured space of the interior. The ground sloping downward in rear of the guns renders the enemy's practice against the interior of the battery more uncertain and difficult, and, a little behind, a green mound rises, which partially protects from the Russian fire those entering the battery from the camp. This may close the left of the picture, the foreground of which consists altogether of green descending slopes sprinkled with stones.

Next, in the middle distance towards the right, is our right attack (right and left attack are the names given to our two sets of batteries and trenches divided by the ravine, the one superintended by Major Gordon, the other by Major Chapman), where Gordon's

Battery is seen traversing the crest of a green knoll, and terminating in a long trench descending out of sight into a ravine in the middle of the picture, where it joins the French lines. The suburban portion of Sebastopol forms the background to our right attack. To the right of it, having the best built portion of the city for a background, is seen a long line of embrasures in an earthen parapet, seemingly forming part of our own advanced works, but in reality separated from them by a hollow 500 yards across. This is the Redan, one of the formidable Russian outworks. Then, on the right, comes the green basin through which the harbour and the three long lines of buildings are visible. To the right of those buildings, and intersected half-way by the rise of the ground, is the square tower called Fort Paul, terminating the mole which juts out on the side of the inner harbour opposite Fort Nicholas. A low battery follows the ascent of the slope which forms one side of the Malakhoff hill—a prominent object, constituting, with the Mamelon on its right, the centre of the view. The ruined tower of the Malakhoff, half of which is pulled down, contains two arched apertures; around stretches an earthen parapet pierced with embrasures, and surrounded on the slope outside with a dark line of abattis, or obstacle made of felled trees and pointed stakes. Between the spectator and the Malakhoff can be traced the winding course of the ravine, which, after separating our lines from those of the French in front of the Mamelon, turns to the left towards the inner harbour. In the dip between the Malakhoff and Mamelon the masts of two large ships, lying in the great harbour, are seen. The Mamelon is a low hill flattened at the top, crowned, like the Malakhoff, with batteries, but having the embrasures wider apart. Its slopes, sweeping towards the spectator, are dotted with the screens of stone behind which the Russian riflemen are posted, and are crossed by the advanced French parallel, lined with tirailleurs. The puffs of smoke between the antagonists are frequent. To the right of the Mamelon the ground falls, disclosing a peep of the upper end of the harbour; then it rises again to two consecutive hills a mile from the spectator, each crowned with a yellow line of earth forming a battery;—that on the right is the hill where the struggle took place between the French and Russians on the 22d February. Again, to the right, is the top of a French battery in front of Inkermann. It is somewhat indistinct, as a descending green slope intervenes, but the smoke of a gun reveals it, and the shell bursts over the Mamelon, while the rush of its course is still reaching the ear. The Mamelon replies ; a gun and mortar in our right attack drop their shells into the work; the Malakhoff supports its companion by a couple of shells, which graze the crest of our parapet, and, knocking up little clouds of dust as they go, burst far up the hill-side. A mortar near the Malakhoff pitches a shell into the parapet of our advanced parallel ; it rolls over and explodes ; a commotion is visible through the glass, and presently two wounded men are borne past to the camp—one struck in the cheek, the other having his leg shattered. Presently a tremendous explosion close behind makes an unprepared spectator start ; another follows — the two 13-inch mortars have been fired. With a rush like a whirlwind the two great shells are hurled up into the sky, growing small as cricket-balls, and audible when no longer seen. As the sound ceases, two clouds of dust rise in the Malakhoff—the shells have dropt there : another moment, and two columns of smoke rise and are slowly dispersed—both shells have burst in the work.

Turning to the right, so as to complete the half circle, you see on the next hill the Victoria Redoubt, made and held by the French, with an indented line of trench in front of it.

Up to the right centre of the view the sea forms the horizon, but between the Mamelon and the new Russian battery on the hill, the country north of the Balbek and Katcha rivers, jutting out into capes, takes up the line of the horizon, and continues it nearly on the sea-level.

The land north of the harbour, forming the distance of two-thirds of the picture, is intersected in every direction by roads. To reveal the details the aid of a telescope is required. Beginning at Fort Constantine, the line of the land is broken for some distance by earthen forts, which are marked on the plans, Sievernaia being the most extensive. In the dip between the Malakhoff and Mamelon appears a low hill over the harbour, surmounted by a field-work encompassed by roads. Not far from this is a vast burying-ground, containing apparently thousands of graves. To the right of the Mamelon, on the cliff above the harbour, are rows of buildings like barracks, with a camp for six battalions behind. Inland, the plains and hills grow bare and wild, and are traversed by the Simferopol road, along which may be seen advancing to the town a large convoy of waggons escorted by troops. All along the edge of the cliff which borders the harbour, and the marsh at the head of it, parties of Russians may be seen working at batteries and intrenchments.

Having thus taken a general view, let us enter the works themselves. The ravine on the right of the mortar-battery is close, though unseen, and a few minutes' walk conducts to it. Here, on both sides, are rows of graves, on one of which two or three men are now employed with pickaxe and shovel. Passing these, the ravine (the same in which Captain Craigie was killed) winds, deepening as it goes, between its green banks sprinkled with fragments of grey rock. Presently you meet a party of Frenchmen bearing a covered form on a stretcher. You stop one to ask if it is a wounded man? "Monsieur, il est mort"—he has been killed by a splinter in the parallel. The next turn shows the right bank of the ravine ahead, covered with the recumbent forms of French soldiers, forming a strong picket, ready, if necessary, to reinforce those in the trenches. Near these the end of our first parallel meets the ravine, and you enter it, casting first a glance to the right, where, high above, a glimpse of the Malakhoff, with its guns, a mile off, is disclosed.

All the trenches are nearly of the same description —two or three yards wide and two or three feet deep, with the earth thrown up to form a parapet towards the enemy. Sometimes the soil is clayey, but oftener bedded with stone, through which the workmen have painfully scooped a cover. After walking some hundred yards, you find two guns stationed on their platforms in the trench which, widened here, and its parapet heightened and strengthened with gabions and sandbags, becomes a battery. Piles of shot are close to the guns, and a thick mass of earth crossing the trench contains the magazine. Through the embrasures or openings in the parapet which the guns fire from, the Mamelon is visible, and these are the guns which you just now saw firing on it. Next, you come to a mortar-battery, where the parapet is very solid, and so high that the enemy's work is not visible to those working the pieces, which are directed by two iron rods, called pickets, stuck upright in the parapet, in front of the mortar. These being placed one before the other so that they form but one object when the eye is directed from behind them on the work, they are so left; a white line is made down the exact middle of the mortar, by a chalked cord stretched and rapped along it; and an artilleryman standing behind the mortar, holding before his eye a string with a plummet attached, causes the mortar to be shifted till the string coincides with both pickets, and with the white line on the mortar, which is then correctly aimed without the necessity of seeing the object.

Then come more guns, separated by traverses or masses of earth, faced with gabions or sandbags : the presence of these generally shows that the battery or trench containing them is in the path of the enemy's shot, to the course of which they form obstacles. The embrasures here look on the Malakhoff. As you regard it, a cloud of smoke is puffed from one of its embrasures; the report is followed by a rushing noise, and a shell, dashing over the parapet near you, buries itself in the ground a few yards behind the battery. All in its neighbourhood stoop to avoid the splinters; after a moment it bursts in a cloud of earth and smoke, and the splinters whirr and jar around. Plenty of pieces of shells, some new, some rusted, are lying about, and the ground is channelled with the graze of shot. Here and there you see one of our own guns half buried in the soil—it has either burst or been struck by the enemy's shot, and rendered unserviceable.

A trench, branching from the first parallel, leads towards the second. This approach, or rather series of approaches, is of zigzag form, the branches in one direction having the parapet on the right, the others on the left. Traverses are frequent here, and the

THE BATTERIES AND WORKS.

necessity for them is shown by the occasional singing of a bullet, and the marks where round-shot have grazed parallel to the trench, and close to it. There are no batteries in these trenches, as they look obliquely on the enemy's works; but in a trench thrown out from one of them a mortar-battery is placed. Further on are the two field-guns looking on the rifle-pits in front of the Mamelon.

Turning to the left, up a steep trench where the parapet is higher, you have to walk circumspectly to avoid treading on the sleeping soldiers who guard the work, their arms, loaded, and with bayonets fixed, leaning against the parapet. This is the point where the Russians penetrated on the night of the 22d March; and on the left of it is the magazine into which the Albanian leader of the sortie discharged his pistol in a desperate attempt to blow it up the moment before he was killed. Close to this is the battery, and the parallel beyond it is lined with soldiers, some of whom are pointing their rifles through sandbag loop-holes at the enemy's riflemen, whom, through these loop-holes, you may discern behind their screens of stone; beyond them, 500 yards off, rises the Redan, a dark line of earth broken by embrasures, where the guns are visible. The complaining sound of the bullets is frequent here, and follows you at intervals along the zigzags by which you return to the first parallel of the right attack, which terminates in the ravine where the Woronzoff road lies.

Crossing this ravine, you gain the parallel of the left attack, which leads into Chapman's Battery. This is similar to the other, but more substantial, owing to the soil being easier to work in. From its embrasures you see the Redan, and a range of batteries extending from it, near which are numbers of small white hovels. Lower down the slope is the Russian Barrack Battery, some of whose guns bear on us, some on the French across the ravine. The buildings of the city are seen to great advantage from here. On the opposite side of the ravine stands the Flagstaff Battery, or Bastion du Mât, protecting the town; and, close in front of it, the advanced French parallel. At intervals, lower down towards the water, are posted other batteries, the chief being that known as the Garden Battery; part of which, as well as some guns of the Flagstaff, looks on our left attack.

The first parallel of the left attack terminates in the great ravine, and advancing along the rocky ledge of it for 200 yards, you reach another parallel, from which branch off approaches leading to the advanced works. Passing along these, you frequently see yourself under the guns of the Flagstaff Battery, but it is not worth its while to fire at individuals. At length our most advanced work is reached—a battery solid and compact, whose embrasures are as yet unopened. In the trenches to the right and left the parapets are lined with our sharpshooters watching their opportunity from the loop-holes. Looking through one of these, you find yourself just above the end of the inner harbour. Across the ravine below the Flagstaff Battery are riflemen, who fire, some on these trenches, and some on the advanced lines of the French.

Returning to the end of the second parallel, you descend the high rocky precipice to the great ravine, which is here divided into two; the left, and shortest, would conduct you to our engineers' camp near the Third Division; the windings of the other and more considerable, lead to a distant point on the plateau. Both lie deep and gloomy between their rocky sides, where layers of grey stone, hollowed by fissures and caves, support a grassy plain, whose green border peers over the verge. The bottom of the ravine, which resembles the dry bed of a river, is threaded by a broken pathway, where shot and shell, fired from the Russian batteries on each side, lie in extraordinary quantities, causing the smaller ravine, which forms the ordinary approach to our works, to be called the Valley of the Shadow of Death.

At the point of junction in the full width of the valley stand the ruins of a white house on a knoll. This was once a pleasant spot surrounded with vineyards and gardens: a remarkably fine willow, shading a well close by, was uprooted in the storm of the 14th November. Crossing by this house, you see at the top of the further precipice an English battery of three guns, climbing to which you find yourself looking down on the head of the inner harbour, where the Russian batteries are posted to defend the approach. Going along the ledge of rock, you enter the French parallel which conducts to trenches and batteries, at first much like ours, but, as they approach the place, of more solid and elaborate construction. The rearmost trenches, like our own, are unguarded and solitary; but the more advanced are full of soldiers, smoking, sleeping, or playing at cards, and pitch-and-toss. In an advanced battery are several French officers on duty with their men, and one or two of them offer to accompany you. Going to the end of the parallel, you find yourself on the verge of the ravine looking down on the inner harbour; the bridge of boats is at no great distance, with planks laid from one to the other by which the Russians are crossing; in the yard of the arsenal close to the water are piles of cannon-shot. Just underneath, in the bed of the ravine, is a Russian cemetery full of white and black crosses, and riflemen are posted in it behind stones. One of the French officers, in his anxiety to point out all that may be seen, gets out of the trench and stands behind it, looking over the parapet, till a friendly corporal tells him that a bullet from the cemetery has shortly before struck just where he stands, when he gets down again into the trench, very deliberately, however, lest the credit of the *grande nation* should be impaired in the eyes of their allies. The bullets which pass over here come from the sharpshooters already seen from the advance of our left attack. In the third, or most advanced

French parallel, the parapet is very high and solid, being overlooked by the Bastion du Mât, which stands on a high hill opposite, distant less than 150 yards, as you may see by looking through one of the loop-holes; taking care, however, not to look too long, as one of the riflemen opposite would think it no great feat to send, from his ambuscade eighty yards off, a bullet into the three inches square of space between the sandbags. The riflemen here were a short time ago in the habit of diverting themselves by sticking up bottles on the parapet for their opponents to fire at. Our commanding engineer, looking through a loop-hole here one day to survey the place, found a great number of bullets striking near him, and, hearing a suppressed chuckle from our worthy allies behind, he looked up, and found they had silently placed a bottle on the parapet over his head. This they considered a very capital joke indeed, and wanting nothing except a bullet through the general's head to render it quite successful.

In the parapet of a trench near is a portal six feet square, opening on a steep path descending into the earth. An officer outside tells you it is forbidden to enter here, but the sergeant who accompanies you obtains the permission of the engineer officer, and, descending, beckons you on. The passage narrows to little more than a yard square, along which you crawl for a considerable distance. A few men are squatting in the gallery, which is lit at intervals by candles. The heat grows stifling as you advance, and the roof seems ready to close on you. The rifle-shots, French and Russian, are now crossing each other unheard above you; and, a few yards farther on, you are actually beneath the enemy's ramparts. The sappers working here can never be sure that in the next minute the Russians, delving "a yard below their mine," will not "blow them to the moon," as Hamlet says; or pour upon them, through a sudden aperture, sulphurous vapours; or drown them with torrents of water. You breathe more freely after emerging from the narrow gallery of the French mine.

The batteries in this parallel are beautifully finished, high, solid, and carefully revetted. The guns have been removed from the opposing Russian battery, having been rendered unavailable by the proximity of the French marksmen.

A long walk through the trenches conducts you back to the first parallel, which you can quit near an enclosed field, in which stands a small house with a bell on the top, known as the Maison de Clocheton, where a French guard is posted. A road from hence traverses the French camps.

Perusing the foregoing chapter with the aid of a plan, the reader may perhaps form some idea of the aspect of the ground before and around Sebastopol.

CHAPTER XXI.

THE SECOND CANNONADE.

THE oft-repeated question, When shall we reopen the fire? was at length answered. On Easter Sunday, the 8th of April, orders were given for commencing the cannonade at daylight next morning. The batteries were supplied with 500 rounds for each gun, and 300 for each mortar, and were fully armed, with the exception of the batteries in the advanced parallels of the English attacks, which were not ready for the reception of the guns and mortars, and which were not to be unmasked till the fire of the rest should have enabled them to open with more security from the enemy's riflemen in the pits and quarries.

The morning of the 9th broke darkly in wind and rain. At the hour of sunrise a heavy mist covered the plains, and objects were so indistinct that in traversing ground I was familiar with I lost my way for a short time, but the sound of the guns guided me towards them. The order to the artillery was to begin as soon as the objects to be aimed at were discernible; and at twenty minutes past six the English guns, as they caught sight of the opposing batteries, opened their fire, and the French soon followed. The Russians were so completely unprepared that it was twenty minutes before they began to reply.

A strong south wind drove a flood of rain and a cloud of mist across the scene of contest. At times the heavy vapour hid the view from the spectators who had issued from their camps; then the fog would lift in parts and reveal the rounded hills crowned with batteries and wrapt in the smoke of cannon, through which the red flashes incessantly darted; again, as a squall passed, the view would dissolve, and the combat seemed transferred to a world of shadows. To us, who remembered the din of the former cannonade re-echoing through the camps, the noise of the present seemed trifling, blown from us as it was by the wind; but to the inhabitants of Sebastopol the uproar that awoke them must have been appalling. Three hundred and sixty French guns and mortars bore on the town defences and parts of the outworks; one hundred and forty English pieces on the Mamelon, Malakhoff, Redan, and Barrack and Garden Batteries. The arrangements for maintaining our fire were much better now than formerly. Caves in the ravine close to Chapman's Battery formed capacious and secure magazines, from whence ammunition was drawn as required for the smaller ones in the batteries, the explosion of which would consequently be of comparatively little importance. The parapets had been heightened and strengthened, and bomb-proof chambers had been constructed in rear of them, to which wounded men were conveyed and their hurts attended to in security. The guards of the trenches were no longer stationed in the batteries, which were exclusively occupied by artillerymen, but lined the parallels, and thus did not on the first day lose a man, the enemy's fire being solely directed on the batteries.

The Russians did not commence or sustain the fire with the vigour that was expected. The dreaded Mamelon fired but few shots, and seemed to be insufficiently manned ; only five or six guns from the Malakhoff opened ; one face of the Redan grew almost silent in a few hours ; while the French breached the central salient in their front, and greatly injured the Bastion du Mât.

The storm of wind and rain continued all day, and through it rushed as steadily the storm of shot. Each uplifting of the curtain of fog showed the same unvarying circle of eddies of smoke drifting from the Allied batteries towards the Russian works. Our guns fired each about eight times in an hour, at which rate no second of time would elapse without a shot. Drenched to the skin, and standing in thick mud, the artillerymen and sailors worked their guns with admirable vigour. Bad as the circumstances were for them, the Russian gunners, fighting with the wind and rain in their faces, must have found the trial doubly severe. The losses in our batteries were not heavy, though the Russian fire was very well directed, and dismounted several guns. At mid-day the desultory fire of the Mamelon altogether ceased, and the work seemed to offer a tempting prize to a bold assailant. The fire of the Allied guns ceased at nightfall, but that of the mortars, depending less on a sight of the object for its efficiency, was continued with great regularity throughout the night, which was filled with the roar of those great engines. The French had nearly 100 mortars, we 28, mostly of larger calibre than theirs. Three large sea-service mortars, which threw their shells into the dockyard and arsenal buildings 4500 yards off, were unserviceable throughout the day, in consequence of the rain rendering the platforms so slippery that the handspikes could not be brought to bear on the vast beds.

Next day the Russian fire was much brisker, though by no means so formidable as in the former bombardment. Lieutenant Twyford of the Naval Brigade was killed on this day.

On the 11th the Russian fire somewhat slackened, and our own was rather diminished, owing to several guns having become unserviceable. The Mamelon scarcely fired at all, the Round Tower only an occasional gun—one, perhaps, every ten minutes. The trenches were still deep in mire. The great ravine by which the left attack was approached was so muddy that it was a labour to traverse it, and it was filled with the reverberations of the cannonade and the sharp jar of splinters. The approaches to the advanced batteries were deep in tenacious mud, and filled with pools. The night before an attempt had been made to take six 32-pounders from the first parallel to the advanced batteries; but they had stuck so fast that 300 men were unable to move one to its destination, the drag-ropes giving way under the strain. The Russians, hearing the noise, opened fire on them, and knocked off the muzzle of one, which, with the others, was left in the second parallel till night, when, the soil being somewhat drained, the battery was armed. Four of its guns opened on the following day, but the Russians replied with so heavy a fire as to silence them for the time. On the 13th the six guns opened again, and disabled some of the Russian pieces in the Garden Battery opposed to them. On the 14th also they continued to be worked throughout the day, though so heavy a fire was concentrated on them that the battery was greatly damaged, and the gun detachments suffered much loss. The advanced battery of the right attack had also been armed with 8-inch guns, which made excellent practice against the Mamelon and Round Tower. The two Russian batteries on the small hills opposed to the French works at Inkermann remained silent.

During the week the Russian fire continued to decrease. Their extensive batteries, far more powerful than ours, never put forth their strength, owing, as was surmised, to the paucity either of artillerymen or of projectiles. Most of their guns were fired in turn, but at slow intervals, as if a few gun-detachments served them all; their practice was very good, and had it been as warm and sustained as it was accurate, would have occasioned us heavy injury and loss.

As the cannonade went on day after day, great impatience was manifested in the English camp. The French had been very urgent with us to begin; and it was asked, with reason, why the fire had been commenced unless to be followed by an assault; and if the assault was intended, why it was delayed when our ammunition was rapidly decreasing, and our gunners worked beyond their strength,—for they passed eight hours in the batteries, then had eight hours relief, and then returned to their guns, and out of the eight hours' remission nearly two were spent in going to and returning from their camp; so that they spent ten hours on their legs, which caused many to suffer so much from sore feet that they performed their duties with difficulty. It was evident therefore that, even if our supply of ammunition had been unlimited, our fire must soon slacken. It had already produced as much effect as could be expected —indeed, the practice was altogether excellent; and as it was impossible to destroy, or even effectually breach the enemy's earthworks at the distance we were from them, by any amount of fire, it seemed that a few hours' more or less cannonade could not materially affect the difficulty of an assault.

However, while we had still ammunition to sustain the fire for some days longer, orders were given gradually to diminish it; and it was soon reduced to its former amount, without the attainment of any appreciable result from this expenditure of men and material.

Our approaches towards the Redan continuing to be pushed, drew near some Russian rifle-pits, one of which stood on ground that would be included in the next night's trench-work, and which it was therefore necessary to take. A detachment of the 77th, under Lieut.-Colonel Egerton, sallied from the advanced trench on the night of the 19th, before midnight, and, without firing a shot, drove out or killed with the bayonet all the occupants of two pits, and repulsed the troops supporting them. Captain Lempriere was killed by the enemy's fire, and, towards one o'clock, Colonel Egerton had returned into the trench bearing the dead subaltern in his arms, and was showing to some other officers a bullet which had been flattened against his own pocket-flask, when the Russians in front reopened their fire. As he hastened along the approach to the open ground, a ball entered his mouth, and, severing the vertebræ of the neck, killed him instantaneously. A man of ordinary stature would have escaped under shelter of the parapet of the trench, over which Egerton's head rose, for he was very tall, and one of the finest men in the army. The Russians, who had returned in force, opened a heavy fire on our men in the pits, by whom it was returned, as also from the advanced trench ; and the enemy, after being in vain exhorted by their officers to close, retreated, leaving a good many dead. We continued to hold one pit. Next night the neighbouring one was entered, its occupants retreating without a contest, and leaving some dead Russians in it, killed on the preceding night : this latter pit was destroyed.

As our trench-works were continued, it seemed that the design now was to advance on the place as in the siege of a regular fortress, where the operations are certain in their progress and result, which are merely questions of time. But here the case was widely different. In advancing on a regular fortress, the works of the besieger are not exposed to the fire of those bastions or salients not attacked, and his attention is directed solely on the two salients before him, and the ravelin or other outwork covering the curtain which connects them, the number of guns in which being determinate, they are always overpowered by the superior number brought against them. The sap proceeds slowly and surely till sufficiently near, when the breaching batteries or the mine open the road through the defences for the stormers.

But the fortifications of Sebastopol, far from being regular, extend along the whole length of the town and harbour. The town itself is to a certain extent isolated by the inner harbour, and the French had made there an attack as regular as the ground admitted of ; but the Barrack Battery from the opposite side of the creek bore on their works, as did the Garden Batteries in rear of the Bastion du Mât.

Great difficulty, therefore, attended the attempt to advance here by sap without attacking or silencing the Barrack Battery, which, in its turn, was flanked by the Redan, which was supported by the Malakhoff, and so on, in a sequence of as many links as that of the House which Jack built. Thus, in a regular attack, an advance on all these points was necessary, and thus was constituted, rather than one siege, a multitude of sieges. The capture of the Mamelon and its two flanking hills beyond Careening Bay, would have been a work of infinite labour and difficulty, carried on under heavy artillery fire, and would have been but a step towards the attack of the Redan and Round Tower, each formidable achievements, and still the town would remain for a separate siege: and this process demanded, if successful in all its separate particulars, many months to accomplish.

In fact, the appellation of siege applied to our operations may almost be considered a misnomer; it may rather be said we were attacking an intrenched position. Under this view we had erred in distributing the fire of our artillery so widely, and should rather have concentrated it on those points intended to be forced; and, when the enemy's guns bearing on the ground to be advanced over were sufficiently silenced, the attempt should have been made to carry these points by assault. As the inner harbour divided the defences of the place, if an assault were made on both sides of it the garrison must have divided their force, when the two bodies could not have mutually assisted each other, the fire of the French having destroyed the bridge of boats, and commanding the whole extent of the creek : or they must have left one point inadequately guarded, the forcing of which would have entailed ultimately the loss of the whole of the defences south of the great harbour. With our very superior numbers so many points might have been threatened that the garrison must have been subdivided into many small garrisons, and the real attacks might have been made with a disparity in our favour which would have promised well for success.

But if the assault were judged impracticable, there would seem to remain for the capture of the city but one alternative; viz., to invest the place, either directly, by marching down upon the north side, or by throwing a sufficient force across the roads from Perekop and the Sea of Azoff to answer the purpose of an investment. This again involved (besides the necessity of large reinforcements) complex and doubtful operations—marches into the interior from a divided or inadequate base, and battles in the field : all which considerations were doubtless taken into account in discussing the question of the assault.

CHAPTER XXII.

SUBSEQUENT OPERATIONS.

ON Thursday the 19th April, at daybreak, I rode down to Kadukoi to accompany a reconnaissance which Omer Pasha, who had arrived from Eupatoria with 20,000 Turks and Egyptians in the preceding week, was about to make towards the Tchernaya. At the barrier-gate of the intrenchment across the Kadukoi road eight hundred Chasseurs d'Afrique were assembled. In the camp of our heavy brigade a squadron of each regiment was drawn up in front of its own tents, and a half troop of Thomas's horse-artillery was issuing from the village on to the plain where the 10th Hussars, who had arrived from India a few days before, were drawn up, making with the heavy brigade, who presently joined it, about one thousand sabres. The French cavalry and guns, together with a few Turkish horse, descended into the plain, and the whole waited the proper moment to advance. This depended altogether on the progress of the Turkish infantry, which, led by Omer Pasha, had issued from the right of our lines far up the hills, and were crossing towards Kamara. A few shots told us when the Russian outposts were driven in, but the ground was more difficult than was expected; and so much time was taken up on the march that I had leisure to ride into Kadukoi and breakfast and feed my horse before the cavalry moved across the plain.

At half-past eight, the Turks having reached Kamara, we moved towards Canrobert's Hill—French chasseurs, Turkish horse, and English hussars forming a line of skirmishers, supported by detachments at a short distance, while the main bodies of cavalry came on in compact columns with the artillery on the flanks. Passing beyond Canrobert's Hill, we found on its rearmost slope a number of burrows, like those bivouacked in by the Turks, roofed with branches and earth; and other similar abodes appeared on the adjoining slopes, all, of course, deserted. Crowning the next ridge, we saw a few Russian horsemen before us in the defile where the charge of the Light Brigade had taken place; on a steep brown hill in front was a body of Cossacks behind an intrenchment drawn across the slope near the summit. Kamara was occupied by the Turkish infantry, whose skirmishers extended down towards those of our cavalry, and the main body of the reconnoitring force appeared on the verge of a high woody rock at the back of Kamara, and thither I (being present merely as an amateur, and not tied to any particular station) accordingly rode.

The only building remaining in the village of Kamara, which stands half-way between the plain and the top of the heights on the Woronzoff road, is the church, and that is in a very dilapidated condition. It stands in a stone enclosure, which was lined with Turkish soldiers, a battalion of whom was drawn up on the slope beneath. Passing this, I ascended by a path like the bed of a torrent throughthick coppice (which showed that the Russians here must have been better off than we for firewood during the winter) carpeted with primroses and buttercups, and enlivened by some wild fruit-trees in full blossom, to the top of the abrupt mountains, where the main body of the Turks had piled arms, and were cooking their victuals, their officers and such of ours as had accompanied them forming breakfast circles, while the Engineers took such notes and sketches of the country before them as were required. The view from this lofty point was extensive and grand ; on the left the Tchernaya might be traced passing our position on the plateau to the distant Ruins of Inkermann ; in the plain below were our cavalry, picturesquely grouped ; and all around were high mountains, grey or brown of tint, with glimpses of green in low-lying spots between.

After a time the infantry descended towards Kamara, where Lord Raglan and his staff were watching the operations, which were directed altogether by Omer Pasha. The venerable appearance which the Turkish commander's white beard and mustache gave him at a little distance completely vanished on a closer view, when the brightness and energy of his face corresponded well with his slender straight figure. He looked about forty-eight. He had two splendid chargers in the field, a chestnut and a bay. The Cossacks still held the hill in front, and two bodies of Turkish infantry were marched towards them, accompanied by doleful music. Long before they got within musket range, however, some rockets were fired by the French at the Cossacks, which pitched and exploded near them, when they at once quitted the intrenchment and hastened off behind the hill, up the steep stony barren side of which we all now moved, the Turkish infantry, already on their way, being first. Presently a volley was heard in front, which was fired by the Russians posted in the valley of the Tchernaya at those who were first over the hill, and which damaged nobody. Steep down beneath us was a bend of the river, which divided into streams, and, uniting again below, meandered here among willows and poplars. On the left stood a stone bridge, higher up the stream than that we had crossed when on the march from Mackenzie's Farm, in September; covering the latter, on the opposite side of the river, was an earthwork for six guns, which was not armed. Other intrenchments were visible at different points, particularly up the main road into the hills in front, where a few Russians were drawn up, and near them was a footbridge over the stream. Nothing appeared to prevent our passage, if we had been disposed to cross the river; but when the Turkish chief had satisfied his curiosity, the troops swept round the hill, and commenced the march home. The 10th Hussars marched past for Lord Raglan's inspection on the plain; and he afterwards rode through the ranks of the Heavy Brigade, which, drawn up in squadrons, looked very soldier-like and splendid, though its numbers were but scanty. The men and horses, survivors of that terrible winter bivouac, had quite recovered from the effects of their privations, and, though not so sleek and shining as of yore, looked as fit for work as ever.

A few days after, Omer re-embarked for Eupatoria, which was said to be threatened with an attack, taking a great part of his troops with him.

On the 25th of April, the ambassador, Lord Stratford de Redcliffe, arrived with his family from Constantinople, and remained more than a week.

On the night of the 1st of May, the French attacked and carried a counterguard before the central bastion covering the town, in which the Russians were preparing to place guns, and from whence some small mortars had begun to throw shells into the trenches. The musketry fire was very hot during the conflict. At four o'clock on the following afternoon, the Russians attempted to retake the work, but were repulsed with loss, some French guns having been brought to bear on them. In the two affairs, the French lost about 100 men killed, and double that number wounded ; and 160 Russian bodies were left on the ground. Nine of the small mortars were among the trophies secured by our allies, and five Russian officers were made prisoners. On both occasions the enemy's officers are said to have displayed great gallantry in leading on and animating their men.

Early in May, I accompanied a friend, who had just joined from England, over the battle-field of Inkermann, now gaily sprinkled with flowers, blue, red, and yellow. From the Two-gun Battery we descended the face of the hill, where the Russians had climbed up to attack the Guards. The valley was filled with a luxuriant growth of grass, quite hiding the marshy soil, and alive with frogs, whose croakings filled the air ; and the trees which fringe the course of the Tchernaya were in full leaf. Passing beyond the farthest French sentinel, we came, amid the bushes on the face of the steep, on the shallow grave of a Russian, where was visible, protruding from the thin covering of soil, a withered clenched hand. The dead man's belt still encircled his bones, and the bayonet-sheath rested outside the earth. A little farther down was a skeleton in Russian uniform, lying on its face ; some light-coloured locks still clung to the skull, and through a hole in the trousers the fleshless leg was visible. Thus it happened, that my friend, who had read in England, months before, an account of the battle, and had learned almost to class it with the famous actions of history, was now face to face on the battle-field with the corpse of a soldier slain in the combat. While we looked at it, a rifleman, on the other side of the valley, sent a bullet at us, which dropped among the bushes some yards below, and some others followed with no better aim.

On the 3d May, an expedition, which had been for some days in course of preparation, consisting of about 7000 French with 12 guns, and 3000 English with 6 guns, sailed for Kertsch, but just after arriving in sight of its destination, was recalled by a message from the French commander. He had received telegraphic instructions from the Emperor to despatch all the transports he could command to the Bosphorus, to convey the French reserves there to the seat of war, and considered the instructions as sufficiently imperative to necessitate the recall of the expedition, which accordingly returned, amid much dissatisfaction. A few days afterwards, General Canrobert resigned the control of the army to General Pelissier, and took the command of the first division, the same he had held under St Arnaud.

Several events marked the change of commanders. On the night of the 22d, the French made a determined attack on the rifle-pits between the Quarantine and Central Bastions, which form part of the earthworks covering the town. At nine o'clock a cannonade, accompanied by volleys far warmer and more sustained than in any previous night-attack or operation of the siege, signalised the commencement of the enterprise, and continued without intermission till three in the morning. The moon rather glimmered than shone upon the scene, and against the cloudy horizon the flashes of the guns, like summer lightning, marked the lines of defence and attack; the rattle of small-arms was almost incessant, and occasional cheers, rising from the gloom, showed some advantage won or charge attempted.

On the following day I visited the scene of combat. Entering the French lines at the Maison de Clocheton, a long walk through the zigzag approaches led to the advanced trench, where glimpses over the parapet, and through loop-holes, rendered precarious by the proximity of the Russian riflemen, who fired incessantly, revealed the features of the ground.

In a green hollow or basin, at the head of the inlet known as Quarantine Bay, was a Russian cemetery, having in the midst a small church, surrounded by crosses and headstones. No English country churchyard, where the forefathers of the hamlet sleep, could, in its trim sanctity, be more suggestive of repose than this peaceful spot, above the occupants of which rude requiems of musketry and cannon had for months broken the silence. Instead of mourning friends, marksmen had crouched in the grass of the graves, or lain in the shadow of the tombstones. On the previous night there had been hard fighting above the dead, on the thresholds of whose green abodes lay others ready to join them. The cemetery was surrounded by a wall, and was about seventy yards square ; the further wall was less than 100 yards from the wall of the town, which was of masonry, upright (those of fortified places are in general strengthened with sloping buttresses, termed revetments), and having no ditch. It was breached in three or four places, though not extensively enough for the assault; but it was evident that, in a few hours, the French batteries could, whenever they pleased, destroy the whole extent of wall, which it would have been impolitic to do until the moment for storming had arrived. Between the wall of the cemetery and that of the town was a line of rifle-screens, strongly constructed of earth and gabions, and capable of holding each at least a dozen marksmen. Only two of these had been taken by the French, and the number of dead stretched on the grass showed at what cost. The cemetery was cleared of Russians, who had retired to their remaining rifle-pits, and its right wall now formed part of the French parapet. The Russian batteries before the town were silent, and the garrison had hoisted a flag of truce, which the French refused to respond to, as it was known the attack was to be resumed in greater force the same night (23d) ; and, on returning in the evening, I met bodies of troops entering the lines. In all, it was said that 30,000 men were to be assembled in the trenches for this new attack. That night at nine o'clock, the cannonade and musketry opened as before, but soon became fainter, and by midnight died away. The Russians, cowed by the slaughter of the previous night, and overpowered by the numbers of the assailants, withdrew within their works, after a short struggle, and left the whole of the rifle-pits to our allies, who connected them by trenches, opened a communication with their nearest approach, and occupied them as a new advanced line. On the 24th there was a truce for six hours to collect the dead. The French lost 1600 killed and wounded, of whom about a fourth were killed. They delivered to the Russians 1150 bodies; 800 more were collected by the burial-parties on the ground, most of whom had been killed by the fire of four French field-pieces, which ploughed through the enemy's dense columns drawn up in support; and the loss of the garrison in the two attacks could scarcely have been less than 6000 men.

On the 23d the expedition again sailed for Kertsch, and this time accomplished the object of its mission. On the afternoon of the 24th, the allied force disembarked at Kamish, a village south-west of Kertsch. About 2000 Russian cavalry showed themselves there, but did not offer to attack; and the garrison, after blowing up their magazines and spiking most of their guns, were seen moving off. Next morning the Allies advanced on Kertsch, and halted for an hour in the town, where they destroyed a large foundry and bullet-factory, and then, advancing on Yenikale, and finding the place deserted, they proceeded to intrench themselves. In all, 108 guns were taken, many of them of large calibre (68-pounders), which in another week would have been mounted in the batteries, offering a formidable defence. Some of our war-steamers of light draught, and gun-boats, immediately entered the Sea of Azoff, capturing 260 boats laden with grain, and proceeding to Arabat, a strong fort at the southern extremity of the long narrow isthmus, by which the land communication with the neighbouring provinces of Russia was maintained, blew up, with the first shell fired, an immense magazine there. A few days afterwards, Genitsch, at the other extremity of the isthmus of Arabat, was set on fire, and eighty-six boats destroyed in its harbour. The whole of the Sea of Azoff was scoured by this light armament. The town of Berdiansk on the north shore was abandoned by the enemy, as was Soujouk-kale, near Anapa; and besides the towns, guns, ammunition, and vessels (including four war-steamers sunk by themselves), the Russians either destroyed or lost grain sufficient for 100,000 men for four months; moreover, the road by which supplies had chiefly been sent to Sebastopol was rendered unavailable.

CHAPTER XXIII.

THE POSITION EXTENDED.

During the month of May the Sardinian contingent had joined us. The appearance of these troops was much admired; they were very neatly and serviceably clothed, those of the line in grey coats, fitting loosely, and leaving the neck free, with a light jacket and trousers underneath; their arms, equipments, waggon-train, and horses, were all in excellent order; the troops looked healthy and cheerful, and the few cavalry that accompanied them were extremely soldier-like and well-appointed.

Besides this addition to our forces, the French had received such strong reinforcements that it was necessary, if only for the ventilation of the army, to extend our position. On the 25th, 20,000 French, 10,000 Sardinians, and 20,000 Turks, quitting the plateau some hours before daybreak, marched towards the Tchernaya, from which the Russians, who were in inconsiderable numbers there, fell back without opposition: the area of our position was thus nearly doubled, the passage of the river secured, with a plentiful supply of water, and a large portion of the army encamped on spots far more eligible than could be found on the bare and trodden surface of the heights.

The Russian supplies from the Sea of Azoff being cut off, and our force thus largely augmented, the campaign assumed a new aspect. The enemy had now to draw their supplies from their depôt at Simferopol, and an allied army advancing from Eupatoria to threaten that place, would have drawn their force thither, as Sir John Moore's advance in the north of Spain drew Napoleon's army from Madrid. A second force of the Allies might have followed them from the Tchernaya, still leaving sufficient troops to watch Sebastopol, and effected a junction with the army from Eupatoria, presenting a force which it was unlikely the Russians could attempt to cope with, and the conquest of the whole province might have ensued. On such grounds the time for actively continuing the siege might have seemed past, as, with our then means, the town might have been obtained on easier terms than at the expense of a bloody assault. Situated as the Crimea is, at the extremity of the empire, and all the northern portion being extremely barren, it appeared impossible that Russia should be able to maintain there an army at all equal to ours, and the form and position of the province rendered it very vulnerable to an enemy who commanded the sea. On such considerations the time seemed to have arrived when the operations of the siege might have given place to new, more extensive, and more decisive enterprises.

On the 25th I rode to our outposts on the Tchernaya, and afterwards completed the circuit of the position. Descending from the plateau by the Woronzoff road with a companion, we crossed the ground where the Light Brigade made their memorable charge, to the low heights between the plateau and the Tchernaya, leaving behind us the hills from which the Turkish outposts were driven in the affair of Balaklava, and which were now again occupied by our Ottoman allies. The plains were in every part covered with luxuriant herbage and flowers, varying in character with the ground, the lower portions being sometimes moist and filled with marsh plants, while a shorter growth clothed the upland slopes. At the base of the low heights, which were now occupied by a French division under Canrobert, six field-batteries were posted, the heights themselves were covered with the French tents, and bowers made of branches; and the guns in the Russian works above the Ruins of Inkermann tried vainly to reach them with shells, which, for the most part, burst high in air midway. A dell in the midst of these heights led to the road along which we had marched from Mackenzie's Farm. The bridge by which we had crossed the Tchernaya was uninjured, and on the further side the French were constructing a *tête-de-pont* or earthen work, the faces flanked by parapets for musketry on the hither side of the river. We rode along the bank, which was lined with Frenchmen and Sardinians fishing, and who appeared to have good sport, pulling out fish something like trout: one soldier caught a carp of a pound and a half. The meadows here, though they must in winter have been deep swamps, contained the remains of many burrows where the Russians had bivouacked, the branched roofs of which had fallen in. At a neighbouring ford several hundred French cavalry were watering their horses, the men in their stable dresses, with carbines at their backs, while a strong picket, fully accoutred, was drawn up beyond the river to protect them from any sudden descent the enemy might make from the opposite heights, where a few Cossacks were occasionally visible. Close by, on the opposite bank, was a tall conical hill held by the Piedmontese, who had here their advanced post of light troops, dressed in green tunics, and hats with bunches of green feathers, like theatrical bandits, and armed with short rifles. The back of this hill formed, with a steep slope opposite, a narrow gorge, where a pretty stone bridge spanned the Tchernaya, and from this point branched the aqueduct which used to supply Sebastopol. Beyond, the valley widened again into meadows sprinkled with trees, and tinted glowingly with flowers; in some places knolls were so covered with purple, red, or yellow, as to look like great nosegays. In the midst of a grove stood the village of Tchergoum, with its large octagonal tower, and up the road behind it a Cossack might be seen sauntering towards some of his comrades who appeared on the heights, and occasionally fired at those who advanced furthest from the outposts. There were plenty of Russian burrows here on both sides of the river, and the Allies in their advance made spoil of abundance of arms and furniture, which they disposed of to visitors, one of whom was offered a piano a great bargain, of which he was unable to avail himself, as it was rather too large to put in his saddle-bags; while in another quarter a post-chaise was for sale. Had the same purchaser got both, he might have taken home the piano in the post-chaise.

Riding back over the steep hills, which in the eastern corner of the position were held by Sardinians, you reached their right outpost near Kamara, where a road swept round the back of the mountain. Here the aspect of the country suddenly changed—for whereas the hills towards Bakshi-serai were bare and chalky, here they were clothed with a thick verdure of tall coppice, with some trees of large growth, spotting with the darkness of their shadowed sides the even sunlit green of the bushes, which was further broken by park-like glades. All was silent here; there were no soldiers visible, and no sound was heard except the thrushes in the leaves, and the murmur of a small stream caught in a stone fountain beside the road. The next turn disclosed a camp occupied by a detachment of our marines, supplying the pickets and sentries who completed the circuit of outposts from Kamara to the sea-shore far south of

Balaklava. Their tents were pitched in a sunny meadow, before which rose a wooded mountain, with craggy peaks breaking through the verdure, on each of which stood a sentry with his red-coat and cross-belts discernible a mile off against the sky. From this camp a wood-path, shaded with fine trees, ascended to the next mountain-ridge, where a turn of the road disclosed a really magnificent prospect. Doubtless the long residence on the dreary heights of Sebastopol enhanced for us the effect of the view, but anywhere in the world it would have been eminently attractive. Below us lay the valley of Baidar, stretching from the edge of the sea-cliffs on our right to the distant mountain range, where it wound round out of sight. Like the fabled vale of Avilion, it was "deep-bower'd, happy, fair with orchard-lawns;" flowery meadows, sprinkled with trees and groves, reminded me, in their fertility and expanse, of the Vega of Granada, as seen from the mountains behind the city. Two red-roofed villages, embowered in trees, stood, at some distance apart, in the midst of the valley, but no inhabitants, nor cattle, nor any kind of moving thing, gave life to the scene—it was beautiful as a dream, but silent as a chart. No corn had been sown for this year's harvest; the only tokens of agriculture were some farm-waggons discernible through the glass at a distant point of the valley. The villages were not only deserted, but, as some visitors had ascertained a day or two before, quite denuded of all tokens of domestic life. Beyond this outpost it was now contrary to orders to pass; a marine officer was in charge of the party, and lay in a kind of nest, under the shade of his blanket and cloak, which hung on bushes.

Turning with regret from this view, we rode back along the sea-cliffs towards Balaklava. The tint of the Euxine was so light in the bright sunshine that it was not easy to distinguish where the sky joined it; and the steamers that crossed to and from Kertsch (one of them tugging a sailing vessel, perhaps a prize) seemed to traverse the air. The cliffs, as I have mentioned elsewhere, were of remarkable beauty, with delicate rosy tints and purple shadows. At length we arrived at the stockaded barrier drawn across the road in the winter, passing which we came to the fortified ridge from whence you look down on the harbour of Balaklava, lying like a small lake in its rocky, tower-skirted basin. Here work-a-day life began again—troops lighting their cooking fires and fetching their water—guards lolling in the sunshine— mules and buffaloes toiling with their loads; and up the hills beyond Kadukoi the bearded pashas, sitting in open green tents like canopies, gazing as they smoked their tall silver nargillys towards the distant mountains which surround Bakshi-serai; while the more devout among the Mussulman soldiers, drawn up in a body, with their faces turned (I suppose) towards Mecca, repeated, with many bendings and prostrations, their evening prayers.

ZOUAVES AT A WASHING PLACE

CHAPTER XXIV.

ASSAULT OF THE MAMELON AND QUARRIES.

NOTWITHSTANDING the extent of our force, great part of which was necessarily idle, our strategical operations seemed to be limited to the expedition to Kertsch, as the preparations for a renewal of the cannonade on Sebastopol, to be followed by an assault, were actively continued. We erected new batteries, accumulated great stores of ammunition, and augmented the number of mortars in the trenches. On the 6th June, at three o'clock in the afternoon, the batteries opened, and after a short space the Russians replied with a fire heavier than in former attacks, but by no means so well directed, owing, perhaps, to the want of reinforcements of good artillerymen. All that afternoon and all night our fire continued, and the next morning that of the Russians, which had begun so spiritedly, was much subdued. The Mamelon, which on the previous afternoon had fired salvos, was reduced to two or three guns, and its parapets, as well as those of the Redan, and the face of the Malakhoff looking towards our batteries, were little more than a shapeless heap of earth, testifying to the excellence of our artillery fire, which was probably unequalled for precision and effect. The practice of our mortars was admirable; scarcely the smallest interval elapsed without a huge shell bursting in the midst of the Mamelon, and the loss of its garrison must have been very severe; of which, indeed, we shortly had proof.

It had been arranged, before opening the fire, that on the second day an assault should be made; by the French on the Mamelon and the smaller works towards Careening Bay, by us on a work known as the Quarries, in front of the Redan. Up to our last cannonade the ground there had been occupied merely by heaps of loose stones and rubbish, where marksmen were posted; but since then the enemy had thrown up an intrenchment surrounding the Redan at about 400 yards in front of it, and had filled it with riflemen; and it was this work which, though quite regular in form, retained the old name of the Quarries. As soon as the French had secured the Mamelon we were to attack this point and establish ourselves; but our attack was for the present to terminate with the success of this operation, because the Redan, if carried, would be untenable so long as the Russians retained possession of the Malakhoff. The time chosen was half-past six in the evening, and for this reason, that as men advance with much more spirit and confidence when they see what is before them than in night-attacks, the assailants would have daylight enough to secure possession of the work, while darkness would descend in time to enable them to throw up the necessary cover against the fire which the Malakhoff (looking on the rear of the Mamelon) would otherwise pour in so hotly as, perhaps, to render the occupation of it difficult and attended with heavy loss.

At half-past five the French columns of attack were formed at the mouth of the ravine which divides the English right from the left of the French at Inkermann—and to each battalion General Bosquet addressed a few words of encouragement, to which they responded with cheers, and straightway plunged, in rather more tumultuous array than English discipline permits, into the ravine. A most conspicuous personage was a *vivandière*, who, well mounted, and wearing a white hat and feather, rode at the head of the column with a little keg slung at her saddle. First went the Algerine Zouaves, tall, lithe, swarthy, and with African features ; next the French Zouaves, who, having obtained precedence over the Green Chasseurs, greeted these latter *braves* as they passed them with screams, howls, and derisive expressions, which were received in silence by the Chasseurs, who followed next, attended by their *vivandière*, a very pretty and smartly-dressed girl, who seemed to possess great control over her feelings ; for, whereas a woman can scarcely be expected to see with indifference even a single lover going to battle, this young lady beheld with equanimity a whole regiment of admirers advancing to deadly conflict. Several regiments of the line followed, and the whole array swept down the ravine to the trenches.

The English light and second divisions were destined to attack the Quarries. Two bodies, each of two hundred men, issuing from the foremost trench of our right attack, were to turn the extremities of the work, drive out the occupants, and, advancing towards the Redan, and lying down there, keep up a fire to cover the operations of eight hundred workmen, who, with pickaxe and shovel, were to throw up a parapet towards the enemy. Besides the guards of the trenches, other detachments were to remain at convenient points, ready to support them against all attempts of the enemy.

By some means the news had got abroad that an assault was to be made, and crowds assembled at different commanding points before the camps. As the hour approached, and the number of the spectators augmented, the greatest excitement prevailed. We could see the French lining their trenches, and the English filing into theirs. The fire from our batteries was hotter than ever, and shells were showered more thickly into the devoted Mamelon. At length three rockets were fired from the Victoria redoubt, which General Pelissier had just entered, and every glass was turned towards the French trenches, from which the assailants were seen to issue and swarm up the slope. Led by one man, who kept considerably in advance of the rest, they passed the line of intrenchment which the enemy had drawn round the front of the work, and in a few minutes were seen at the edge of the ditch, firing into the embrasures. Presently some climbed the parapet; large columns pressed in at the left; and, almost without a struggle, the Russians hurried off towards the Malakhoff, while the tricolor was hoisted in the captured work. The smaller works towards Careening Bay had been simultaneously assaulted, though the conflict there was disregarded in the absorbing interest of the attack on the Mamelon, and they also were carried after a short struggle; but the one nearest the sea, being exposed to the fire of batteries on the north side of the harbour, was found too hot to remain in, and the French quitted it.

Possession of the Mamelon being obtained, it was necessary to cover the operations of the workmen by a further advance, and the foremost assailants dashed out in pursuit of the Russians, who made for the Malakhoff. Flushed with their easy success, the French did not content themselves with a demonstration against this formidable work, but actually assailed it. It immediately became a hornet's nest; every gun opened; its parapets sparkled with musketry; and the garrison of the Redan, not yet assailed by the English, were seen leaving their post, probably to succour the Malakhoff.

The French pressed on gallantly till stopped by a belt of abattis—an obstacle composed of trees with the branches pointed and sharp stakes. A few men penetrated through this, and, advancing to the edge of the ditch, fired on the defenders. At this time the Malakhoff became wrapt in smoke, which, drifting across the scene, dimmed the view of the struggle. The guns fired wildly ; shells exploded in all parts of the ground, and shot came bounding up among the spectators, one of which, later in the evening, killed an unfortunate civilian who was looking on. After the lapse of about a quarter of an hour, during which the French, unable to penetrate into the Malakhoff, gallantly held their ground on the slope before it, the Russians, reinforced by several battalions, drove them back amidst a tremendous uproar of musketry and cannon, and they retired into the Mamelon, behind which a considerable body of their comrades were drawn up. Here they made a stand against the enemy, and commenced a struggle which wore an unpromising aspect ; for while some of the French supporting force held their ground, others retired to the intrenchment midway down the slope, and began to fire from thence. At length the French gave way, and ran down the face of the hill to their own trenches, where their reserves were drawn up. Upon these they rallied, and, after a breathing space, were again led to the assault, and successfully. Again they rushed into the Mamelon, drove out its defenders, and pursued them to the Malakhoff, around which their musketry continued to crackle long after darkness set in, while their comrades intrenched themselves in the Mamelon, which was found strewn with dead from the effect of our shells.

Meantime our men, issuing from their trenches, had entered the Quarries, which they found unoccupied, and advanced toward the Redan to cover the operations of the working party. Their movements were not so plainly visible from the rear as those of the French, owing partly to the nature of the ground, partly to the dense smoke which overhung the scene; but Lord Raglan, who remained at a point about half-way between the ridge before our camps and the batteries of our left attack, received occasional notices of the state of affairs. Some of our men had entered the Redan and found it empty, the garrison having, as before said, probably gone to reinforce the Malakhoff; but they speedily returned in force, and our reserves advanced to support the assailants. When darkness set in, the line of musketry marked the disputed points, but the artillery fire had almost ceased, except from our mortars, which threw shells into the Redan and Malakhoff. The latter work seemed to be still assailed by the French; the former was silent. All was darkness, except where the sparks of musketry were scattered as from a forge; then, with a flash and roar, a shell would climb the sky, passing the ridge of clouds lying on the horizon, mingling confusedly amid the stars, and then rotating downwards, when, as it disappeared behind the parapet aimed at, for a moment all was dark, till the explosion lit up the work, making it stand out in transient red relief from the surrounding blackness ; or a shell from a gun would traverse the ground at a low angle, the burning fuse rising and falling in graceful curves as it bounded on, till its course ended in a burst of flame. Sometimes a bugle sounded shrilly in the still night ; once or twice there was a cheer ; and these sounds and the rattle of the small-arms showed the chief part of the combat, in which so many of our comrades and friends were darkly engaged, to be in the ravine of the Woronzoff road. Sometimes the sound of strife died almost away, and then was renewed with great warmth. These sudden outbursts marked the onsets of the Russians, who made vigorous efforts to retake the work, and even drove our men out of it, but were again repulsed. Towards morning they advanced on our trenches, and penetrated into some of the approaches, but were driven back with loss.

The next morning the Russian works, beaten into uneven heaps, were almost silent, firing only an occasional shot. The French had intrenched themselves in the Mamelon, and had placed some small mortars there, while we had made good our footing in the Quarries. Both the English divisions had suffered severely ; in the second, the report up to ten o'clock in the morning showed fifty killed and 270 wounded ; while, in the light, the 7th and 88th had suffered severely. In the afternoon several Russian mortars were directed on the Mamelon, and must have caused loss to the French in it.

Before and during the assault no feint or demonstration was made at any other point of the line to mislead or distract the enemy, who took advantage of the directness of the attack to collect their troops in the Malakhoff in sufficient numbers to drive back the French, as before described, from that work, and even temporarily to retake the Mamelon. Our allies attacked with great gallantry, and the Russians, taken as they were by surprise, and having already suffered much from our heavy fire, showed more stubbornness in the defence than was generally anticipated. Next day the expectation was very strong, in the English camp, that the attack was to be renewed in the course of the day, and that this time the whole south side would be ours; but the sun went down without any preparations for a second assault.

CHAPTER XXV.

THE CONFERENCES AND DEBATES.

THE conduct of the Vienna conferences, and the tone of the parliamentary discussions on the war, were not such as to inspire respect either for the politics or diplomacy of the age. Europe fixed its attention on the former, and, while failing to receive any lessons of wisdom, was not even gratified by an exhibition of skill. The three greatest nations of the earth were at war, and before either side had obtained a decisive advantage, all had agreed to treat for peace. Seldom has diplomacy had such a field for display, and seldom has it appeared in a less respectable light. No cunning of fence was shown, and the advantages obtained were of the paltriest description, and not worth the playing for, such as when Russia suspended the conferences to consider the request of the other powers that she would originate a proposition, and then, after securing unnecessary delay, declined to propose anything. The negotiations and the war seemed mutually to await each other's chances, and there appeared no man of sufficient political or military foresight to afford his colleagues the means of adopting a decided course. Perhaps the most curious feature in the spectacle was the lofty bearing of beleaguered, distressed, and defeated Russia. When at the conference Lord John Russell, as a precedent for Russia to consent to limit her power in the Black Sea, quoted (not very happily) the cession of Dunkirk by Louis XIV.,—" Ah!" said the Russian plenipotentiary, with extraordinary assurance, " but we have met with none of his disasters, and the case does not apply." Met with no disasters! when the banks of the Danube were strewn with dead Russian armies, when the despised Turks had defeated them in every action, and when a fortress like Silistria had defeated their whole power deliberately cast on it! Met with no disasters! when the defenders of the soil were beaten from their strong position at Alma, when they had been repulsed from our weak point at Inkermann, when half the Black Sea fleet was at the bottom of the harbour of Sebastopol, and the other half penned therein as in a trap!—when a daily augmenting force was establishing itself in the Crimea, and preparing for fresh assaults on the city!—when Bomarsund with its fortifications was demolished, and the Baltic equally with the Euxine blotted from the highways of Russian commerce! Yet such effrontery passed without the obvious rejoinder, because the English nation had proposed to itself the capture of Sebastopol as the true and only meed of victory; and the wily Russian, adopting the absurd assumption with which we had ourselves furnished him, asserted that, while Sebastopol had not fallen, Russia had suffered no disaster.

But, in truth, the whole conference was an absurdity. The terms offered by the Allies, so far as their vagueness allowed them to be intelligible, were ridiculously easy, and, on the other hand, Russia was insane to refuse them. She might have accepted them, have procured an armistice, have secured a seeming triumph; and then, when it suited her, and if still disposed for war, she might have broken off the negotiations on a question of details. All this would have been quite consistent with the usual course of her policy, and with the diplomatic resources of her ministers. Instead of this, she assumed the airs of a conqueror—condescendingly agreed to treat —was undisguisedly insolent in conference; and when she deigned to make any proposals, they were such as were insulting from their absurdity. And this was at a time when the Allies were accumulating a force sufficient to take the Crimea in a month; when her own army was pressed for supplies, and its communications so ill-secured that a detachment cut their main branch irremediably without a struggle; when her coasts were threatened, her towns burnt; and when the fortresses which she had acquired, with great expense and trouble, were so ill provided for defence that, at the first approach of an enemy, the garrisons abandoned them. Yet her envoys could comport themselves as if her great credit for resources and strength were unblemished; could not merely veil discomfiture, but assume the tone of undoubted success, and half Europe was disposed to admire their supercilious demeanour. If such finesse is admirable, great empires may be dexterously lost.

But, whatever the disasters of Russia, she at least enjoyed one advantage over us. Whether her councils were directed by wisdom or presumption, they were secret, while all our elements of weakness were laid bare in the national discussions, and were paraded far more ostentatiously than those resources and successes which should have bid us be of good cheer. Every shade of policy between vigorous prosecution of the war, and peace on any terms, found its spokesman, and such want of unanimity could not but give confidence to the enemy.

Of the Four Points discussed at the conference, the Third was the only one bearing directly on the circumstances of the war. In the parliamentary debates on this point, it was asserted that Russia never would consent to such humiliation as a limitation of her fleet in the Black Sea. The objectors spoke as if that fleet were still riding the Euxine unmolested; in which case it might, indeed, be derogatory to the dignity of the Czar to consent to its diminution. But force had already confined the few remaining ships of the Russian fleet to their port, dooming them to hopeless inaction; and, whatever turn the affairs of the Allies might take by land, it was evident that Russia could never, during the war, by any effort or any success, regain her naval supremacy in the East. A more reasonable objection against the Third Point was, that it left the essential article of limitation indefinite and dependent on the chances of the war.

Mr Disraeli found an easy task in criticising the conduct of the Government and its envoy, but was by no means so successful in amending the plan of the campaign as in exposing its errors. He denounced the aggressive movement of the war as the cause of all our disasters, maintaining that a purely defensive policy would have been the true one, and, like some other speakers of great reputation, assumed that Russia was invulnerable.

Since to blockade the ports of Russia is in itself an aggressive movement, it is to be presumed that Mr Disraeli meant that our operations by land only should have been restricted to the defensive; that our troops should have occupied Turkey in sufficient force to render her territories secure against the armies of Russia.

But, to maintain in Turkey a force sufficiently large to be effective, would be almost as costly as to make war in the Crimea; at any rate, it is difficult to see how occupying Turkey could shorten the war, or cripple Russia more effectually than assailing herself. To capture Sebastopol was to solve the knottiest question of the war; it was to give security to the shores of Turkey, to deliver her capital from the apprehension of invasion, and to enable her to concentrate her powers on her land defences. It has been said that we could have no security that Russia would not rebuild her fortifications and renew her fleet; but it is not likely that the war, if concluded to-morrow, would leave the finances of Russia in a condition so flourishing as to enable her immediately to set about accumulating expensive means of aggression.

The assumption that Russia is invulnerable by land, is surely a mistake; to an enemy commanding the sea, the Crimea is especially an assailable province. Far removed from the heart of the empire, her ponderous powers cannot be vigorously transmitted to so distant an extremity. In any season it would be almost impossible for her to maintain there a force sufficient to cope with ours; the losses in marching an army into the Crimea are necessarily great, and still greater in maintaining it. Our fleets ought to give us an incalculable advantage in moving from point to point of the coast, threatening and harassing the enemy, and enabling small bodies to check large ones; and with such a force and such means as the Allies possessed, Russia had no right to calculate on calling the Crimea hers for two months. Once ours, the difficult question of how we were to dispose of it remained; but as that consideration was not broached in the debates, it need not be alluded to here, though it may not have been without important influence on the war. But, however that might be settled, the Crimea ours, and Sebastopol dismantled as a sea-fortress, we should hold the guarantee we needed, and might withdraw, besides the greater portion of the army, all our fleet, except a few war-steamers to watch the coast. With the Crimea lost, with the Circassians on their old frontier, with the trade of the Sea of Azoff cut off, and its towns ruined, and with the Baltic blockaded, it is difficult to see what end Russia could propose to herself in continuing a war in which she could assail none of her enemies but Turkey, who had already repelled her single-handed.

We, on the other hand, would have obtained by force of arms what Russia had refused to diplomacy, the security of Turkey; and while suffering far less from the war (which might then become a blockade) than our adversary, we could have no more reason than she to wish to prolong it. It would be a question of endurance, where Russia would have most to endure.

The facts of Sebastopol being yet uncaptured, and the Russian army in the Crimea still able to oppose us, do not alter the real state of the case, because the vulnerability of the Crimea depends, not on a chance combination of military and political circumstances, but on its natural and unalterable features. A temporary failure does not lessen our chance of ultimate success, nor give Russia greater security of retaining the province. While we are able to encompass its shores with our ships, and to land and supply our troops; while the internal resources of the peninsula are insufficient to maintain large armies, and the barrenness of its northern portion forbids Russia to supply adequately, by convoys, those necessaries which the country does not afford; so long must the Crimea remain an arena where the chances are all in our favour, and where alone are neutralised the advantages which our enemy derives from her enormous military power; and nothing is wanting to secure the prize, but a man able to grasp it.

Such is the aspect which the present conjuncture wears to some of those whose thoughts have necessarily been deeply intent on it, and than whom none can be more powerfully interested in a creditable termination. But in England, while our most resolute statesmen have laid far less stress on the "vigorous prosecution of the war," than on its inevitable associate phrase, " a safe and honourable peace," there are many of spirit so abject, that it would be quite consistent with their views if six of our most venerable commanders were to present themselves, like the citizens of Calais, before Sebastopol, in their shirts, and with halters round their necks, and humbly beseech the best terms the enemy might please to allow us. The puzzled public is busily patching the body and members of the prostrate political and military machine, while the defect is in the brain. There is sufficient strength and completeness, but the Promethean spark is wanting. Meantime, amid councils so varied and irresolute, the nation, like the Prince in the Arabian Nights, pressing onward to its goal, is stunned and bewildered by so many voices warning it against false dangers, that it pauses, looks back, and is turned into stone.

Of all the arguments used against the war, none reflects so much discredit on its propounder, as one by Mr Bright, who, in the course of a clever and much-applauded speech, put it to the House, "whether they believed that when the capital of the greatest banking-house in Lombard Street can be transferred to the United States on a small piece of paper, in one post, the imposition of £75,000,000 of taxation over and above the taxation of an equal population in the United States, will not have the effect of transferring capital from this country to the United States—and if capital, then trade, population, and all that forms the bone and sinew of this great empire?"

Had this been merely a warning to Government of one of the difficulties they would have had to provide against, by rousing the feeling of patriotism till self-interest should be in great measure lost in the nobler sentiment, such a reminder would have been timely and politic. But the whole tenor of the speech showed that the speaker, in all whose views there is an ignoble consistency, believed that no capitalist could be actuated by any higher motive than the desire to make the most of his money; and that to transfer one's self with one's property to another country, when our own was engaged in a struggle which rendered it no longer capable of affording profitable investment, was a natural and sensible act, such as British merchants might acknowledge without reproach.

If a man's first duty is to think of himself, and if his best interests are centred in the increase of his capital, then Mr Bright's argument was just, and worthy the applause of the representatives of the nation. The Carthaginian women who cut off their hair to serve as bowstrings for the defenders of their beleaguered city, had much better have sold it to make wigs for the Roman ladies. But if there be anything to admire in the sacrifices a nation makes to sustain a contest with a powerful enemy; if it be more heroic to struggle to the last than to submit ; what can be found worthy of applause, at a time when Mr Bright's countrymen are spending their energies and blood to uphold the honour of England, in an appeal to a principle which, however legitimate in commercial questions, or in the ordinary transactions of life, can never obtrude itself either in public or private affairs, where higher interests than money are concerned, without the risk of fettering justice and staining honour.

CHAPTER XXVI.

ATTACK OF THE MALAKHOFF AND REDAN.

THE cannonade subsided with the capture of the Mamelon and Quarries, and trenches were pushed out from these works towards the Malakhoff and Redan. From the Quarries, zigzags led to a trench sixty or seventy yards in advance, where riflemen incessantly exchanged shots with the garrison of the Redan, while a battery for guns and mortars was constructed close in rear of it. When this was armed, the guns swept so completely one of the communications of the Malakhoff, that the enemy could scarcely use it, and the 8-inch mortars dropped their shells into the Redan with great accuracy. But neither the advanced trench, the Quarries themselves, nor the communications in front and rear, were by any means secure, against either the cannon or riflemen of the Redan and its flanking batteries, and many casualties occurred there every day—insomuch that, except securing the favourable position for the battery, the possession of the Quarries did not seem to bestow any advantage adequate to the loss suffered in their capture and occupation. But it is probable that, when the French resolved to attack the Mamelon, we considered ourselves bound to make some corresponding advance, without nicely balancing the advantages to be gained. Such is one of the difficulties attending the combined operations of an allied army.

On the 17th the cannonade recommenced. For three hours the fire was warmly returned, and then the Russian batteries grew almost silent. Several causes might exist for this : their ammunition might be failing ; their guns might be disabled by our fire ; or the losses in the batteries might be so great that the enemy could no longer man them. But this slackening of their fire, from whatever cause, seemed favourable to the success of another assault, which had been planned to take place on the following day, as follows :—

After two or three hours' cannonade, the French were to assault the Malakhoff. That work carried, the English were immediately to assail the Redan, which would not be tenable by us unless the Malakhoff were first captured. Three columns, of 400 men each, were to be ready in the Quarries and advanced work, with strong supports in the trenches and approaches close behind. At the signal they were to rush out : the one on the right was to attack the angle at the left face and flank of the Redan ; the one on the left, the angle of the right shoulder of the work ; and the centre column was to advance on the salient, and make a lodgment there. Twenty artillerymen under an officer were to accompany each column, to spike the guns or turn them on the enemy, and parties of sailors were to carry the scaling-ladders. The right and left columns, uniting in rear of the Redan, were to drive the garrison towards the water, and to attack the Barrack Battery should the enemy make a stand there, in which operations they were to be assisted by a brigade under General Eyre, which was to descend the great ravine towards the inner harbour, and, when their first attempt had succeeded, effect a junction with them.

This plan was changed, at the instance of the French, on the evening of the 17th, when it was resolved that the assault should be made at daybreak without a previous cannonade. The other arrangements remained the same. This change was regretted by the English artillery officers, who were very confident of rendering the Russian batteries nearly harmless in a fire of three hours. Notwithstanding this alteration of the plan, which, made at the eleventh hour, seemed to betoken indecision, confidence was at a high pitch in the Allied camp. At length we were to close with the enemy; the dreary vigils in the trenches, the wearisome life on the heights, were to be at an end, and, with the assured capture of the city, a new era would dawn for us and for Europe.

At two o'clock on the morning of the 18th, we rode towards the lines. It was very dark; the camps were still silent as we clattered through them, and we were near the trenches before a faint glimmer of daylight tinged the gloom. A point in an advanced trench, which commanded a near view both of the Redan and Malakhoff, had been selected as Lord Raglan's post of observation, and he was already there.

Day broke rapidly, and we could see our troops destined for the assault in the Quarry and advanced trenches, while the supports occupied the lines in rear. The interval of suspense was short before the rattle of musketry showed the French to be assaulting. It continued, increased, and seemed to encompass the Malakhoff, though we could not see the actors in whose success we were so deeply interested. After a few minutes the guns of the Malakhoff deepened the din, and covered the ground with the spray of their grape, the steadiness of their fire showing that the work was not yet entered in force by the French.

However, their success seems to have been considered sufficient to warrant the giving of the signal to attack the Redan. The party of rifles and 33d, who who were to lead the stormers on the right, at once quitted their cover, and, gallantly led by the engineers and their own officers, ran across the smooth grassy slope between the Quarries and Redan, till, reaching the abattis which surrounded the latter at a few yards in front of the ditch, they lay down there and fired on the embrasures, which now began to pour forth grape. Probably, on the previous day, the guns had been run behind the parapet for security from our fire, which they could not effectually return, and were thus preserved from its effects ; for, warned by the attack on the Malakhoff, they were already run out, and opened on our men with a violence that nothing could withstand. In vain the officers stood up amid the iron shower and waved their swords ; in vain the engineers returned to bring up the supports ; the men could not be induced to quit the parapets in a body. Small parties of half a dozen, or half a score, ran out only to add to the slaughter. The party of artillerymen, whose business it was to follow this column and spike the guns, sallied forth, led by their officer, and, of the twenty, only nine returned unwounded ; and the sailors who carried the scaling-ladders, and the naval officers who led them, also suffered very severe loss. Sir John Campbell, calling to the nearest troops to follow, left the trench, led the way to the abattis, and was shot dead under it. The men drawn up behind the Quarry suffered almost as severely as those who had advanced ; and the remainder of these latter, after continuing for nearly a quarter of an hour under this tremendous fire on the ground before the abattis, ran back to the trenches.

The point where Lord Raglan stood was the focus of the fire of the Malakhoff and Redan, and such a storm of shot of all kinds came over and through the parapet, which was low and thin, as rendered it a very indifferent post of observation. First a soldier was wounded by a grape-shot ; another struck General Jones on the forehead, ploughing the skin; then a shot, entering a neighbouring embrasure, carried off the head of an artilleryman, killed a sapper, and struck off the right arm of Captain Brown of the 88th; and the fire rather increasing, his lordship was recommended to exchange this position for one in the first parallel.

The musketry still continued to rattle around the Malakhoff, and, from the eight-gun battery in our third parallel, which now began to fire, I saw several hundreds of the French clinging to scarped spots in the ground before the Malakhoff, and firing on the parapets, which were lined with Russians. The French guns in the Mamelon (where General Laboussinière, of the artillery, had been killed) were silent, while our artillery now opened both on the Redan and Malakhoff, principally on the latter. The practice was admirable. The Russians speedily left their parapets, where whole sections of them must have been swept away, and our shells, bursting just after grazing the edge of the work, must have been most destructive to the troops drawn up in its defence. A couple of the guns of the Malakhoff were directed on the French still clinging to the hill, and the grape rattling among them put them to flight; but the vigour of our artillery fire enabled them to retreat with but little loss from the enemy's guns, which, in their own defence, were now directed on our batteries.

When it was known that the French did not

mean to repeat the assault, the greatest disappointment prevailed. On our part the disaster was rather a blunder than a repulse; for an attack so feeble against such a work as the Redan could not be called an assault. Probably its garrison of thousands never beheld from their ramparts more than three hundred enemies advancing upon them, and they must have been puzzled to account for such a futile attempt, taking it, perhaps, for an ill-concerted feint. The French attack, though made in greater numbers, was no better managed than our own. The business of the stormers was to lose no time in reaching the ditch of the enemy's work, and, collecting there in sufficient numbers, to swarm over the ramparts. Instead of this, they appear to have lain down and commenced firing their pieces at the embrasures and parapets, and the supporting columns, of course, stopped also, instead of pressing into the work, and driving out its defenders with the bayonet. It is doubtful whether any French soldiers got inside the Malakhoff, though two battalions are said to have held their ground in it for a short time; but had that been the case, the guns of the work could scarcely have fired so unremittingly as they did.

It was not till the afternoon, and while we felt the first soreness of disappointment, that it became at all generally known that Eyre's brigade (consisting of 1800 men of the 9th, 18th, 28th, 38th, and 44th regiments), which, as before said, was to proceed down the great ravine towards the Dockyard Creek, had actually advanced into the suburbs, and had been all day hotly engaged with the enemy. Turning a corner of the defile, just in advance of the Allied works, the head of the column came on a small cemetery occupied by Russian sharpshooters, whom they drove out, and, pushing on, occupied the houses which skirt the course of the ravine. A little further on, the Woronzoff ravine joins this one, and a broad flat piece of ground extends to the water, near the edge of which is a long low battery, sweeping the approach. At the junction of the two ravines, and resting against the slope of the high ground which separates them, are a number of houses sufficient to rank as a small town, some mere hovels, some of better appearance, and these were taken possession of; while the advanced parties extended in front of the low battery, and, scaling a hill on their left, reached a battery for three guns on a shoulder of the cliff-like side of the ravine, from whence they saw no obstacle to their advance on the town, which stands on a rounded hill, bounding the Dockyard Creek. They had now reached a point from which they could operate on either side of this Dockyard Creek or inner harbour. If the attack against the Redan were successful, they could, by scaling the cliff of the Woronzoff ravine on their right, effect a junction with the stormers; or, had the French penetrated into the works covering the town, they would have received powerful help from Eyre's brigade. This latter contingency, however, there was no reason to provide for, as it was never contemplated ; and it is one of the most unaccountable features of these operations, that, with our immense forces, no diversion, far less any real assault, was made on this point. Even the artillery of the French lines before the town was silent.

To meet Eyre's force, the Russians, issuing from the Garden Batteries which crown the left cliff of the ravine, descended some distance to a long low breastwork, from whence they began to pick off our men. Growing excited, they stood upright on the parapet, and exchanged volleys with our troops, who poured on them so destructive a fire as in half an hour forced them again to have recourse to the shelter of their work. The guns in the Garden Batteries above sent round and grape shot through the houses and low walls of the gardens and enclosures ; the stones from which, as well as from the tombstones in the cemetery, flying in all directions, caused a great number of casualties. A shot, however ill-directed, seldom failed to dislodge stones enough to give it all the effect of a shell, and none of the walls were thick enough to resist the heavy missiles, which riddled them through and through, so that the wounded, laid in houses for shelter, were covered with dust and fragments, and sometimes killed. The riflemen, who occupied the ground in front of the Barrack Battery, descended towards the ravine, to oppose our people there ; and the fire, thus almost surrounding the assailants, searched through them with deadly effect.

General Eyre was wounded in the head early in the action, withdrew into a house, where he got his wound dressed, and returned to his post. The brigade was dispersed in small parties, wherever cover was to be obtained ; the regiments were mixed, and all unity of action was lost, as indeed no attainable object remained to strive for. In front was the low battery before the creek, some guns from which (luckily it was not fully armed) swept along the course of the ravine ; on their left, the Garden Batteries, whose shot plunged into them, extended towards the Bastion du Mât, which appeared far in rear ; and on the right rose the cliff, by ascending which they might indeed communicate with our works before the Redan, but the whole intervening space was swept by the formidable Barrack Battery, as well as by the flanking fire of the Garden Batteries across the ravine. Nothing could be finer than the spirit displayed by the troops under these circumstances. Ignorant of the fortunes of the day at other points of the line, they probably imagined they were destined to carry the town, and their eagerness to attempt it was so great that they were with difficulty restrained from pressing forward beyond a point from whence extrication would have been impossible. All day the fight continued, and whatever the French (whose parapets to the right of the Bastion du Mât looked down upon the arena) may have thought of the prudence of the movement, the manner in which our troops maintained themselves throughout the day, in so desperate a position, must have excited great respect for their gallantry. Uncheered by any hope of solid achievement or success, the brigade held its ground, and at nightfall withdrew unmolested, with a loss of 600 killed and wounded. We continued to hold the cemetery, and thus the contest was not entirely barren of result; while the valour of the troops engaged brought some consolation for the loss, and rendered this the least painful to dwell on among the unhappy mistakes of the day.

Supposing, for the sake of argument, that to prosecute the siege actively was the right strategic policy, and that the Malakhoff and Redan were the best points to assault, yet the execution of the measure was such as to invite failure. I have already mentioned how feeble were the attacks in themselves, and how much it was to be regretted that the original plan, by which the artillery was to fire for some hours before the infantry advanced, should have been changed. But, though the immediate cause of failure is to be found less in the plan of assault than in its very defective execution, yet it seems extraordinary that, with the vastly superior force which the Allies could command, attacks were not made on points so numerous as to bewilder and divide the garrison, especially on the bastions before the town, from whence, if the enemy had been induced to place there a large proportion of troops, they could not have been easily transferred across the creek. But, so far from making any demonstration which might induce the enemy to believe that point menaced, the French batteries in that quarter did not open in the first day's cannonade till afternoon, and on the day of the assault scarcely fired at all. The small number of Russians who opposed Eyre's brigade, and the circumstance of the riflemen in front of the Barrack Battery leaving their post to meet our people in the ravine, seem to warrant the conclusion that the great mass of the garrison was placed in support of those works which alone were threatened.

Faulty as the assault would seem, the general plan of which it formed part, or rather which was absorbed into it, is no less open to criticism. Whatever reasons may have dictated our mode of operations, it is not easy to deny that, in assembling so large a force on the extremity of the peninsula, in allowing a great portion of the army to remain idle while the remainder pressed the siege on the old plan, and in concentrating our efforts on the strongest of the Russian outworks, where numbers were neutralised to a great extent by the defences, we were doing what the Russians themselves would most wish us to do. Notwithstanding our altered circumstances, our plans were unchanged, and were of the most simple and unscientific character. With an army of 200,000 men, we persisted in staking success on the attack of two works which 10,000 men might defend, and by the failure in which attack these hosts were for a time paralysed. If we gained Sebastopol we gained nothing more, for the Russian army could then retreat upon its communications. We had far more troops than were necessary to conduct the siege and to defend the plateau, yet the superfluous force attempted no enterprise of importance, while the heats of summer were at hand, and the more anxious and farseeing began already to anticipate another dreary winter here as inevitable. Meanwhile the Russian army was invisible, and its movements and state unknown; but it seemed as if the mere *vis inertiæ* of a force like ours must press the enemy back, and that any forward movement, however blind, must cause us to blunder into victory.

About this time death was busy among the chiefs. Admiral Boxer, whose great energy and activity had established order in the crowded harbour of Balaklava, and created commodious wharves there, had been dead of cholera some weeks. General Alexander La Marmora, brother of the commander of the Sardinian forces, had fallen a victim to the same disease; and a few days after the attempt on the Redan, our Adjutant-General Estcourt, a man of remarkably kind and courteous disposition, died after a short illness. At the time of his funeral it was known that Lord Raglan was indisposed, and next day he kept his room; but although the symptoms caused his medical attendants to be apprehensive, he did not appear in immediate danger till the afternoon of the 28th June, when he rapidly sank, became insensible, and expired at half-past eight in the evening, tranquilly and without pain.

On the afternoon of the 3d July his body was conveyed to Kazatch Bay for embarkation. The funeral was a very strange and splendid spectacle. The generals, staffs, and numbers of officers of the four armies—French, English, Turkish, and Sardinian—assembled at the appointed hour in the large courtyard of the house which had been the headquarters of the deceased marshal. Before the porch waited, with its team of bay horses, a horse-artillery gun, destined to be the appropriate hearse of the old soldier. The courtyard was crowded with the uniforms of the different nations—the gaudy colours and laced Louis-quatorze hats of the French staff—the green plumes and dresses of the Sardinians—the red skull-caps of the Turks, unadorned, except Omer Pasha's, in the front of whose fez blazed a large ornament of diamonds—and our own costumes, in all the diversity of cavalry, infantry, and artillery. The Guards furnished the guard of honour, drawn up fronting the house to salute the body of their general, which had been enclosed in coffins of lead and iron, with a plain wooden one outside. It was brought out, placed on the gun, covered with a flag, and the procession moved on through the garden and vineyard surrounding the headquarters. As it appeared round the corner of the house a battery on the opposite slope saluted with nineteen guns, which were echoed by the desultory fire of the batteries in the trenches and the guns of the enemy. The road from the house to Kazatch Bay was lined throughout its extent on each side with infantry, French and English, the men standing a few feet apart. First the procession passed between our own men, who had been last night fighting in the trenches, till it reached the French headquarters, when a French battery saluted, and our own troops were succeeded by those of our Allies: first, the Zouaves, wearing to-day green turbans; then the Imperial Guard, with their tall bear-skins and long blue frocks; and then regiments of the line—each corps marked by its colours inscribed in gold letters with the victories of the Consulate and the Empire. A body of cavalry and artillery escorted the coffin, the white pall of which, with its cross of St George, was conspicuous at the head of the long procession, which covered miles of the road. Crossing the ridge of a slope beyond the French headquarters the sea appeared, and, upon the right, the now familiar puffs of smoke and sound of the guns marked where the siege still dragged on its weary length, to the cares, the honours, and the disappointments of which, so all-absorbing to us, he whom we escorted was now insensible. Slowly we journeyed along the plains, the dust rising in clouds from the dry soil, till at sunset we reached Kazatch. The water of the harbour was almost hidden by the number of boats thronged with seamen in their white frocks, whose uplifted oars looked like a grove. At the end of one of the wooden piers a crane had been erected, under which the gun-carriage was drawn—bareheaded sailors slung the coffin to the crane, hoisted it, and lowered it into the boat destined to take it to the Caradoc, the steamer in which Lord Raglan had come from England, and which was now to take home his remains. A parting salute was fired as the boat left the pier, and we had seen the last of our kind and gallant old chief. To most of us he appeared as the relic of an age now historical, and his name, associated with the Peninsular victories, caught a large share of the lustre reflected on all the companions of the great Duke. During the long period in which he transacted business at the Horse Guards, his reputation for suavity and kindness spread widely through the army, and was amply supported by his demeanour as commander-in-chief in the present campaign. His rank, his dignified manners and appearance, his former services, and his long experience, combined to gain for him the respect and willing co-operation of our allies; and the regret felt throughout the allied armies for his loss, proved how sincere was the regard he had inspired in his associates and followers.

On the day of Lord Raglan's death, Sir George Brown, the next in seniority, had embarked for England at the recommendation of a medical board; and on the 1st of July a telegraphic message from England confirmed General Simpson, late chief of the staff, in the command of the army, which had devolved on him by seniority.

During the early part of June the successes of the Kertsch expedition continued without any check. At Taganrog and Berdiansk, on the north shore of the Sea of Azoff, the public buildings, stores, and grain were destroyed, as well as at Genitsch, at the upper extremity of the Isthmus of Arabat. The fort of Arabat was fired upon by our gun-boats, and a magazine was blown up, but no landing was attempted there; and, intimidated by the presence of the force which thus ravaged the coast without hindrance, the garrisons of Soujouk-kale and Anapa, blowing up their magazines and destroying the fortifications, abandoned their posts.

On looking at the map, the reader will perceive that the peninsula of Kertsch narrows to a neck of land between Kaffa on the Black Sea, and Arabat on the Sea of Azoff, the distance across being about twelve miles. When Kertsch and Yenikale had been so easily captured, the garrisons of those places, in number about 5000, marched unmolested towards the interior of the Crimea. It is evident that had Kaffa been attacked immediately after we had secured an entrance into the Sea of Azoff, on capturing it, a force might have marched on Arabat, with which our gun-boats could have co-operated from the sea. The experience we had gained during the enterprise, warranted the belief that those places would have fallen at once; and, the neck of the peninsula thus occupied by a sufficient force of the Allies, the enemy's troops remaining in it must have laid down their arms, and whatever resources the country from thence to Kertsch afforded, must have been lost to the Russians. As it was, the expedition terminated with the conquests already enumerated. Six thousand Turks, one English, and one French regiment, remained to garrison Yenikale and St Paul's, the points commanding respectively the two entrances to the straits; lines were constructed for the defence of those places against an attack by land, and guns were brought from Constantinople to arm the batteries, as the Turkish gunners were not sufficiently familiar with the construction of the Russian ordnance to work the captured pieces with confidence. Kertsch itself, which stands retired within the bay, was occupied merely by a guard for the protection of its inhabitants; and the presence of a few Cossacks hovering nightly outside the town, showed that the enemy had not entirely withdrawn from the peninsula. The town of Kertsch, which had been a flourishing and pleasant place, containing 17,000 people, presented a melancholy spectacle; the houses had been broken open, ransacked, and in part burnt, and the inhabitants were not secure from ill treatment.

CHAPTER XXVII.

PROGRESS OF THE SIEGE.

DURING July and August the interest of the siege was concentrated in the attack of the Malakhoff, as little progress could be made with the works before the Redan, owing to the nature of the ground; while the French attack on the bastions before the town had been for months stationary. In Chap. XXI., speculating on the various methods of continuing the contest, I remarked that, if the attack by regular siege operations were persisted in, the siege would resolve itself into several sieges, each demanding much labour and time; and that a consecutive attack on the different outworks would require months to accomplish. It appears, however, that this objection of long delay was held less powerful than the obstacles to more prompt and comprehensive designs, and the advance on the Malakhoff had been patiently prosecuted for a quarter of a year; and now, for the first time, the operations, thus confined by the suspension of the other attacks to a point, presented the appearance of an ordinary siege.

On its own right, the works crowning the Malakhoff hill are extended down the slope in a series of batteries to the ravine which separates it from the Redan. On its left, other works extend to the great harbour, terminating at a point below Careening Bay, on the opposite side of which the French had placed batteries. Thus the Russian line of intrenchment, from the salient of the Malakhoff to the harbour, about the middle of which was a smaller work (called the Little Redan by us, by the French Redan de Carenage), was to a certain extent enclosed by a larger arc of attack; and the captured Mamelon became the base of the attack of the Malakhoff. These two hills are about 500 yards apart, the slope of the Mamelon being rather more abrupt than the opposing one, which rises in a gentle, gradual glacis to the foot of the ditch. Down one slope, and up the other, the French sap was pushed in a network of trenches, advancing on the two salients of the Malakhoff and the Little Redan, and connecting the advances by parallels. It is a general rule that a second parallel cannot be formed till the artillery of the assailed work, and of those that flank it, is silenced. Such was not the case here. Had a fire been concentrated on the Malakhoff for the purpose of silencing it, the Redan would have supported it by opening on the aggressive batteries: these and others would have replied in their own defence, and so the cannonade would become general along the whole line; and to expend ammunition which cost so much labour to accumulate on so extensive a scale, was a serious consideration : therefore the French continued to advance under a fire which, though desultory, and held in check by the English batteries as well as their own, never ceased to annoy them. A loss of a hundred men a-night, and sometimes greatly exceeding that number, testified that the rules of military science, the result of long experience in war, cannot be disregarded with impunity. But there was no help for it ; the bloodless method of conducting approaches detailed by Vauban is based on the certainty that the enemy's guns, silenced or disabled by an overpowering fire, cannot be replaced, as they were here, from a full arsenal, and the damaged works easily repaired ; so the French had to make the best of it. The fire of the Malakhoff itself was in some degree kept down by riflemen in the advanced trenches ; but a few guns in the low batteries on each side dropped missiles into the parallels and batteries, from whence they were often themselves unseen. In spite of these, the approaches continued steadily to advance on the salients, and to be connected by long parallels and communications, till, on reaching a certain point about eighty yards from the ditch, it was found impossible to proceed without first silencing some guns whose fire generally destroyed in the day the work of the preceding night. With this view our batteries were to be opened again on the 17th, not in a general cannonade, but directed to this special object. The battle of the 16th did not retard the execution of the design, and the English guns opened next morning; but as the French on our left hardly fired at all, the Russians were enabled to concentrate their guns on our most advanced batteries, some of which suffered considerably, and where we lost some valuable artillery officers. Captain Oldfield, who had shown the greatest energy throughout the siege, and entirely devoted himself to the trenches, was killed by a piece of shell striking him on the temple; Commander Hammett, R.N., by a round shot; and Major Henry, R.A., promoted for previous service in the trenches, lost his right arm. The object of the cannonade, which was steadily maintained, was quite secured by the damage done to the enemy's batteries. At six in the evening a magazine blew up in a work between the Malakhoff and Redan, and a number of shells there accumulated were hurled into the air, exploding in all directions; the occupants of the battery were seen leaping outside their parapets in consternation, and the mortars which the shells were intended to supply were completely silenced; and the guns whose fire had been so mischievous being also quieted, the French were enabled to continue their approaches on the night of the 18th and following day. On the night of the 18th it became known to us that large bodies were assembled within the enemy's works, and a heavy fire of mortars was directed on them, which must have proved very destructive. They lined the parapets and opened a heavy musketry fire, which was replied to by us and the French; but no sortie was attempted, and the fire of small-arms soon ceased. On some subsequent nights the same incident occurred; but whether the enemy's troops were placed in the works to resist an anticipated attack from us, or to make a sortie, which was not afterwards found practicable, we did not learn.

On the 20th, some rockets from the advance of our right attack fired the Karabelnaia suburb, situated behind the Malakhoff, which consists of a great number of small houses adjacent to though not adjoining each other, in which the troops for the defence of this part of the Russian works reside. When the alarm of fire was given there, a great number of soldiers thronged out in disorder, and a multitude of carts made their appearance. At first only one of our guns bore on the crowded space between the houses, from whence the troops attempted to pass towards the Malakhoff after each discharge. By widening an embrasure, a second gun was brought to bear on them with spherical case, and proved very destructive—prostrate men, broken carts, and runaway horses marking its effect. The fire continued to burn all day, and destroyed several houses, and others were frequently set on fire afterwards by rockets, while the guns continued to enfilade the streets of the suburb whenever a few persons were visible.

Towards evening on the 20th, the French batteries on our left before the town suddenly opened, without warning, and in a short time the Russians replied from the bastions covering the town, and from the Creek and Barrack Batteries. On both sides the firing was extremely violent till dark. I was in the third parallel of our left attack at the time, and never beheld a more splendid spectacle than the setting of the sun behind the Bastion du Mât. Purple masses lay on the horizon, becoming luminous as the sun passed behind them, till the whole western sky was in a softened glow of orange, with red and crimson of every gradation in the cloudy glories around and above the orb. Against the fiery space was sharply cut the purple line of the enemy's rampart—

"A looming bastion fringed with fire,"

whence the smoke from the cannon curled upward in dark blue wreaths with rosy edges. Sometimes a shell, bursting high, left a compact rounded cloud tinged with light, till it was slowly dissipated in streaks as of blood, while the din of the cannonade, reverberated from all the ravines in prolonged peals, filled the air. On leaving the batteries at dusk, I found that my horse, which I had left tied up in the ravine below the second parallel, had broken loose, frightened by the uproar and by some shells which burst near him, and made off. The ravine, besides being about three miles long, has several branches, some towards the French camp, some towards our own, and on the side of one of the latter the sailors are encamped; so that, besides the walk home late and hungry, there was a very good prospect of my horse being stolen, or, at any rate, if fortunately recovered, yet without saddle or bridle. The sailors had long been notorious horse-appropriators, while the public, including everybody whose horse was not stolen, had agreed to look on the proceedings of "Jack," and the "honest tar," as they affectionately term our naval friends, as rather eccentric than felonious, so that, considering the indulgence with which these speculations in horse flesh were regarded, they may on the whole be praised for their moderation. On reaching home, however, I found the knowing animal had arrived a short time before me (having stopped to water on the road), bringing his saddle and bridle with him, and creating some doubt as to the probable fate of his rider.

A few days before this opening of the batteries, I visited the Mamelon and the advanced batteries before the Malakhoff. A broad road passed over the rampart of the former work, where the guns had once looked on the French lines, while what had been its gorge or rear when the enemy held it, was now a formidable battery, as yet unmasked, but completed, armed, and ready to open on its old ally the Round Tower. The interior was still in a state of great confusion; Russian guns were lying dismounted and half-buried, platforms shattered, gun-carriages with their trucks in the air, and the numerous traverses which the Russians had thrown up for protection from our shells, were pounded and blown by explosions into shapeless heaps, making the interior of the redoubt look like a newly opened quarry. From one of its angles a path led to the advanced trenches and batteries, the latter beautifully finished and revetted with fascines, the guns already in them, and nothing wanting but the removal of the screen of earth still hiding the embrasures to enable them to open. The work was greatly facilitated by the nature of the soil, which was clayey, and might be cut like a cheese to the required depth, while, in most other parts of our extensive lines, the trenches had been quarried with infinite toil through solid rocks, and among huge pebbles and imbedded flints, where the tools were broken and blunted, the arms of the workmen jarred, and the weary night's work scarcely afforded the satisfaction of a perceptible advance. In one part of these lines a kind of watch-tower, indistinguishable from without, had been erected, where the French generals, looking through three loop-holes, rendered quite bullet-proof with timber and sandbags, might conveniently watch the progress of affairs ; and near at hand was a spacious subterranean chamber, cool as an ice-house though the day was very hot, where the commanding officers of the trenches might sit unmolested by shot and shell, ready to issue such orders as might be needful. In a beam over the entrance stuck a large shot, there arrested in its flight. As we entered the Mamelon, a French mortar-battery on the right was throwing shells which probably galled the enemy, for on pausing in it in returning, to make some sketches of the works and men in the interior, such flights of shells from the Malakhoff alighted and exploded within as rendered the operation of drawing somewhat difficult and interrupted.

On the night of the 27th, the whole camp was aroused, shortly after midnight, by a tremendous explosion, and beyond the Mamelon might be seen, in the moonlight, a huge white cloud, casting acres of shadow as it spread and slowly dispersed. A magazine made by the Russians in the Mamelon, in which the French had placed 15,000 pounds of powder, had been blown up by a shell—more than a hundred Frenchmen lay prostrate, bruised or scorched, of whom about thirty were killed on the spot; and beams were hurled through the air to a distance of 700 yards, wounding men in our trenches. Time was when the Russians would have seized the opportunity to pour shot and shell on the scene of ruin, or have followed up the accidental success by a sortie; but perhaps imagining this to be the explosion of the mine that was to breach their own ramparts, they remained silent; while the English artillery opened on the Malakhoff, in order to anticipate a sally or a cannonade, and to cover the necessary confusion of their allies. Beyond the loss of life, no serious damage was done by this explosion, which left, in token of its occurrence, a vast crater like a quarry in the middle of the Mamelon.

VALLEY OF TCHERGOUM

CHAPTER XXVIII.

BATTLE OF THE TRAKTIR BRIDGE.

INTELLIGENCE of an intended attack had reached the camp of so reliable a nature that, on the morning of the 13th August, the whole army was under arms before dawn, pursuant to the orders of the night before. The trenches were fully manned, strong columns guarded the ravines, and other bodies lined the rear of the ridge in support, in expectation of a sally from the town; and shortly after midnight light sleepers might have been roused by the rumble of wheels, as the field-artillery passed through the camps towards its appointed position in the front. The expected attack was eagerly awaited, in full confidence that the enemy would be driven back shattered and discomfited to their defences; but day broke, and showed the line of works silent, and no preparation apparent, on the side of the Russians, for an action. When it became evident that the attack, if designed, was postponed, our troops returned to their encampments. Still the impression continued strong that the enemy, who had, as we knew, been largely reinforced, were about to try their fortune in an assault on our position. There could be but one object in sending troops in any considerable numbers to the south of the Crimea, where it must be so difficult to maintain them even for a short time, and that object must have been a sudden and powerful attempt to raise the siege ; and the truth of this general impression was soon confirmed.

The cluster of heights on our side of the Tchernaya, which have before been described as dividing part of the broad valley extending from the harbour of Sebastopol to that of Balaklava into two defiles, were occupied, when General Pelissier assumed the command of the army, by the French, at first under Canrobert, and when that General returned to France, under General Herbillon, an old officer, commonly called by the troops Le père Herbillon. These heights, lower than the plateaus, and of insignificant elevation compared with the surrounding mountain-ranges, are ascended by easy slopes, are smooth and grassy at the top, and are furrowed by deep chasms, in one of which lies the road to the Traktir Bridge over the Tchernaya, which the French had fortified. Other and more abrupt hills rise to the right on both sides of the river, and these were crowned by Sardinian advanced posts ; but in front of the French the ground, beyond the Tchernaya, extends in level meadows to the wide plain which winds round the base of the great plateau of Inkermann.

Down this plain a Russian army of 6000 cavalry,

five divisions of infantry, and twenty field-batteries, was marched from the heights of Mackenzie's Farm, and drawn up in the night of the 15th, while a smaller force of infantry and guns appeared near Tchergoum. At daybreak the attack was opened by the Russian guns, drawn up at long range, and the Sardinian outposts being at once driven in, the hill they had held across the river was occupied by a Russian field-battery. These were opposed by the French batteries drawn up, some across the heights, some along the bank of the river, in which latter position a battery of horse-artillery suffered very severely.

The Russian infantry advanced to the attack in columns, and reached the river, now an inconsiderable streamlet, knee deep, which some crossed, while others assailed the *tête-de-pont* or field-work covering the bridge. After a sharp conflict the Russians carried this, and the whole advanced to the heights which rise almost directly from the river's bank at this point; but to the left and right of the bridge a second obstacle remained to be crossed in the shape of the aqueduct, a small canal, six feet wide and three deep. Numbers of Russians fell on the bank of this; but others, crossing and joining those who had forced the passage of the bridge, passed along the road and up the heights on each side. Here the French infantry met them, and after a short struggle, the enemy, leaving 300 or 400 dead and wounded, fled tumultuously down to the river, mixed up with the pursuing French, plunged in and crossed it, and continued their flight across the meadows beyond, pursued by the fire of the infantry, who halted at the stream, and of the French guns, which ploughed through the fugitive masses, killing hundreds. If the French cavalry, crossing the river above, near the Sardinians, had charged along these meadows, multitudes of prisoners might have been made ; but the position of the Russian battery on the hill before occupied by the Sardinians was probably what prevented this movement. A feeble attack made on the Piedmontese in the valley of Tchergoum was also easily repulsed, with the co-operation of some 8-inch howitzers we had lent to the Sardinians, and an English battery of 32-pound howitzers, which compelled a Russian battery of lighter metal to withdraw. An attempt against the left of the heights, where they look towards the Ruins of Inkermann, was also made, the Russians advancing to the white house near the pond at their base; but it met no better success than the others.

At eight o'clock A.M. the enemy's infantry, entirely repulsed, had withdrawn behind the line of cavalry and guns, and there re - formed in deep square columns, out of cannon - shot. Their artillery on the heights still continued to exchange shots with the opposite French batteries, while some French rockets from the plateau flew to an extraordinary distance, exploding among bodies of the enemy so far off, that it was difficult to ascertain through the telescope whether they were cavalry or infantry.

Large reinforcements arrived at this time for the French, including the Imperial Guard, which had left the plateau a short time before. A considerable number of French troops were crowded down the road to the bridge, when the enemy suddenly discharged salvos from some heavy guns, on a knoll forming one of the roots of the cliff of the plateau of Inkermann, and some of the shells pitched with good aim on the *tête-de-pont* and the slopes around. This, repeated twice or thrice, was the last effort of the enemy to revenge their defeat; their battery on the Sardinian height was withdrawn, together with the cavalry supporting it, and the Piedmontese lancers immediately advanced, some on to the meadows of the plain, and others (consisting of a troop supported by a company of riflemen) followed the enemy as they quitted the heights. Joining the advance of this troop, I passed through the intrenchments taken from the Sardinian outposts, where the struggle had been but slight, for I saw only three dead Russians, and one ammunition waggon, blown up afterwards by a shell, remaining as traces of conflict. Advancing along these heights we came on the coverers of the Russian rearguard, distant about a carbine shot, in a line of single horsemen. Behind appeared a larger body; and on our left on the plain, still drawn up as before, awaiting, perhaps, a charge which they hoped to make as disastrous to the Allies as that of Balaklava, were the cavalry and guns, those nearest, close enough for the colour of the horses and the uniforms to be discernible; and on the right were what looked like cuirassiers, with two long standards flying. Along the plain, and all the way up the dusty chalky road that leads to Mackenzie's Farm on the plateau, filed the retiring infantry. It certainly appeared to me that, if the attention of the enemy had been engaged by a feint in front, a strong body of cavalry and light guns might have formed on these heights, the slopes of which to the plain are of easy descent, and thence have poured down on the enemy before they could have changed their front, and rolled them up and cut them to pieces long ere the infantry could have returned to their support. However, the opportunity, whether good or objectionable, was allowed to pass, and the enemy here, as well as in the valley of Tchergoum, retired unmolested. The latter force was to have been supported, it is said, by another Russian division, which, however, halted at Aitodor; and rumour goes on to say that its general was disgraced, and the division, as a punishment for its non-appearance, sent to form part of the garrison of Sebastopol.

The Russians, who were commanded by Prince Gortschakoff, left, according to the French returns, 2700 dead on the field, some on the slopes of the heights held by the French, most on the meadow beyond the river, and a good many had fallen between the river and the watercourse, which here branches off as the aqueduct of Sebastopol, for the crossing of which many of the Russians were provided with small portable bridges of plank. Including the wounded, 2200 prisoners remained with the French, and the enemy's loss was estimated, in all, at 10,000. The French lost less than 800 killed and wounded (many of the latter slightly) and the Sardinians 200.

The immediate object of this attack was to obtain possession of the heights held by the French. This would have conferred on the enemy the advantage of the river as a watering-place for the cavalry and troops, of which we should have been deprived; it would have enabled them to act against the Sardinians on the right, and our detachments at Baidar, whose position would have been somewhat awkward, though they would probably have effected their junction with the army by the road along the cliffs; and it would have served as a point to make an attack against the plateau, in co-operation with a sortie from the town. A detailed plan of attack on these bases, including also the capture of Balaklava, was found on the body of General Read, a Russian officer. But the enemy never at any time had any prospect of success, and the attempt seems to have been dictated by desperation.

While the French were removing the wounded of the enemy from the battle-field, the Russian batteries did not cease to fire on that part of the ground;

General Pelissier therefore sent to say that he would not bury the Russian dead, but, if they pleased, they might have a truce for the purpose. On the 18th a party of Russians, escorted by a detachment of Cossacks, mounted on shabby ill-fed ponies, came down to the Tchernaya to inter the bodies.

CHAPTER XXIX.

A CRISIS IN THE CAMPAIGN.

As our prospects changed with the advance of the works, so did new features disclose themselves in the operations of the enemy. Thrown from the shore of the north side of the harbour opposite Fort Nicholas, the rudiments of a bridge appeared, made of rafts, moored side by side. After the battle of the 16th, the work proceeded with increased diligence, and about the 26th or 27th it stretched completely across to the point of rock on which Fort Nicholas is built, and was speedily put into operation, great trains of vehicles moving incessantly across, conveying articles, apparently of furniture, to the north shore. We had looked attentively for the completion of this bridge; rumour said that, as soon as large bodies of troops should be enabled to move across with ease and celerity, a simultaneous attack would be made from the town, and by the army on the heights, the latter aiming at Balaklava, while the force sallying from the town would distract our attention, and, if successful, effect a junction with their comrades across the plateau.

This comprehensive scheme was perhaps the same that had been so early blighted in the attack of the 16th, when the sanguine expectations of our opponents met with something the same fate as those of Alnaschar, the barber's brother, who saw his way clearly, by successive steps, to the post of grand vizier and son-in-law to the caliph, till he was roused from his dreams by the shattering of the basket of glass which was to be the foundation of his fortunes. On that memorable occasion Pelissier might truly have remarked to Gortschakoff, " C'est le premier pas qui coute." However, the belief remained strong that the Russian army had been reinforced for the special purpose of immediately attacking us, that the Czar's orders so to attack were imperative, and that the condition of the enemy's troops, too numerous for their supplies, and threatened with starvation, or a retreat in winter, admitted of no alternative, but at once to attack, or at once to retire. Several false alarms placed the army under arms at daybreak, and on three or four occasions the onset was confidently looked for by the generals. On the first of these, staff-officers, warned over-night, were ready to issue forth before dawn, each with a feed of corn hanging from his horse's crupper, and biscuit and brandy in the leather pocket attached to the saddle, that both steed and rider might be prepared for a long day's work. Living a little apart, I missed the others, and followed in the darkness, not knowing which road they had taken, till, as I descended a hill, I saw on the rise over me, against the sky, the dark shapes of the detachment of lancers forming the commander-in-chief's escort, their weapons, with the square pennons blown out by the night wind, giving them, in the gloom, the appearance of the bannered towers of a castle. As we gained the verge of the plateau, the first salmon-coloured streak of dawn appeared; all was silent, and no light visible beyond the sparks, like fireflies, which marked the clustered lines of French and Sardinians on the mounds of the valley; and, as day broke, the only object in front of the Allies was a thin white mist steaming up from the river; but no sign of a foe. This was repeated on several subsequent occasions, but—except the opportunities afforded of studying different specimens of sunrise—without any notable result.

On the 5th September the cannonade re-commenced, slowly and steadily at first, on our part and on the part of the French before the Malakhoff; but on the works before the town with a vigour greater and more sustained than in any previous fire from the French batteries. At night a frigate in the harbour was set on fire by a shell from the French, and burnt to the water's edge, lighting up the whole harbour. On this day the Russians made a reconnaissance in force (10,000 to 15,000) at Tchergoum. There they could find little to encourage them for another attack. The French position, which they failed to take on the 16th, was now greatly strengthened. The *tête-de-*

pont was thickened and revetted, lines of trenches surrounded the bases and summits of the heights ; on the left, towards Inkermann, a watercourse from the Tchernaya which fills a reservoir had been bordered with a parapet. A battery for guns had also been constructed there, another on the middle of the heights, and others looked on the bridge, especially one for 12 guns, in the road leading down to the bridge, which, as well as the approach from beyond the river, was completely swept by it.

On the 6th the French before the town continued to fire vigorously. Sometimes, after a lull of an hour or two, all their batteries would suddenly open together, and the volleys of smoke would increase and mingle till the whole ground presented the appearance of the burning of a hundred farm-steads with all their stacks and barns. The Russians on these days, and on the 7th, replied but feebly. On the afternoon of the 7th one of the two-deckers in the harbour was set on fire by a shell from a mortar, and burnt all night. This was the eve of the assault, the orders for which, detailing the divisions of attack, were issued in the afternoon, and the hour fixed for noon.

Thus it seemed as if all the efforts of Russia to raise the siege had only enabled her to collect a number of military spectators at the final struggle for the prize. And, supposing the war destined to continue, it would have been better for her had Sebastopol been carried in 1854 by a *coup-de-main*. The efforts to reinforce the garrison, and to maintain the army outside, must have been most exhaustive. Every man, every shot and barrel of powder, and every sack of grain that reached Sebastopol, must have been transmitted at ruinous cost, and the maintenance of the garrison and the army on the heights must have been as expensive as that of a five-fold force on the frontiers of Turkey, Austria, or Poland. The want of roads in Southern Russia, from the clayey nature of the soil, where no stones, or even pebbles, are to be met with for a hundred miles together, the fewness of towns, and the sparse population, all render the collection and transmission of convoys more difficult in Russia than in any other country of Europe. It is less easy to create a road in a boggy steppe than to carry one over the Alps. Hence the maintenance of Sebastopol was a perpetual and debilitating drain on the resources of Russia, in men, money, and material.

It has been said that the credit of holding Sebastopol against all the efforts of the Allies must have an important effect on the relations of Russia with the Asiatic powers. When it is remembered that Sebastopol, never a trading port, was inaccessible to the ships of other nations, and that it had never made its influence actually felt as dominant in the Black Sea, the political importance of its defence seems much overrated; and after the Sea of Azoff was occupied by the Allies, and Anapa abandoned, the small portion of prestige yet remaining to Russia, in the possession of Sebastopol, seemed scarcely worth the ruinous efforts made to maintain it. More, if the object of France and England were to exhaust as speedily as possible the defensive resources of Russia, and to protract the war till their enemy should be shorn of his vast military powers, it would even have been wise policy (but for the impatience for results manifested by the two nations) to delay the assault of the town, secure that it must eventually be theirs, and that every supply sent to the garrison was another jet of lifeblood from the arteries of Russia. In continuing to hold Sebastopol, hers was the policy of the speculator who, living beyond his means, will not retrench lest the world should suspect him of insolvency. To maintain a province which (except through some unforeseen political chance) it was beyond her power to preserve, she squandered the resources which, rightly applied, would have rendered her empire elsewhere unassailable. If the Czar had been able to say "attack the Crimea if you will ; I acknowledge it to be my vulnerable point; but in that case I will retaliate on your weak points," there might have been good argument for defending it to the last, while aiming at the joints of his adversary's armour. But the territories of England and France were beyond menace ; and, meantime, the vitality of the Russian Achilles was frittered away by the irritation of the incurable and poisoned wound in the vulnerable heel, when timely excision would have left the vast frame, though maimed, yet potent for defence.

For the sake of all the powers engaged, and of the world, it is to be hoped that, when Sebastopol has fallen, Russia will see the necessity of concluding peace. But if glory be worth fighting for, it is scarcely to be desired that the war should soon terminate, while the idea of England's military deficiencies, so strongly impressed of late on the mind of Europe, is yet undispelled by an adequate exhibition of her real power. Through the clouds of gossip, twaddle, lamentation, and foreboding, which form part of the conditions of our national existence, the fact will at length become lustrously apparent, that the nation which forty years ago found itself, at the termination of a long war, not only unrivalled by sea, but possessed of as complete and formidable an army as any country of Europe, has, since then, with her advances in wealth, science, and the arts of peace, grown also in military resources in greater proportion than her neighbours. With each successive year her preponderance will increase, till, at her full development, attained not without distraction, sacrifice, and internal disquietude, she shall wield a power capable of stilling the world's convulsions, and of securing for herself at once pre-eminence and peace. Then she will, as before, trust only to her splendid reputation, till the trumpet will again startle her amid her bales and machinery, and she will find her arms rusted, her sinews relaxed, and her great name endangered by the feebleness with which her first blows are delivered; and she will be more fortunate than she deserves, if her latent strength can yet be called forth in time to redeem her reputation.

CHAPTER XXX.

THE GENERAL ASSAULT.

THE day before the fire opened, the generals of the two armies had finally settled the duration of the cannonade and the hour of the assault. The French were decided by the consideration that the nature of the ground would not allow them to push their approaches on the Malakhoff and the Little Redan closer without great loss, and the operation of running a gallery beneath the enemy's counterscarp, or rampart, would take up eight or ten days, which delay, it was considered, would be prejudicial to the success of the assault. The enemy had begun a second line of works behind those of the Malakhoff, and, if permitted to finish them, a troublesome obstacle might still exist after the Malakhoff was taken. Therefore, on the fourth day of the cannonade, at noon (Sept. 8), the attempt was to be made.

A strong gale, which had on the previous day blown towards the enemy, now changed round straight in our faces. The smoke drifting and eddying in thin veils before the city and its defences, rendered them almost invisible. The fine earth of the trenches, dried to the lightness of sand by the sun, was blown in clouds from the parapets, rendering it difficult and even painful to look over them. The fire of the French on the left was as fierce as ever; ours, which, though very sustained, had not, owing to the delay of ships with ammunition, hitherto exerted its full vigour, was increased to the utmost from daybreak; and the Mamelon, the batteries before it, and the White Works, all opened, thus completing the semicircle of fire which enveloped the ramparts of the city. The enemy replied only by an occasional gun.

Shortly before noon, General Simpson and his staff entered the first parallel of our left attack. From hence a view was obtained of the Malakhoff, which, together with the Curtain and the Little Redan, was to be first attacked; and the tricolor hoisted on it, and repeated in the Mamelon, where General Pelissier had stationed himself, was to be the signal that the French had made good their footing, when a simultaneous attack on the Redan and on the Central Bastion covering the town would compel the enemy's attention to those points.

A short description of the works on the French right, comprised between the Karabelnaia Ravine and the Ravine of Careening Bay, will render the details clearer.

The Malakhoff hill is an eminence towering over all the rest. The stone building known by us as the

Round Tower, which was of semicircular form, had originally an upper storey, and on the flat roof a battery was mounted. In the first urgency of defence this tower had been regarded as the citadel of this part of the works, and the earthen rampart covering it, following its shape, was also made semicircular, and was called by the French and Russians the Kornileff Bastion. Eventually an entire enclosed work, in the form of an irregular redoubt, had been made in rear of the tower, communicating with the left flank of the work covering it. The upper part of the tower, rendered ruinous in our first bombardment, had been long since pulled down, and only a small portion of the masonry of the lower storey appeared over the ramparts.

From the right of the tower a line of rampart, known as the Gervais Battery, extended to the Karabelnaia Ravine. On the left, towards Careening Bay, at 500 yards from the Malakhoff, was a smaller eminence crowned with an irregular work, known by the Russians as Bastion No. 2, by us as the Little Redan; and a line of intrenchment connected these two salients, known in military phrase as the Curtain. Finally, the Russian line of defence was completed by a rampart extending from the Little Redan to the Great Harbour, at the junction of which with Careening Bay was Bastion No. 1, one of whose batteries swept the ground in front of the Little Redan.

The first parallel made by the French in advance after they gained the Mamelon, extended from the

Karabelnaia Ravine to that of Careening Bay. The second, 100 yards in advance of this, touched the Careening Ravine, but extended on the left only far enough to embrace the works of the Malakhoff; and from this, two lines of zigzag trench were pushed, the one on the Kornileff Bastion, the other on the inner or proper right face of the Little Redan. The former approach had reached within fifteen yards of the Malakhoff ditch, the latter to about thirty yards from the Little Redan, where the ground became so stony that there was great difficulty in working.

As a precaution to deceive the enemy, the French had, the night before the assault, broken out the commencement of a new sap, and had also, in the morning, exploded two or three mines, which they were accustomed to do to loosen the earth where they intended to work; and the Russians were thus induced to believe that they meant to advance closer before the assault. The French troops were also assembled in the trenches with all possible secresy; moreover, the Russians, knowing we had always assaulted either in the morning or evening, considered themselves safe during the middle of the day; and so completely unexpected was the assault, that, at the moment it was given, the troops in the Malakhoff were just being relieved. The usual mode of doing this is to introduce the new garrison before withdrawing the old; but so hot was the fire of our shells, that, during the bombardment, they marched out the old troops before introducing the relief; and thus it happened, that at this most important moment the work was unusually ill-prepared for resistance.

The French columns of attack, numbering, reserves and all, 24,000, being all ready in the trenches, precisely at twelve o'clock the assault began. There were three points to be assailed,—1st, The middle of the Kornileff Bastion ; 2d, The Curtain, near its centre ; 3d, The inner face of the Little Redan,—and all were attacked and entered almost simultaneously.

The first column, throwing some planks across the ditch of the Kornileff Bastion, at the point where the circular form prevented it from being seen from the flanks, rushed through that work and got possession of the redoubt almost without a struggle. But some of the garrison were, at the moment of attack, in the bomb-proof chamber at the base of the Round Tower, whose loop-holed wall looks on the rear of the interior, from whence they began to annoy the French extremely, and kept a large space clear from the assailants. A reminiscence of their Algerine experience helped our allies in this difficulty. General MacMahon, collecting a quantity of gabions from the works around, heaped them round the tower, and set them on fire, when the garrison made signs of surrender. But no sooner had this measure succeeded than it occurred to the general that there might possibly be mines in the neighbourhood which would be exploded by the burning gabions, and he looked hastily round for some means of extinguishing them. Fortunately intrenching-tools were at hand ; a trench was dug along the course of the fire, and the earth heaped on it, which put it out. And here occurred a singular chance; the trench thus dug laid bare the wires placed by the Russians to fire a mine, which were immediately cut and rendered useless. After this, though the battle raged hotly round the Malakhoff, and several desperate attempts were made to retake it, the French never found their possession of it endangered.

When the columns entered, the French officers in the trenches, believing the victory secure, fell to embracing one another, in token of congratulation. These rejoicings, however, were premature. The two right columns presently returned from the Curtain and Little Redan, having found the fire of musketry from the retrenchment, and of field-artillery posted on various commanding points of the interior, too hot to be supported. The crowded trenches were ploughed through by the enemy's shot; numbers were killed among the reserves in rear; and three Russian steamers coming up near the mouth of Careening Bay, in spite of a French battery lately erected on the opposite point, the guns of which could not probably be sufficiently depressed to bear upon them, also enfiladed the approaches, and killed men and officers in the Mamelon. To support the attack of the infantry, some field-artillery was brought on the scene. In anticipation of such a measure, a road had been levelled straight across the trenches, and the gaps filled with gabions; these were thrown down by sappers posted behind them as the guns approached, and a troop of French horse-artillery, galloping by from the rear, and losing a good many horses as it went, emerged on the level space between the French works and the Curtain, and its six 12-pounders came into action against the ramparts. It was a deed of great daring; the ground was swept by the Russian guns as well as those still serviceable in the works, and the musketry of the Little Redan and Curtain fired at a range which rendered their aim deadly. In taking up such a position, these field-guns achieved a novel and brilliant exploit, and one which will no doubt be commemorated with pride in the annals of the French artillery: but their gallantry was unavailing; they were immediately crushed by the tremendous fire, and withdrew, having lost a great number of officers, men and horses, besides the captain, who was killed.

The French supports advancing when the stormers were repulsed, a continual stream of men poured for several hours between the French and Russian works. The inside of the assailed angle of the Little Redan was heaped with dead, over whose bodies others constantly advanced and retired, till the struggle ceasing at sunset left the Russians in possession of this work and the Curtain. In the course of the afternoon a mine had blown up near the Malakhoff, and appeared to those in the trenches to explode in that work, creating great uncertainty for its tenure; and some French officers, headed by General de Cissey, leaping from the trenches, made a movement to succour it ; but as the dust cleared, the tricolor was seen still floating on the ramparts.

The attacks on the Little Redan cost the French near 4000 men. But, though the work remained uncaptured, it must not be supposed that this heavy loss was altogether fruitless of result, as, had the French desisted from the attack, a large Russian force would have been set free to join in the attempt to retake the Malakhoff.

In ten minutes from the commencement of the attack, the signal-flag, anxiously looked for from the English trenches, was hoisted, and the storming party of 800 men of the 62d, 41st, 90th, and 97th regiments, with a detachment of the 3d Buffs, carrying ladders, and another of Rifles, to keep down the fire from the ramparts, issued from the trenches. First went the Rifles, and, closely following them, the ladder party, who had been posted in the most advanced trench, an unfinished one, about 150 yards from the Redan. While crossing the intervening space, a number of men were wounded by grape from the flanks, where several guns opened fiercely, and a great many ladders were dropt as the bearers fell ; but about six reached the ditch, into which they were let down, and four were transferred to the opposite side. Though an assistance in descending and mounting, they were not absolutely essential, as many officers and men passed over the work without their aid, so ruined was the slope by the artillery fire. The stormers advanced without a pause, though the grape thinned them as they went, and part of them entered at once, when the Russians within, seemingly surprised, fled without resistance. Had the whole of the storming party now pushed on, followed by efficient support, it is probable that we might have secured possession of the work. But an opinion which I had previously heard from our engineers, that the long period of duty in the trenches would be found, without diminishing the intrepidity of the troops, to impair their dash, and make them unduly careful of obtaining cover, was now confirmed. Most of those who reached the parapet lay down there and began to fire, while those officers and men who had entered extended over a space reaching to the third or fourth gun on each side. Recovering from their first panic, the Russians began to return, and large reinforcements constantly arrived, emerging, probably, from the subterranean chambers of the work. These began a hot fire, standing partly across the open space thirty or forty yards from the salient, partly behind the traverses and embrasures. This desultory combat lasted about a quarter of an hour, during which many officers and men distinguished themselves by gallant attempts to head a rush against the enemy, ending in the immediate fall of the leaders; then our supports advanced in a large square column, and the former scene was renewed. Small parties of men led by their officers got over the parapet, but the number actually within the work was never sufficient for its capture, while the enemy received constant reinforcements from the rear.

All this time the rattle of small-arms was incessant, and showed a great number of men to be engaged in and about the Redan ; but the duration of the struggle created unpleasant doubts in the minds of those in the trenches. We saw the stormers first, then the supports, advance, disappear in the ditch, and reappear on the parapet ; then all became smoke and confusion. The guns in the faces of the Redan were almost silenced, but those in the flanks continued to fire, while several other Russian batteries suddenly opened, and sent shot thickly over all parts of our trenches. After a time we could see Russian soldiers standing in the embrasures of the faces of the Redan, loading, and firing into the interior of the work. At the end of an hour, the number of men seen hastening back proved that we had suffered a repulse. The enemy had come up in overpowering numbers, and the assailants suddenly gave way ; all rushed from the place at once, carrying their officers with them, many of whom were swept off their feet by the tide of fugitives. Numbers fell on the way back, and all the advanced trenches were thronged three or four deep by those who flocked into them.

There had been two brass field-guns in the Redan when our men entered, and these the Russians, immediately after the repulse, placed in embrasures, where their green wheels were plainly visible, and began firing on our trenches, and on the French on the slope before the Malakhoff. Two or three of our guns were directed on them, and struck and silenced both. The heavy guns of the Redan, some of which had been spiked by our people, scarcely fired at all after the attack.

Messengers came at intervals from General Pelissier, to report the progress of the French, saying they had made good their footing in the Malakhoff, and could hold it, but were hard pressed on the right. How the day had gone with them on the left was not known till afterwards.

At the same time as the English attacked the Redan, the French on the left attempted to enter the Central Bastion. The guns along the front of the Russian works here had been almost silenced by the vigour of the French fire, and the stormers reached the ditch without difficulty. But the obstacles here were even more formidable than on the right; and though 200 or 300 Frenchmen succeeded in penetrating at one point of the Bastion, and remained there some time, they were unable to support the fire from the interior defences, or to make head against the overwhelming force of the Russians, and retreated to their trenches, with a loss on this side of about 600 killed and wounded. One regiment (the 42d) lost thirty officers out of forty-five, and two generals were killed here. The Russians exploded a mine in this attack, which caused great loss to the assailants.

The smoke from the Russian batteries clearing after the repulse, we could see the salient of the Redan heaped with red-coated dead. When our men first issued forth to assault, I saw a rifleman knocked over half-way across. As soon as he dropt, he began rolling over and over, till, reaching a hollow, he lay still there. Towards evening he lifted up his head, and looked cautiously round, and, rising, ran a short distance, when a bullet striking near him, he dropt behind a bush. After a time he rose again, and this time got over the nearest parapet, where a comrade received and assisted him. Far away to the right we could see some Russians clinging to the houses of the Karabelnaia suburb, close up to the ditch of the Malakhoff, till they were scattered by shells from our guns in the Quarries; while on the French extreme right, which we could not see, a continued fire of small-arms told that the struggle which ended in the repulse of the French from the Little Redan was still undecided. The sun went duskily down, and darkness found us doubtfully speculating on the results of the day. The general opinion was that the Russian defence, though now hopeless, would be protracted till the French guns from the Malakhoff should open; but no one guessed that the enemy was at that moment abandoning the place, though General Pelissier at one time appears to have thought so, for I heard one of the messengers who came from him to General Simpson state that the Russians were passing the harbour in great numbers, apparently in full retreat. These, however, were supposed to be parties conducting prisoners to the north side.

The Russians committed, in constructing their most important defences, those of the Malakhoff, two considerable errors. First, they adapted the trace of their intrenchment to the shape of the stone tower it was intended to cover, which was the arc of a circle: thus, at the middle of the arc, the ditch could not be seen from the flanks, as it could have been if the salient had been carried out to an angle; and a most important point was left without other defence than the direct fire from its own parapet; that is to say, there was one spot where, standing on the edge of the ditch, you could see no other portion of the works than the part of the rampart immediately before you; and this was the point at which the French threw their bridge.

The other error was even more fatal; it was that of making the Malakhoff an enclosed work. The first error enabled the French to penetrate the work, the second to hold it. Had it, like the Redan, been open in rear, the defenders might have returned in force and maintained the struggle; but, once lost, it became as great an obstacle to the Russians as it had been to the French.

My faith in historical narrative, founded in anything else than personal observation, has been greatly shaken by the numerous instances in which, during the present campaign, anecdotes, apparently trustworthy, have subsequently appeared untrue. The information I collected to add to my own observation of the events just narrated, did not always bear sifting, and several particulars were given me by eye-witnesses, who had the best opportunities of watching the course of events, which an examination of the ground convinced me were erroneous. In these moments of intense interest and excitement, the imagination has undue sway, and gaps are filled up by suppositions adopted merely for their plausibility and convenience, till it is difficult to separate fact from fiction, and the whole assumes the coherent and circumstantial air of perfect truth. Unfortunately, the prettiest and most poetical incidents are such as frequently dwindle to nothing under a strict scrutiny, and I have often been sorry to relinquish the agreeable fictions.

CHAPTER XXXI.

THE LAST HOURS OF SEBASTOPOL.

THERE was but little sleep that night in the camps. Successive explosions of the most tremendous description shook the whole plateau, making tent and hut quiver as if in an earthquake. The information thus loudly given, that the enemy was about to abandon the place, was confirmed soon after midnight in a singular manner.

An officer had lost a friend in the assault of the Redan, and his regiment being one of those occupying the advanced trenches, he prevailed on twenty volunteers to accompany him in the search for the body. Not finding it among the dead in the open ground, he advanced towards the ditch. All was silent; he entered the ditch, which was of easy descent, and still finding no obstacle, and no sign of the presence of the enemy, he and his men went softly up the rampart. There was no token of life or motion; the guns were there, the iron guardians of the city, but they alone remained.

It was intended that the Highland regiments,

which had relieved those of the Light and Second Divisions in the advanced trenches, should at daybreak repeat the assault. But, in case this attack also should fail, and an advance by sap become ultimately necessary, the trenches were meanwhile pushed forward. The engineer conducting them suspected, from the silence, that the enemy had deserted the work, and a corporal of sappers, creeping stealthily forward, returned with the intelligence that all was still within. This being reported to Sir Colin Campbell, he called for ten volunteers from each of the Scotch regiments to ascertain the truth. These, advancing at a run, crossed the ditch; a 93d man standing on the rampart shouted out his name in token that he was the first to scale it; and, entering, they found the place empty.

On the night before the assault, two considerable fires—one near Fort Nicholas, the result of shells from our 13-inch mortars, the other in the town—had burnt briskly, and the conflagration continued next day. These the garrison tried to stop. In the evening of the 8th the figures of many men might be seen darkly hovering on the roofs of a large building, where they were trying to extinguish the flames that lit up the whole interior, and burst from every window. But now their efforts were all for destruction. After every explosion the fires augmented, till, towards morning, the whole city and its suburbs were in flames, sending one vast column of smoke upward, which leaned heavily, from the pressure of the wind, now almost lulled by the cannonade, towards the head of the harbour, over which it hung in a vast canopy. Soon after daybreak, one terrific explosion, surpassing all the rest, pealed through the camp, and a cloud, which seemed like the upheaving of the whole promontory, rose in earthy volumes, and hung for a space a blot upon the landscape, pierced murkily by the rays of the rising sun. The harbour gleamed of a dusky yellow amid the dark-grey hazy capes and buildings. Fort Paul, veiled in smoke, but visible, remained standing on its jutting mole till afternoon, when a fire in a building near communicated with its magazine, and it was hurled into the air. When the dust of the explosion subsided, nothing was left of it but a heap of loose stones.

The continual explosions by no means prevented enterprising Frenchmen from searching the town for valuables. I met one party who had been plundering a church: one man had an immense bible bound in green velvet, another displayed a white altar-cloth with a gold cross embroidered on it, a third was partly attired in the vestments of a priest. I told the adventurer with the altar-cloth that the bishop would excommunicate him; to which he replied by a gesture by no means flattering to episcopacy.

The motives of the Russians in setting fire to the city are not quite clear, or, at any rate, are questionable in point of expediency. At the conclusion of the war, they might look on it as likely that they would resume possession, and this consideration might have restrained them. But their traditionary stroke of policy in burning Moscow seems to have impressed on the national mind a general idea of the virtue of incendiarism ; and the catastrophe of Russian towns and fortresses, like that of a Vauxhall entertainment, would appear incomplete without a general conflagration.

The whole garrison withdrew unmolested under cover of the night, and destroyed the end of the bridge of rafts on our side of the harbour. The bursting mines and blazing streets prevented an entrance in the dark, and it was not till after daybreak that the Allies were within the works in any numbers, when the only Russians captured were a few—some of them wounded—who were found lurking in pits and holes, and who had perhaps remained to fire some of the mines.

The bodies of those slain in the assault were collected in the ditch of the Redan. Riflemen and soldiers of the line lay together in all postures, some shattered, some with their wounds not visible; here a bearded sergeant, there a boy-recruit lying on a tangle of blood-stained bodies, fragments of limbs, and protruding stumps ; amid which appeared here and there, in frightful contrast to such ghastly pillows, a face calm as in calmest sleep. The dead Russians were placed together at one end, and when all were collected, the earth of the slope was shovelled over, and the rampart they had fought for formed above assailant and defender a common funeral mound.

The interior of the Redan was a wide level space, filled with debris of all kinds—fragments of gabions, broken guns and carriages, beams hurled from exploded magazines, and chasms made by bursting shells. Parallel to the faces of the work, and in rear of the guns, were mounds of earth in the form of traverses, revetted with gabions, containing splinter-proof chambers for a part of the garrison; but the greater part of these found shelter underneath the surface of the whole interior space, where a kind of subterranean barrack, capable of holding many hundred men in its low, flat cells, and entered by several short descending galleries, had been constructed. From the Redan a continuous line of batteries extends down the hill almost to the Karabelnaia Ravine, where the pass is defended by a ditch and parapet for musketry; and the end of the ravine, instead of sweeping, as might be supposed, down to an inlet, slopes curiously upward to a point at the edge of the harbour-bank, where a battery looks along its course. The guns in these batteries and in most of the defences were worked, as on board ship, with breechings to prevent recoil, and these breechings had been cut through before the enemy abandoned them. At two or three places a heap of slain Russian gunners were collected behind their batteries, whose bodies wore terrible marks of shot and shell; numbers were headless, some cut absolutely in two, with the upper or lower half wanting; some torn open, some with great holes in their skulls; and detached from the group might be sometimes seen a human thigh or shoulder. All the way down, the underground habitations were continued, showing how terrible must have been the fire which rendered works of such labour necessary, and giving a lamentable idea of the life of the wretched occupants, whose moments of relief from the service of the batteries were thus passed in dark, crowded cellars. Crossing the ravine, you are at the foot of the steep hill or mound of the Malakhoff, whose redoubt stretches across the summit, one side of its rampart looking along the interior of the more advanced Redan, and sweeping the whole space down to the Inner Harbour. The battery extending up the slope to the redoubt is the Gervais Battery; and here the French stormers, quitting the Malakhoff, had attempted to pass down the hill, and bodies of Zouaves and Chasseurs were scattered about. In some places numbers had been engaged hand to hand, in others men had fallen darkly and unnoted, and lay unseen till, in some narrow passage, you stumbled over their bodies. A Frenchman lay in one of these spots, near a magazine, from the door of which protruded a pair of boots: the wearer, a Russian, lay dead in the dark receptacle, into which he had probably crept when wounded, and perished close to his enemy. In this battery near the Malakhoff, was a small chamber hollowed in the rampart, which had apparently been a surgery, for a Russian soldier, half-stript, as if to get at his wound, lay dead on his back on a table of plank. A Russian lay in one of the passages between a traverse and the rampart, his face covered by the cape of his coat. Fancying I saw him breathe as I passed, I stooped to uncover his face; but he silently resisted, as if desirous of dying in peace. I pointed him out to some Frenchmen engaged in removing the wounded.

The Malakhoff redoubt was a large enclosed work, its interior crossed by huge traverses, with a row of open doorways along one side of each; stooping to enter which, you found yourself in a long, low, narrow chamber, extending along the length of the traverse, with soldiers' pallets spread on the floor as thickly as the space allowed, for the garrison to repose on in the intervals of relief. In two open spots were collected the ordnance injured and dismounted by our fire —guns of all sizes, some half buried, all dragged there out of the way. From the Malakhoff to the Little Redan, behind the Curtain, is a wide open space terminated towards the harbour by the retrenchment which the Russians had begun to throw up. All this space, almost paved with iron, so thick lay the fragments of shells, was covered with bodies of Frenchmen and Russians, some of the latter still alive; and two *vivandières* were moving about giving water to those who needed it. In the corner of the Little Redan, which also, notwithstanding its name, is an enclosed work, had been the principal struggle, and French and Russians lay heaped there together in great numbers. In another corner was a chasm made by an exploded mine; planks had been thrust down the side of it, and the Russian bodies, brought to the edge, were placed on the planks, down which they rolled, rigidly vibrating, to the bottom of their ready-made sepulchre. The most frightful spectacle of all was in a corner of the Malakhoff: it was the corpse of a man who had been killed by the explosion either of a mine or a large shell, probably the former. Not a vestige of clothes remained on the body, from which the hair and features had been also burnt; the legs were doubled back, the chest torn open and shrivelled, and the whole figure blasted into the appearance of an ape or mummy.

Outside the Curtain, between it and the French trenches, burial-parties brought the dead Frenchmen and laid them side by side on the grass. Even here the peculiar national taste for effect was visible in the arrangement of the rows of bodies in symmetrical figures. About one thousand lay there, and all had not been collected—Chasseurs, Indigènes, and soldiers of the line; but no Zouaves, for these last had attacked the Malakhoff. Lord George Paget, passing the place at the time, saw one of the bodies move, and pointed out the circumstance; the man was examined, found alive, and conveyed to the hospital, and thus preserved from a fate the most horrible.

Mines and magazines left by the Russians continued to explode at intervals, and there were some others which the fire failed to ignite. I had been asleep about an hour that night, having lain down in full confidence of getting the first night's sound rest

I had enjoyed for a week, when I was roused by a summons to convey directions for the swamping of a mine, which had been discovered in the cellar of a large building in the barrack. As I rode across the dark plains on this errand, a fringe of clear flame marked the outline of the hill the city stands on. Two deserters or prisoners had told of the existence of this mine, which was a large magazine of powder-barrels in a cellar, surrounded by loose powder to catch any stray sparks : it was rendered harmless by a party of artillerymen.

A cordon of sentries had been drawn round the whole place, and none but general officers, or those having passports, were at first allowed to enter the town or works, except on duty. On the 10th I accompanied Sir Richard Dacres into the place. We entered the Centre Bastion, where the French had been repulsed, and afterwards made a circuit of the walls nearly down to the sea, passing the scene of contest of the 22d and 23d of May, and re-entering the place at a large folding-door in a wall of masonry rising from the ditch. Here we were in a suburb of ruined hovels, roofless and windowless, and pierced with shot ; and, from an eminence, looked across the ravine at the best-built portion of the skeleton city. Some houses were still smoking, and one or two were in flames, especially near Fort Nicholas. The streets of the suburbs, far from being paved, were rough and rocky as a mountain-path, but in the heart of the city itself were several wide streets, extending in long perspective towards the harbour, having *trottoirs*, and bordered by houses of a better stamp than the others, though by no means equal to the average habitations in an English town of the same magnitude. The churches, and most considerable buildings, stood along the crest of the hill, looking, on one side, to the Black Sea, on the other to the Inner Harbour. Towards the latter a large garden extended down the hill. Two buildings which had often fixed our glances from the trenches, the one surrounded with a colonnade, the other bristling with pinnacles, were both churches. The columns of the former, which were not of stone, but of some composition, had been struck by shot in several places, and huge pieces knocked away. From the colonnade, at one end of this building, nearly the whole scene of contest was visible,—the Garden Batteries, the Creek Battery bordering the head of the Inner Harbour, and sweeping the ground where Eyre's brigade had suffered so severely on the 18th June, the interior of the Redan, and the hill of the Malakhoff, and, beyond, the plains furrowed with our trenches. Passing down a road parallel to the Inner Harbour, we crossed on a wharf between the Creek Battery and the water, and entered the arsenal, which lay along the edge of the inlet, and contained many rows of ordnance never used, cast, as our own used to be, at the Carron Foundry. The road from thence to the barracks behind the Redan, lying at the foot of the steep hill, was pitted with shell holes.

The barrack in rear of the Redan was a huge quadrangle of several storeys, with smaller buildings interspersed, the walls pitted with shot, with gaping chasms here and there, and the roofs perforated like a cullender. Along the ground between this and the Malakhoff was the Karabelnaia suburb, a large collection of insignificant stone houses, with a few of better class among them, the whole smashed into one shapeless mass of ruin, and for the most part completely uninhabitable. A great many cats and a few dogs, nevertheless, adhered to their ancient homes, the latter skulking and downcast, the former making for their retreats in a great hurry when any one approached. Behind the suburb, at the edge of the dockyard basin, was a loop-holed wall plentifully marked with shot. The docks were in the deep dry basin at the head of the Dockyard Creek, a small branch of the Inner Harbour. Along the water's edge was a very spacious well-built barrack left unconsumed amid the surrounding flames, the reason of which became apparent on the afternoon of the 10th, when a steamer came across with a flag of truce, to ask for the wounded left in these buildings when the garrison retreated; and this was the first intimation we had of their presence on our side of the harbour.

The scene that ensued was a climax of the horrors of war. In these vast apartments, and in the cellars beneath, not less than two thousand desperately wounded men had been laid. It is scarcely possible to conceive a situation more horrible than theirs, for two days and nights lying here, helpless, and tortured by wounds, without assistance, and without nourishment, surrounded by flaming buildings and exploding mines. When the place was entered, about five hundred remained alive, and were transferred in a lamentable condition to the steamer. The corpses of the rest were buried by our troops. In one room alone seven hundred dead were counted, many of whom had undergone amputation. The sudden revealment of the secrets of a churchyard would disclose nothing half so horrible as the spectacle of this cemetery above-ground, where the dead lay in every posture of agony, on and beside their beds. One small cellar was altogether filled with the bodies of Russian officers. Three English officers, wounded and taken in the assault, were found here, two of whom lived to be removed to camp, where they lingered for a few days.

On the night of the 11th, the Russian steamers were burnt; those line-of-battle ships not destroyed before, had been sunk on the night of the 8th, one close to Fort Paul, where its huge masts and tops projected high above the water, a kind of satire on the Third Point of the Conference, respecting the limitation of the Russian naval power in the Black Sea; and the fleet of Sebastopol thus became utterly extinct. The captain of the Vladimir, who came with the flag of truce, boasted to Captain Keppel of the speed of his vessel, and, it is said, avowed his intention of running the gauntlet of our fleet, and trying to make his way to Odessa; but the gale which prevented our fleet from weighing to take part in the assault, also defeated his project, and the Vladimir was burnt with the rest.

So ended amid death and destruction the great siege of Sebastopol. The drama, with its many dull tedious passages, and its many scenes of intense and painful interest, extending over nearly a year, had for actors the three greatest nations of the earth, and all the world for an audience. The catastrophe solved many difficulties, quieted many doubts, and falsified many prophecies. Besides those foreboders who founded their prognostics on reason, there were some seers who traced in the campaign and siege the fulfilment of revelation, and who must now search elsewhere for the great valley of Armageddon, a name which they found to be merely Hebrew for Sebastopol, with such nicety did their expositions correspond with Scripture. But, indeed, so great were the interests involved, so massive the events, and so dark the uncertainty which shrouded them, that others besides visionaries have read in the progress of affairs the manifestations of Divine interference; and I have heard of a French general, who characterised the taking of the Malakhoff as a thing beyond expectation, "which was to be, because else the flags of France and England would have been trailed in the dust." Pelissier's mode of expressing his sense of the fortune of war was by a comparison drawn from écarté : " Nous étions quatre à quatre, et j'ai tourné le roi."

So ended, too, our first campaign. Hitherto I, and doubtless most others my contemporaries, had viewed in a kind of epic light the men of Wellington's campaigns, beside whose rich and stirring youth ours seemed pale and empty. Now we, too, had passed behind the scenes ; we, too, had been initiated into that jumble of glory and calamity, war, and had been acting history. In one step we had passed from civilisation and luxury, such as our fathers knew not of, to a campaign of uncommon privation. We, too, knew of the marshalling of hosts, the licensed devastation, the ghastly burden of the battle-field, and the sensation of fronting death ; and, henceforth, the pages of military history, hitherto somewhat dim and oracular, were for us illuminated by the red light of experience.

The barren plateau, with which the army of the East is now so wearily familiar, has for France and England an interest deeper than their most cherished possessions. There are few communities in either country with whose memories it is not associated by the sad link of a citizen's grave. The bones of a mighty host are scattered here, Russian and Turk, Frenchman and Englishman ; and if, as our Saxon forefathers believed, the spirits of the departed hovered above their resting-places, no dreary dell, no hill, or plain, or trench-furrowed slope, would be without its troop of shadows. When these great armies have departed, when the cities of tents have vanished, and the last echoes of the tramp of troops, the hum of camps, and the roll of artillery, have died away, these solitudes, tenanted only by the fox and the eagle, will continue for us and our descendants a colony of the dead.

CHAPTER XXXII.

A RETROSPECT.

Thus by main force, strength matched against strength, "in plain and even shock of battle," France and England had pushed Russia from her stronghold. Such has been the course of the campaign, so peculiar and exceptional, that it is not easy to say what military lessons have been derived from its incidents, or what advance in soldiership has been gained by our army, beyond the experience of encamping in the field in presence of an enemy. But from our present stand-point of an appreciable result we may at least survey comprehensively and clearly the events of the campaign, and trace with something like certainty the circumstances which produced them.

The questions of the merits of the policy pursued up to the time of the departure from Varna, and the amount of neglect attributable to the Government in allowing the expedition to depart with such slender preparation, are such as persons conversant with public business at home are most competent to decide. Admitting that the state of public feeling in the summer of 1854 rendered some enterprise necessary, and that the capture of Sebastopol, as solving one of the principal problems of the war, was an object of first-rate importance, we may, by pursuing the course of affairs from the commencement of the expedition to its crisis, compare the means with which the attempt was made with the chances of success.

No objections have been made to the conduct of affairs up to the battle of the Alma. Some critics have objected to the tactics of the Allies on that occasion. Certainly nothing could well be simpler or less scientific than the plan of attack; but the moral effect produced on the Russians by the gallantry of the advance, preventing, as it probably did, the defence of either the Katcha or the Balbek, may well be held to compensate for the absence of brilliant manœuvring. The next error imputed is in the assertion that the Allies should have advanced immediately after the battle. But this would have left not only our dead unburied, but our wounded at the mercy of the Cossacks, who hovered round in sufficient numbers to overpower any small detachment left as a guard, and a large one we could not spare. We had no superfluous troops to detach, because our deficiency in transport compelled us to leave several thousand French at Varna, and nearly all our cavalry, which would have been inestimable in such a country as we advanced over.

The next point of debate is whether the north side of Sebastopol should not have been threatened instead of the south. Now, there are no harbours on the north side; the possession of the forts there would not have secured the immediate capture of the city; and, in case of a repulse, the position was greatly inferior in security to the southern plateau. But the true grounds on which the flank march was decided on I believe to be these: The French, after passing the Balbek, found a strong fort on their right, which it would have been necessary to take before advancing upon the north side; this our allies were not prepared to attempt, and the design was changed accordingly.

Meanwhile the Russian commander, unable to make a stand on the Katcha or Balbek, would have found himself, supposing we had occupied, as he expected, the ground to the north of the town, cut off from Bakshi-serai and Simferopol, and dependent almost altogether for the subsistence of his army on the stores of the fortress, while he could not have attacked or even annoyed us without crossing the harbour or the deep valley of the Tchernaya. Therefore, to keep open his communications with the northern depôts, and to enable him to act on our flank and rear, he made the movement during which we came on his rearguard at Mackenzie's Farm, and we took possession of Balaklava and the southern heights unmolested.

Thus, then, with far less loss than could have been anticipated, the expedition found itself close to its object. Fifty thousand men were on the heights before the city, its garrison were panic-stricken, its defences feeble, the beaten army in retreat, and the Allied fleets at the harbour's mouth. Here we have the conditions, if not of absolute success, yet of great advantage on our side, and those who most strongly objected to the enterprise would have been silenced could they have foreseen a juncture so favourable. But Menschikoff's wise measure of sinking part of his ships across the harbour to bar the access to our fleets, totally changed the aspect of affairs. The *coup de main* so strongly insisted on became simply impossible, because no troops could have continued on the ground within the Russian lines of defence, under the fire of ships' batteries incomparably more powerful than anything we could oppose them with. The presence of a siege train proves that the contingency of a siege had been anticipated; but, no doubt, whether the assault was to be given at once or after a cannonade, a combined attack by sea and land was always contemplated. Thus the design of the campaign was frustrated by the sinking of the ships, a measure which critics have not sufficiently taken into their calculations; and since then no event has occurred which could within its possible limits have altered the course of events. That caused all subsequent doubt and disaster; and, but for that, the attempt promised well for success. Then it was that the character of the enterprise was totally changed, from a brisk advance followed by a sudden assault, to a permanent occupation of the plateau and a protracted siege.

THE CHARACTER OF THE CAMPAIGN.

On these grounds, a review of the past convinces me that, with the means we had, the course taken was a right one, and that we may consider ourselves fortunate in having been impelled into it. Throughout the war very little foresight is apparent, if any has been used; there has been little opportunity for free action, and once begun, all seems the result of sheer necessity, like the descent of a Montagne Russe. The chance character of the campaign is notably illustrated by the state of the weather on the day and hour when I write this—noon, on the anniversary of the Alma. Last night, the anniversary of our bivouac on the Bulganak, was a night of winter's cold, storm, and rain, and to-day the dreary drenched plains are thick with mud, while over them still whistles a chilling wind driving sharp showers before it. Had that season been as this, we should have advanced upon the foe, not as then with a bright sun and a firm soil, but over boggy plains, our limbs, cramped by the stresses of the previous night, scarcely enabling us to lift our mud-laden feet to the margin of the Alma, where we should have found a turbid, swollen flood instead of a clear stream, while the vineyards on its overflowed banks would have been a vast swamp. Such circumstances might well have changed the fate of the day and of the war.

The garrison, relieved from the apprehension of an attack from our fleets, now occupied itself in the rapid construction of the most essential of those gigantic defences, the conception and execution of which would have been alike beyond the reach of an ordinary engineer. A man of genius was called for, and he was at hand in Totleben. It is true that nature, in surrounding the south of Sebastopol with a line of commanding eminences between deep ravines, has made the position eminently defensible; but the advantage was unimproved by art, till we were before the place, when, in an incredibly short space of time, massive ramparts armed with formidable batteries rose opposite our trenches; and were added to from time to time, till they assumed the completeness and extent which now surprises the spectator. I have already spoken of the interior aspect of the Malakhoff and Redan; but, of all the defences, the Bastion du Mât, or Flagstaff Bastion, on the left of the line covering the town, was the strongest. Its rampart was the highest and most massive, its escarp alone was faced with a strong stockade, and its ditch was defended by a *caponnière* or small flanking battery extending across it. Galleries and countermines threaded in a labyrinth towards the French lines. Within the work the large space was heaped with mounds, marking the sites of blindages or subterranean chambers for the troops, and all the numerous lengthy approaches from here to the termination of the Garden Batteries above the head of the Creek were lined with these cells, or rather dens, with apertures so frequent that it must have been difficult for each individual to recognise his own abode. Heavy beams laid across each excavation supported the roof of gabions, fascines, and earth. The number of troops capable of being thus accommodated, proves how anxious the enemy were to be prepared on this side against a sudden attack; but the openings to the chambers were so narrow, frequently indeed so difficult of entrance, that a rapid advance would have surprised them before they could quit their burrows. The lines of the Allies are extensive beyond precedent, but these defences of the Russians are stupendous. The long lines of rampart are, throughout, of enormous thickness, with no weak points, and bearing the signs of a presiding genius everywhere. These alone would have been far beyond the powers of any ordinary garrison of a fortress of this stamp; but they are surpassed by the subterranean labours which cause the spectator almost to believe that some band of gnomes, such as mine in the Hartz mountains, must have volunteered to act as auxiliaries. Fighting was the least part of the work of this indefatigable garrison.

In the chapter headed "Exculpation," I have attempted to show how unreasonable was the public indignation during the disasters of our troops in the first part of the siege; and it is unnecessary to recapitulate the view I took, which subsequent events have not induced me to modify; besides, public opinion, which then found such strong expression, has since changed. It will be instructive for men in authority, at the commencement of a future war, to mark the fate of those who conducted this campaign. Lord Raglan, his Quartermaster and Adjutant Generals, his Commissary-General, Admiral Boxer, the naval superintendent in the Bosphorus, and Captain Christie, superintendent of transports at Balaklava, bore for a time the most unpopular names in England; names gibbeted like dead kites and magpies nailed to a stable-door. They were reviled, ridiculed, menaced; the culpability so freely attributed to them was, to a great extent, credited by the country; their imputed crimes were hotly debated in Parliament; and the contest was in some instances continued over their graves. It seemed as if nothing but their immediate and ignominious dismissal from the public service could satisfy the country. Yet, "in a little month," all this clamour died away, and the advocacy of their friends was favourably listened to.

A great deal has been said and written by military critics of the faultiness of our position on the plateau. It is very true that the formation of an army *en potence*—that is, with a salient angle towards the enemy—must, generally, be weak and dangerous. It is clear enough that, on ordinary ground, a formation which enables the foe to throw all his force on a single point, or a single face, of your line, must be objectionable. But if the nature of the position be such, that its apex is unassailable, or capable of being made so, and its wings so posted that the enemy can only advance to the attack at a disadvantage more than counterbalancing the superiority of force he can bring against that face, all objection ceases; and such a position was ours. It was endangered, it is true, on the 5th November; but redoubts and intrenchments subsequently made this the strongest point of our line. The left wing faced the town, and must be attacked either up ravines, deep, narrow, and easily defensible, or in the teeth of our siege-batteries; moreover, in a repulse, the pursuers might pass within the defences along with the flying enemy, and the prize might fall into our hands. The other wing could not be directly attacked, because, opposite it, across the valley, rises an impassable mountain barrier. Thus an enemy's force entering the valley had Balaklava in its front, the troops on the plateau on its right flank, a mountain on its left, and the Tchernaya in its rear. For these reasons I have always considered Liprandi's attack on the 25th October a mistake. His success, such as it was, proved of no eventual benefit to him, and during the winter he abandoned the position, which was one of great hazard. It is true that we committed an error in occupying the outposts which he took from the Turks on that occasion; but it was an error only because our force did not admit of such extension. When our reinforcements warranted the step, the line of the Tchernaya was taken up; and thus Balaklava was secured by triple lines of defence, against the foremost of which the Russians cast their whole weight in vain on the 16th August.

Spring found us still in the strong position to which circumstances beyond control had conducted us. Considering the impatience for a result manifested at home, and the bad condition of the army, I was among those who thought that we should before then have assaulted, with all the force we could command, the defences before the town. Experience has shown that such an attempt, unless aided by some happy chance, would have failed. In May, our circumstances altogether changed, and again the campaign assumed a new aspect. Large reinforcements of French and Turks, besides a Sardinian army, had arrived; Kertsch was taken; and newer and more extensive operations than those of the siege were apparently feasible. Two movements offered themselves; the one from Eupatoria or along the Bulganak; the other from Kertsch. In advancing from Eupatoria, the want of water would always prevent other than a rapid movement, followed, if not at once successful, by as rapid a retreat. At the same time, with our force of cavalry, and with our fleet on the coast, besides Eupatoria itself to fall back on, there could be no great risk in case of an attack by the enemy; while even a very short interruption of the stream of supply to the garrison or army—such as the presence of a strong cavalry force on the road for two days—might have been fatal to the defence of Sebastopol. The advance from the peninsula of Kertsch, involving the capture of Kaffa and Arabat, would have been a safer and more sustained operation, and its consequences more destructive to the enemy.

On the other hand, it must occur to every one, that a man like the French Emperor does not require to be told that, in a military point of view, it is better to attack the flank of an enemy's line of operations than its extremity. The eager interest with which his attention has for so long been riveted on the theatre of war must have rendered him at least as capable of judging of the merits of an obvious plan as any of the critics. In a former chapter I have said, that had we, in 1854, succeeded in a *coup de main* against Sebastopol, it would have been fortunate for Russia. Soldiers naturally look to military successes as all-important in war, but the glance of a ruler comprehends other considerations. Louis Napoleon is a far-seeing genius, capable of distinguishing between the interests of the army and those of the alliance—of separating military from national success. I can imagine such a man saying, "It is true I can take the Crimea, and with it Sebastopol, when I please; but, besides the loss of town and territory, I will drain Russia of whole armies. Pride will not allow her to abandon a contest which it is ruin to her to maintain, and I will not do her the favour to precipitate its termination." To those who reckon up the losses of Russia since the siege commenced, and compare them with those of the Allies, such language will not seem unreasonable nor inconsistent with the

Y

character of a man so calculating in his aims, so persevering in pursuing them.

How deeply Russia has felt the evil of our presence here is proved by the attack at Traktir, which seemed the result of desperation. From that time, the beaten army remained merely spectators of the siege, the termination of which Prince Gortschakoff's preparations showed to be approaching. The bridge was completed across the harbour, and stores of all kinds removed to the north side; while the tenor of some of the Russian commander's previous despatches pointed to the evacuation of the place. The tremendous fire of the Allied artillery, searching through the town and works with an enormous destruction of life, could not be much longer supported; and it is probable that the capture of the Malakhoff only precipitated a measure already resolved on. The Prince's subsequent despatches, and the Czar's proclamation, place the abandonment of the town in a peculiar light—as a great stroke of generalship, and rather advantageous than otherwise to the Russian cause; so that, unlike the loss of fortresses in general, the event seems to have given satisfaction to everybody.

Although long service in the trenches is undoubtedly prejudicial to the discipline of troops, yet any detriment of this kind the armies have suffered will soon be repaired now that the siege is over. In another campaign they will take the field seasoned to the climate, inured to hardship, and familiar with all the exigencies and shifts of life in the bivouac and camp. What is most to be regretted is, that the course of the campaign has not been such as to develop what of military genius England may possess. Russia has her Totleben, the good soldier who, in her hour of need, was equal to the emergency; the creator of the vast works that have so long repelled us. Should peace not shortly ensue, we may see whether his genius is as potent in the open field as in defence of a city, and how far generalship and science can avail against French vivacity and British firmness. To us opportunity has been denied for showing pre-eminence, and the coming general is still unrevealed.

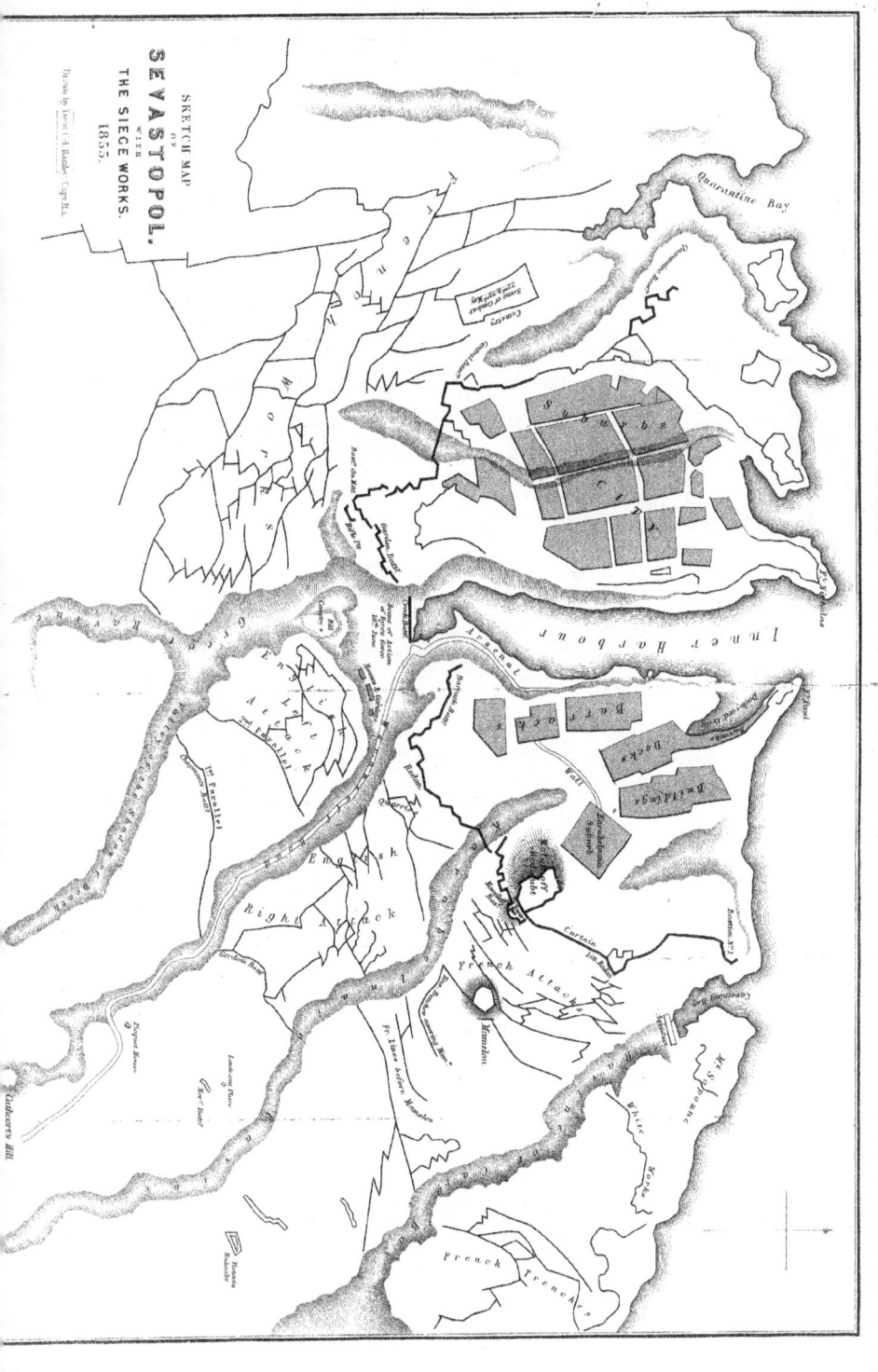

www.ingramcontent.com/pod-product-compliance
Lightning Source LLC
Chambersburg PA
CBHW031132160426
43193CB00008B/112